Mastering Kafka Streams

From Basics to Expert Proficiency

Contents

Introduction

In today's rapidly evolving technological landscape, real-time data processing has become paramount for a wide range of applications, from enhancing user experiences in real-time analytics to ensuring timely responses in distributed systems. Apache Kafka has already established itself as a robust distributed event streaming platform, capable of handling large-scale data streams. However, the need to process and analyze these streams in real time led to the development of Kafka Streams, a powerful stream processing library integrated with Apache Kafka.

This book, "Mastering Kafka Streams: From Basics to Expert Proficiency," aims to provide a comprehensive guide to Kafka Streams, catering to both beginners and advanced users. Whether you are new to Kafka Streams or looking to deepen your understanding and proficiency, this book will serve as a valuable resource.

Kafka Streams is designed to simplify the development of real-time data processing applications. By leveraging the capabilities of Kafka Streams, developers can create applications that continuously process input streams of data, generate derived streams, and produce results in real time. The library abstracts much of the complexity associated with stream processing, providing a high-level Domain Specific Language (DSL) for common operations as well as a lower-level Processor API for more advanced use cases.

Throughout this book, we will explore the core concepts, architecture, and features of Kafka Streams. We will delve into its capabilities for stateless and stateful transformations, windowed operations, error handling, and logging. Practical examples and hands-on exercises will be provided to reinforce theoretical concepts and ensure a firm understanding of how to build and deploy Kafka Streams applications.

We will begin with an overview of Kafka Streams, highlighting its core concepts, terminology, and the distinctions between Kafka and Kafka Streams. This foundational knowledge will set the stage for understanding the more advanced topics covered later in the book. From there, we will guide you through the process of setting up your Kafka Streams environment, including necessary installations and configurations.

The architectural aspects of Kafka Streams will be thoroughly examined, providing insight into how streams, state stores, and processors interact within a Kafka Streams application. Understanding these components is crucial for designing efficient and scalable stream processing solutions.

Subsequent chapters will focus on the practical aspects of working with streams and tables, performing stateless and stateful transformations, and leveraging windowed operations to handle time-based data processing requirements. We will explore different strategies for error handling and logging, ensuring that your applications are robust and reliable.

Testing is a critical component of any software development process, and Kafka Streams applications are no exception. We will cover various testing methodologies and best practices to ensure the correctness and performance of your applications.

Finally, we will address performance tuning and optimization techniques, providing guidance on how to monitor and enhance the performance of your Kafka Streams applications.

By the end of this book, you will have gained a deep understanding of Kafka Streams and its powerful capabilities for real-time stream processing. You will be equipped with the knowledge and skills necessary to build, deploy, and manage Kafka Streams applications effectively, from basic implementations to complex, enterprise-grade solutions.

We invite you to join us on this exploration of Kafka Streams, confident that the insights and knowledge presented in this book will empower you to harness the full potential of real-time data processing with Kafka Streams.

Chapter 1

Introduction to Kafka Streams

This chapter provides a comprehensive introduction to Kafka Streams, beginning with an overview of its capabilities and the differences between Kafka and Kafka Streams. It covers core concepts and terminology essential for understanding Kafka Streams, discusses the advantages and use cases of the library, and compares Kafka Streams with other stream processing frameworks. The chapter concludes with a step-by-step guide to getting started with Kafka Streams, including a 'Hello World' example to illustrate its fundamental operations.

1.1 Overview of Kafka Streams

Kafka Streams is a client library provided by Apache Kafka for building real-time, scalable, and fault-tolerant stream processing applications. It provides higher-level stream processing capabilities atop Kafka's core primitives, such as producers and consumers. Kafka Streams is designed to make it easy to write applications and microservices whose data is continually derived from, or enriched with, streams of data.

At its core, Kafka Streams enables developers to perform real-time computation on data streams. A stream is an unbounded sequence of events or records. These records are immutable and append-only, meaning that records can only be added to the end of the stream. This provides strong guarantees on the order of data processing and repeatability of the computations.

Unlike traditional batch processing systems, which gather records over a period before processing and producing results, stream processing systems like Kafka Streams process records as they arrive. This low-latency processing model is vital for use cases that require real-time analytics and instant decision-making.

Architecture of Kafka Streams

The Kafka Streams architecture is designed for distributed processing and built-in fault tolerance. Each Kafka Streams application consists of multiple stream processing nodes organized into a topology. A topology is a directed acyclic graph (DAG) of stream processors (nodes) and state stores, representing the processing logic.

- **Stream Processors**: This is the fundamental processing unit in Kafka Streams. Each processor receives one input record at a time, applies its processing logic, and may emit one or more output records.

- **State Stores**: These are used to store any intermediate state required by the stream processors. They support persistent, fault-tolerant storage, ensuring that state is available even after application restarts.

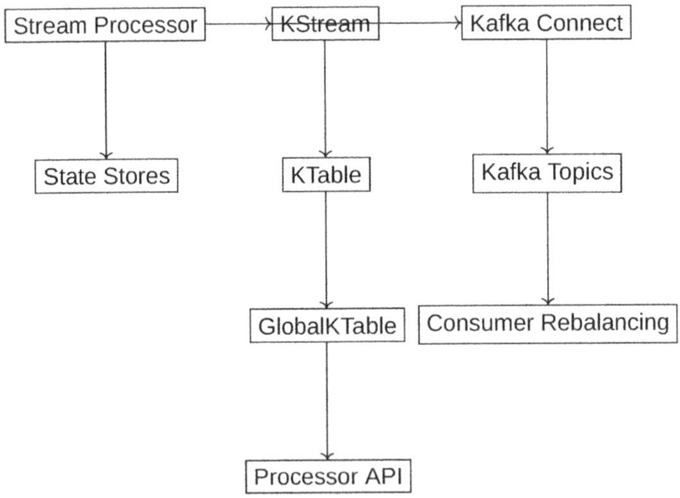

Stream processors in the topology can be stateless or stateful. Stateless processors do not need to store any information between records, while stateful processors maintain intermediate computations and require state stores to manage these computations. An example of a stateful processor is one performing aggregations or windowed computations.

This architecture allows Kafka Streams applications to process large volumes of data efficiently, scale out across multiple instances, and recover from failures automatically.

Building Blocks of Kafka Streams

Several core elements provide the foundational building blocks for creating a Kafka Streams application:

- **KStream**: A KStream represents a continuous stream of records. Each record in a KStream is a key-value pair. Operations available on a KStream include transformations, such as filtering, mapping, and flat-mapping.
- **KTable**: A KTable is a continuously updated view of a table based on a changelog stream. It represents the latest value for each key. Operations on KTables include joins with other KTables or KStreams and aggregations, such as counting and summing.
- **GlobalKTable**: This is a special kind of KTable that is globally replicated across all instances of the Kafka Streams application. It is useful for join operations where lookup latency must be minimized.
- **Processor API**: In addition to the DSL-based KStream and KTable, Kafka Streams offers a lower-level Processor API that provides more fine-grained control over processing logic. It allows the creation of custom processors and offers flexibility for advanced use cases.

Each of these building blocks interacts seamlessly, allowing developers to create complex processing pipelines with minimal boilerplate code.

Integration with Kafka Ecosystem

Kafka Streams is tightly integrated with the Kafka ecosystem, leveraging Apache Kafka's robustness, high-throughput, and distributed nature. Kafka Streams applications inherit the scalability and fault-tolerance properties of Kafka. The integration includes:

- **Kafka Connect**: This provides connectors to easily integrate Kafka with various data sources and sinks, allowing Kafka Streams applications to ingest data from external systems and output results to other systems.

- **Kafka Topics**: Kafka Streams applications consume data from and produce data to Kafka topics, ensuring that data pipelines are decoupled and independently scalable.

- **Kafka Consumer Rebalancing**: Kafka Streams can dynamically redistribute workload across instances during rebalancing events, ensuring load balancing and high availability.

Fault Tolerance and Exactly-Once Semantics

One of the key features of Kafka Streams is its fault tolerance and support for exactly-once semantics. Fault tolerance is achieved through the use of Kafka's transactional capabilities and the state management provided by state stores.

Exactly-once semantics ensure that each record is processed exactly once, even in the case of failures. This is crucial for financial applications where duplicate processing can lead to significant errors. Kafka Streams achieve this by employing idempotent producers and transactional writes to Kafka topics.

The state stores maintain their state using changelog topics in Kafka. If a failure occurs, the state can be rebuilt by replaying the changelog, ensuring that no data is lost.

Kafka Streams offers a powerful, flexible, and scalable toolkit for building real-time stream processing applications. It ensures robust fault-tolerance and exactly-once processing guarantees, making it suitable for critical applications requiring precise and timely data processing.

```
Properties props = new Properties();
props.put(StreamsConfig.APPLICATION_ID_CONFIG, "streams-application");
props.put(StreamsConfig.BOOTSTRAP_SERVERS_CONFIG, "localhost:9092");

StreamsBuilder builder = new StreamsBuilder();
KStream<String, String> source = builder.stream("input-topic");
KStream<String, String> transformed = source.mapValues(value -> value.
    toUpperCase());
transformed.to("output-topic");

KafkaStreams streams = new KafkaStreams(builder.build(), props);
streams.start();
```

Output of the given topology on the input of "hello world":

HELLO WORLD

This simple example demonstrates the essential components and operations of Kafka Streams, providing a solid foundation for more complex stream processing tasks. It highlights the ease with which developers can create robust and scalable stream processing applications using Kafka Streams.

1.2 Differences Between Kafka and Kafka Streams

Kafka is a distributed streaming platform that provides the fundamental backbone for building real-time data pipelines and streaming applications. It is primarily known for its ability to publish, subscribe to, store, and process streams of records in a fault-tolerant manner. Kafka Streams, on the other hand, is a client library for building applications and microservices, where the input and output data are stored in Kafka's clusters. Both Kafka and Kafka Streams are integral parts of the Apache Kafka ecosystem, but they serve different purposes and operate at different levels of abstraction.

Kafka's core architecture revolves around several key components:

- **Producers:** Applications that publish data to Kafka topics.
- **Consumers:** Applications that read data from Kafka topics.
- **Brokers:** Kafka servers that store and serve data.
- **Topics:** Categories or feed names to which records are published.
- **Partitions:** Horizontal scalability units of a topic.
- **Consumer Groups:** A grouping mechanism that enables load balancing among consumers.

In contrast, Kafka Streams abstracts much of the low-level details involved in stream processing and provides a higher-level API for defining stream transformations. Here are some of the primary distinctions between Kafka and Kafka Streams:

Level of Abstraction: Kafka operates at a lower level of abstraction, providing the basic infrastructure to store records, and manage message offset. Kafka Streams builds on top of Kafka, offering a higher level of abstraction to deal with data streams and processing them in a continuous and scalable manner.

Programming Model: Kafka follows a straightforward publish-subscribe model where producers write data to clusters of brokers, and consumers read from them. Kafka Streams, however, introduces a functional programming model inspired by Java 8's Stream API, where developers can define complex transformations over streams using operations such as map, filter, and join.

```
KStream<String, String> textLines = builder.stream("inputTopic");
KStream<String, Integer> wordCounts = textLines
    .flatMapValues(value -> Arrays.asList(value.toLowerCase().split("\\W+")))
    .map((key, value) -> new KeyValue<>(value, 1))
    .groupBy((key, value) -> key)
    .reduce((aggValue, newValue) -> aggValue + newValue);
wordCounts.to("outputTopic");
```

State Management: Kafka by itself does not provide built-in state management capabilities for processing streams. Kafka Streams introduces state stores and provides out-of-the-box mechanisms for state management. State stores enable maintaining state information which can be queried and updated during stream processing. This allows implementations of operations such as aggregations and joins that require knowledge of previous records.

Fault Tolerance: Kafka ensures fault tolerance by replicating logs (topics) across multiple brokers. If one broker fails, another broker that holds the replica can continue serving the data. Kafka Streams, on the other hand, leverages Kafka's inherent fault tolerance and supplements it by enabling transparent handling of stateful processing, which includes reprocessing events, state recovery, and committing results to Kafka topics.

Operational Complexity: Running and managing a Kafka cluster involves handling configurations, replication settings, partition management, and broker maintenance. Kafka Streams applications are relatively simpler to operate. They run as standard Java applications and utilize Kafka clusters without needing additional infrastructure for stream processing logic.

Integration with Kafka Connect: Kafka natively integrates with Kafka Connect, a tool for scalably and reliably streaming data between Apache Kafka and other systems using source and sink connectors.

This allows Kafka to serve as an intermediary real-time data pipeline. Kafka Streams naturally complements this by enabling transformation and enrichment of streams within the same ecosystem.

Use Cases: Typical use cases for Kafka include building robust messaging systems, managing real-time event streams, log aggregation, and data integration across various systems. Kafka Streams is geared towards application-level stream processing such as real-time analytics, monitoring, and building event-driven services.

The delineation between Kafka and Kafka Streams clarifies their individual roles while highlighting their interoperability within the larger ecosystem. Understanding these differences is critical for designing effective real-time data processing architectures and leveraging Apache Kafka's full potential.

1.3 Core Concepts and Terminology

Kafka Streams, a library designed for building real-time applications and microservices, leverages Apache Kafka as its underling messaging system. Understanding the fundamental concepts and terminology related to Kafka Streams is crucial for effectively using this technology.

Streams and Tables

A foundational concept in Kafka Streams is the difference between streams and tables:

Stream: A stream is a continuous, append-only sequence of records. Each record consists of a key, a value, and a timestamp. Streams can be thought of as unbounded datasets, where data keeps flowing in, akin to a log file that is continually appended.

Table: A table, also known as a *state store*, represents a collection of key-value pairs, where each key is unique. Tables are mutable and can be updated over time, allowing them to represent the latest state of data.

Duality of Streams and Tables: Kafka Streams promotes the idea of *stream-table duality*, meaning that a stream can be interpreted as a table and vice versa. A stream of changes can define a table, while each change in a table can be seen as a new event in a stream.

Topology

A Kafka Streams application defines its computational logic via a *topology*, which is essentially a directed acyclic graph (DAG) of stream processing nodes:

Source Processor: Nodes in the topology where streams are read from Kafka topics.

Processor: Nodes where streams are processed, transformations are applied, or data is aggregated.

Sink Processor: Nodes where the results of stream processing are written back to Kafka topics.

The topology defines how data flows through the processing pipeline from sources to sinks, with intermediate transformations and aggregations handled by processors.

Transformations and Operations

Kafka Streams offers a wide range of transformations and operations to manipulate and analyze streams:

Map and FlatMap: The map operation applies a transformation to each record in the stream, returning a new stream with the transformed records. The flatMap operation, in contrast, can produce zero or more records for each input record, allowing for more complex transformations.

```
KStream<String, String> uppercasedStream = inputStream.mapValues(value -> value.
    toUpperCase());
```

Filter and SelectKey: The filter operation allows for records to be included or excluded based on a predicate. The selectKey operation changes the key of each record in the stream, enabling re-keying of data.

```
KStream<String, String> filteredStream = inputStream.filter((key, value) -> value.
    length() > 5);
KStream<String, String> rekeyedStream = inputStream.selectKey((key, value) ->
    value.substring(0, 4));
```

Aggregate, Count, Reduce: Aggregations, such as aggregate, count, and reduce, operate on windows of data to perform stateful transformations. Aggregations are stored in state stores and can be queried to retrieve results of the computation.

```
KTable<Windowed<String>, Long> wordCounts = inputStream
  .groupBy((key, value) -> value)
  .windowedBy(TimeWindows.of(Duration.ofMinutes(5)))
  .count();
```

Stateful Processing and State Stores

Kafka Streams allows for stateful processing, which involves maintaining state information across multiple records:

State Store: A state store is an internal database used to store persistent state information required by stream processing applications, such as intermediate aggregation results.

RocksDB: By default, Kafka Streams uses RocksDB, a high-performance embedded key-value store, to manage state in state stores.

Queryable State: Kafka Streams supports queryable state, which allows for querying of state stores. This is useful for applications that need to expose stateful results for external query and interaction.

Windowing

Windowing is a critical concept for handling time-based operations in streams:

Tumbling Windows: Non-overlapping, fixed-size windows where each record belongs to exactly one window.

Hopping Windows: Overlapping windows with fixed size and a specified advance interval.

Session Windows: Dynamic windows based on activity gaps, where records are grouped by periods of inactivity.

Using these windowing techniques, Kafka Streams applications can perform time-based aggregations, allowing developers to create complex stream processing solutions capable of real-time analysis.

```
KTable<Windowed<String>, Long> hoppingCounts = inputStream
  .groupByKey()
  .windowedBy(TimeWindows.of(Duration.ofMinutes(5)).advanceBy(Duration.
      ofMinutes(1)))
  .count();
```

These foundational concepts and terminologies provide the basis for understanding and utilizing Kafka Streams effectively. By grasping these elements, developers are better prepared to build sophisticated stream processing applications that leverage Kafka Streams' robust capabilities.

1.4 Use Cases and Benefits of Kafka Streams

Kafka Streams serve as a versatile and powerful library for stream processing, enabling the real-time processing of data streams with minimal overhead and configuration. The flexibility and efficiency of Kafka Streams make it applicable across a broad spectrum of use cases, each leveraging the robust capabilities of the library to manage and analyze data in motion. This section explores the diverse scenarios where Kafka Streams excels and highlights the key benefits it brings to stream processing workflows.

Kafka Streams is particularly adept at handling the following use cases:

- **Real-Time Analytics:** By enabling the analysis of data as it arrives, Kafka Streams facilitates real-time analytics. This capability is crucial for industries such as finance, telecommunications, and e-commerce, where timely insights can drive better decision-making and enhance competitiveness. For example, Kafka Streams can be used to monitor stock prices, detect fraudulent transactions, or analyze customer behavior in real time.
- **Event-Driven Applications:** Kafka Streams supports the development of event-driven applications that respond to real-time events. This is especially useful in microservices architectures, where services often need to react to events generated by other components. Events such as user actions, system notifications, and state changes can trigger immediate processing and workflows.
- **Data Enrichment:** Kafka Streams can enrich incoming data streams by joining them with additional reference data. This is commonly used in scenarios where raw data needs to be augmented with metadata, historical information, or external sources to provide more context and value. For instance, enriching transaction data with customer profiles or product catalog information enhances subsequent analyses and business intelligence tasks.

- **Continuous Transformations:** Kafka Streams allows for the continuous transformation of data as it flows through the system. Transformations like filtering, mapping, and aggregating can be applied to modify data streams dynamically. This is beneficial in data cleaning processes, where incomplete or erroneous data is corrected on-the-fly, and in business logic implementations that require consistent data format adaptations.
- **Session Management:** In scenarios where knowing the context and sequence of events is critical, Kafka Streams can manage sessions effectively. By aggregating events based on time windows or session windows, Kafka Streams helps in understanding user sessions on websites, tracks durations of interactions, and analyzes sequences of actions.
- **Real-Time Monitoring and Alerting:** Kafka Streams is used to monitor the operational status and metrics of systems generating events. It facilitates the detection of anomalies, trend analysis, and the creation of alerting mechanisms to respond to significant events instantly. For instance, in the context of IT infrastructure, Kafka Streams can monitor server logs for error patterns and trigger alerts before issues escalate.

The benefits of Kafka Streams extend across several dimensions, enhancing the stream processing landscape significantly:

- **Scalability:** Kafka Streams is natively scalable. By leveraging the distributed nature of Apache Kafka, Kafka Streams can scale horizontally to process high-throughput data streams. Workloads can be partitioned across multiple instances, ensuring that the processing capacity grows with the data volume.
- **Fault Tolerance:** Kafka Streams provides fault tolerance by utilizing Kafka's distributed logging capability. Kafka Streams applications can recover from failures seamlessly, with state stores and changelogs ensuring no data loss. This resilience is crucial for mission-critical applications where downtime must be minimized.
- **Exactly-Once Semantics:** One of the standout features of Kafka Streams is its support for exactly-once semantics. This ensures that every record is processed exactly once, even in the presence of failures, thus maintaining data integrity and mitigating the risks of duplicate processing typically associated with distributed systems.

- **Operational Simplicity:** Kafka Streams abstracts much of the complexity typically involved in stream processing. Developers can leverage a high-level DSL (Domain Specific Language) to define stream processing topologies, making it accessible for individuals without deep expertise in distributed systems. The integration with Kafka also simplifies the deployment and management of stream processing applications.

- **Integration Capabilities:** Kafka Streams seamlessly integrates with other components of the Apache Kafka ecosystem, such as Kafka Connect and Kafka Producer/Consumer APIs. This interoperability allows for the creation of comprehensive data pipelines, from ingestion to processing to delivery.

- **Low Latency:** Kafka Streams processes data with minimal latency, enabling real-time applications that require immediate data processing and response. The combination of in-memory processing and efficient network communication contributes to maintaining low latency across the entire processing pipeline.

- **Flexibility in Deployment:** Kafka Streams applications can be deployed in various environments, from on-premises data centers to cloud infrastructures. The library's lightweight nature allows it to run on a wide range of systems, accommodating diverse enterprise architectures and deployment strategies.

```
StreamsBuilder builder = new StreamsBuilder();
KStream<String, String> source = builder.stream("input-topic");
KTable<String, Long> counts = source
    .flatMapValues(value -> Arrays.asList(value.toLowerCase().split("\\W+")))
    .groupBy((key, value) -> value)
    .count(Materialized.as("Counts"));

counts.toStream().to("output-topic", Produced.with(Serdes.String(), Serdes.Long()));
KafkaStreams streams = new KafkaStreams(builder.build(), props);
streams.start();
```

```
Example Output:
{
  alert: {
    trigger: "unusual behavior detected",
    timestamp: "2023-10-09T14:30:00Z",
    details: "Sudden spike in transaction volume."
  }
}
```

This example demonstrates how Kafka Streams can be employed to perform real-time analytics by counting occurrences of words in an input stream. Through a combination of transformations and aggregations, the stream processing topology provides insights that can be acted upon immediately or further enriched and stored. The real-time responsiveness and built-in fault tolerance of Kafka Streams make it an invaluable tool for modern data processing requirements.

1.5 Kafka Streams vs Other Stream Processing Frameworks

Kafka Streams stands out among stream processing frameworks by providing a lightweight, yet comprehensive library integrated into Apache Kafka. Distinguishing it from other prominent frameworks requires an examination of architectural nuances, feature sets, and performance benchmarks.

Traditional stream processing frameworks such as Apache Flink, Apache Spark Streaming, and Apache Storm offer extensive capabilities yet operate on different paradigms. Kafka Streams, integrated tightly with Apache Kafka, emphasizes simplicity and ease of embedding in Java applications, thus setting it apart.

Apache Kafka Streams is built on Kafka, leveraging its distributed, scalable, and fault-tolerant architecture. This synergy ensures robust integration, making it adept at processing real-time data streams without the need for separate clusters or extensive configurations. Kafka Streams operates as a client library within an application, enabling seamless development and deployment.

Apache Flink offers a unified stream and batch processing architecture, capable of handling high-throughput, low-latency workloads. Flink's inherent state management and fault tolerance are sophisticated, but it demands a dedicated cluster, including job managers and task managers, which introduces additional operational overhead.

Apache Spark Streaming employs micro-batching to process streams of data, which differs fundamentally from Kafka Streams' record-by-record processing. Although effective for many use cases, Spark Streaming's approach results in higher latency compared to Kafka Streams. Additionally, Spark Streaming relies on a separate Spark cluster, which increases the complexity of deployment and resource management.

Apache Storm provides low-latency processing by using a topology-based model. Each application defines a graph of computations (spouts and bolts), facilitating real-time processing. Storm's architecture requires careful management to handle state and ensure fault tolerance, unlike Kafka Streams where state management is integral and simplified by the Streams API.

To further elucidate the contrasts, consider the following technical comparison:

Feature	Kafka Streams	Apache Flink	Apache Spark Streaming	Apache Storm
Deployment	Embedded within application	Requires dedicated cluster	Requires dedicated cluster	Requires dedicated cluster
Processing Model	Record-by-record	True stream (record-by-record)	Micro-batching	Tuple at a time
State Management	Built-in with Kafka's state stores	Advanced state management	Intermediate state management via RDDs	Custom solutions for state
Latency	Milliseconds	Milliseconds	Seconds	Sub-millisecond
Fault Tolerance	Kafka-backed	Exactly-once semantics	Micro-batch-based recovery	Tuple replay
Complexity	Low for Java developers	High due to complexity	Moderate due to batch integration	High due to topology management
Use Case Suitability	Ideal for Kafka-centric pipelines	Versatile; batch + streaming	Good for batch-oriented workflows	Suitable where low latency is critical

Table 1.1: Technical Comparison of Stream Processing Frameworks

Kafka Streams' lightweight nature does not compromise performance. Its tight integration with Kafka means that data processed by Kafka Streams retains the resilience and distributed nature of Kafka topics. This contrasts with the operational models of Flink, Spark Streaming, and Storm, where external coordination services are frequently necessary.

A typical Kafka Streams application includes several core concepts such as the Kafka Streams DSL (Domain Specific Language), which offers high-level operations like map, filter, and join. This streamlines the development process compared to the often lower-level APIs of other frameworks.

```
public class WordCountApp {
    public static void main(final String[] args) throws Exception {
        Properties props = new Properties();
        props.put(StreamsConfig.APPLICATION_ID_CONFIG, "wordcount-app");
        props.put(StreamsConfig.BOOTSTRAP_SERVERS_CONFIG, "localhost:9092"
            );
        props.put(StreamsConfig.DEFAULT_KEY_SERDE_CLASS_CONFIG, Serdes.
            String().getClass());
        props.put(StreamsConfig.DEFAULT_VALUE_SERDE_CLASS_CONFIG,
            Serdes.String().getClass());
```

```
        StreamsBuilder builder = new StreamsBuilder();
        KStream<String, String> source = builder.stream("streams-plaintext-input");

        KTable<String, Long> counts = source
            .flatMapValues(value -> Arrays.asList(value.toLowerCase().split("\\W+")))
            .groupBy((key, value) -> value)
            .count(Materialized.as("counts-store"));

        counts.toStream().to("streams-wordcount-output", Produced.with(Serdes.String
            (), Serdes.Long()));

        KafkaStreams streams = new KafkaStreams(builder.build(), props);
        streams.start();
    }
}
```

Upon execution, the above program will produce output similar to the following:

```
(word, 1)
(count, 2)
(app, 1)
(word, 3)
```

This approach contrasts with the operational intricacies and learning curve associated with frameworks like Flink, Spark Streaming, and Storm. Each framework's strengths cater to different needs, but Kafka Streams' distinctive design philosophy and seamless Kafka integration position it uniquely in the domain of stream processing.

1.6 Getting Started with Kafka Streams

Kafka Streams is a powerful library for building real-time, event-driven applications. Understanding how to start with Kafka Streams involves setting up the necessary environment, configuring the Kafka Streams application, and developing a basic stream processing topology. This section will guide you through these steps with meticulous detail to ensure a robust foundational understanding.

A typical Kafka Streams application consists of a source, a processing logic, and a sink. The source reads from Kafka topics, the processing logic transforms or enriches the data, and the sink writes the processed data back to Kafka topics. We will start by setting up the environment required to run Kafka Streams applications.

- Install Java Development Kit (JDK)

- Install Apache Kafka

- Set up a Maven project

To begin, ensure that you have installed the Java Development Kit (JDK) version 8 or later. Kafka Streams is a Java library; hence, JDK is a prerequisite.

To install Apache Kafka, download it from the official Apache Kafka website. Extract the archive and navigate to the Kafka directory. Start the ZooKeeper service and Kafka broker by running the following commands in separate terminal windows:

```
bin/zookeeper-server-start.sh config/zookeeper.properties
bin/kafka-server-start.sh config/server.properties
```

Next, set up a Maven project. Maven will manage the Kafka Streams dependencies. Create a new directory for your project and navigate to it. Use the following command to generate a new Maven project:

```
mvn archetype:generate -DgroupId=com.example -DartifactId=kafka-streams-
    quickstart -DarchetypeArtifactId=maven-archetype-quickstart -DinteractiveMode
    =false
```

Navigate to the project directory and open the pom.xml file to add Kafka Streams dependencies:

```
<dependencies>
    <dependency>
        <groupId>org.apache.kafka</groupId>
        <artifactId>kafka-streams</artifactId>
        <version>2.8.0</version>
    </dependency>
    <dependency>
        <groupId>org.apache.kafka</groupId>
        <artifactId>kafka-clients</artifactId>
        <version>2.8.0</version>
    </dependency>
    <dependency>
        <groupId>org.slf4j</groupId>
        <artifactId>slf4j-api</artifactId>
        <version>1.7.30</version>
    </dependency>
    <dependency>
        <groupId>org.slf4j</groupId>
        <artifactId>slf4j-log4j12</artifactId>
        <version>1.7.30</version>
    </dependency>
</dependencies>
```

Once the dependencies are included in your pom.xml, build the project using:

```
mvn clean package
```

Now, proceed to develop the Kafka Streams application. Create a Java class called KafkaStreamsExample inside the src/main/java/com/example directory:

```
package com.example;

import org.apache.kafka.streams.KafkaStreams;
import org.apache.kafka.streams.StreamsBuilder;
import org.apache.kafka.streams.StreamsConfig;
import org.apache.kafka.streams.kstream.KStream;

import java.util.Properties;

public class KafkaStreamsExample {
    public static void main(String[] args) {
        Properties props = new Properties();
        props.put(StreamsConfig.APPLICATION_ID_CONFIG, "kafka-streams-
            example");
        props.put(StreamsConfig.BOOTSTRAP_SERVERS_CONFIG, "localhost:9092"
            );
        props.put(StreamsConfig.DEFAULT_KEY_SERDE_CLASS_CONFIG,
                org.apache.kafka.common.serialization.Serdes.String().getClass());
        props.put(StreamsConfig.DEFAULT_VALUE_SERDE_CLASS_CONFIG,
                org.apache.kafka.common.serialization.Serdes.String().getClass());

        StreamsBuilder builder = new StreamsBuilder();
        KStream<String, String> source = builder.stream("input-topic");
        source.to("output-topic");

        KafkaStreams streams = new KafkaStreams(builder.build(), props);
        streams.start();

        Runtime.getRuntime().addShutdownHook(new Thread(streams::close));
    }
}
```

Within this class, we configure the Kafka Streams application through StreamsConfig. The APPLICATION_ID_CONFIG parameter uniquely identifies the streams application. The BOOTSTRAP_SERVERS_CONFIG points to our Kafka broker.

In this example, first, we create a StreamsBuilder instance, which is used to construct the processing topology. KStream<String, String> source = builder.stream("input-topic"); reads data from the input-topic. Finally, source.to("output-topic"); writes the data to the output-topic.

To run the Kafka Streams application, execute the KafkaStreamsExample's main method. The application will start processing records from the input-topic and write them to the output-topic.

To test the integration, create the Kafka topics if not already available. In a separate terminal window, use the following commands to create input-topic and output-topic:

```
bin/kafka-topics.sh --create --topic input-topic --bootstrap-server localhost:9092 --
```

```
    partitions 1 --replication-factor 1
bin/kafka-topics.sh --create --topic output-topic --bootstrap-server localhost:9092 --
    partitions 1 --replication-factor 1
```

Produce some messages to the input-topic:

```
bin/kafka-console-producer.sh --topic input-topic --bootstrap-server localhost:9092
>hello
>world
```

Consume messages from the output-topic to verify that the Kafka Streams application processes them correctly:

```
bin/kafka-console-consumer.sh --topic output-topic --bootstrap-server localhost:9092 --
    from-beginning
```

hello
world

You should see the same messages hello and world in the consumer terminal window that you produced into the input-topic.

By ensuring each component is correctly set up and understanding the flow from source to sink, you now have a Kafka Streams application up and running, capable of reading data from a topic, processing it, and writing the result back to another topic.

1.7 Hello World Example

To illustrate the fundamental operations of Kafka Streams, we will develop a simple "Hello World" application. This example will demonstrate the basic workflow of reading data from a Kafka topic, processing the data via a Kafka Streams topology, and then writing the processed data back to another Kafka topic.

We begin by setting up the project structure and dependencies. Create a new Maven project, ensuring the necessary dependencies for Kafka Streams are included. Your pom.xml file should contain the following dependencies:

```
<dependencies>
    <dependency>
        <groupId>org.apache.kafka</groupId>
        <artifactId>kafka-streams</artifactId>
        <version>${kafka.version}</version>
    </dependency>
    <dependency>
        <groupId>org.apache.kafka</groupId>
        <artifactId>kafka-clients</artifactId>
```

```
        <version>${kafka.version}</version>
    </dependency>
    <dependency>
        <groupId>org.slf4j</groupId>
        <artifactId>slf4j-api</artifactId>
        <version>${slf4j.version}</version>
    </dependency>
    <dependency>
        <groupId>org.slf4j</groupId>
        <artifactId>slf4j-log4j12</artifactId>
        <version>${slf4j.version}</version>
    </dependency>
    <dependency>
        <groupId>log4j</groupId>
        <artifactId>log4j</artifactId>
        <version>${log4j.version}</version>
    </dependency>
</dependencies>
```

Next, configure the necessary Kafka Streams properties. These properties include information about the Kafka broker, the application ID, the default key and value serializers, and deserializers. These properties are critical for connecting our application to the Kafka cluster and correctly serializing the messages.

```
Properties props = new Properties();
props.put(StreamsConfig.APPLICATION_ID_CONFIG, "hello-world-app");
props.put(StreamsConfig.BOOTSTRAP_SERVERS_CONFIG, "localhost:9092");
props.put(StreamsConfig.DEFAULT_KEY_SERDE_CLASS_CONFIG, Serdes.String()
    .getClass());
props.put(StreamsConfig.DEFAULT_VALUE_SERDE_CLASS_CONFIG, Serdes.
    String().getClass());
```

The fundamental structure of a Kafka Streams application revolves around a streams topology. This topology defines the processing steps of stream data which flow from sources (Kafka topics) to sinks (another set of Kafka topics). In our example, we will read data from an input topic, transform the data, and then write the processed data to an output topic.

```
StreamsBuilder builder = new StreamsBuilder();
KStream<String, String> source = builder.stream("input-topic");
KStream<String, String> uppercased = source.mapValues(value -> value.toUpperCase
    ());
uppercased.to("output-topic");
```

Explanation of the code snippet:

- The StreamsBuilder object is responsible for constructing the stream processing topology.
- The builder.stream("input-topic") call specifies that the source of our stream is the "input-topic".

- The mapValues function applies a transformation to the values of each record in the stream. In this case, we convert each value to uppercase.
- The to("output-topic") method specifies the destination topic where the processed records will be written.

To run this Kafka Streams application, we need to create and start a KafkaStreams instance with the configuration properties and topology defined above. The following code initiates the Kafka Streams instance and starts the stream processing:

```
KafkaStreams streams = new KafkaStreams(builder.build(), props);

// Attach shutdown handler to catch control-c and stop the stream cleanly
Runtime.getRuntime().addShutdownHook(new Thread(streams::close));

// Start the stream
streams.start();
```

This code initiates a Kafka Streams instance, attaches a shutdown hook to ensure the streaming process stops gracefully when the application is terminated, and starts the stream processing.

To verify that your "Hello World" Kafka Streams application functions as expected, ensure Kafka is running and create the appropriate input and output topics using the Kafka CLI tools:

```
bin/kafka-topics.sh --create --topic input-topic --bootstrap-server localhost:9092 --replication-factor 1 --partitions 1
bin/kafka-topics.sh --create --topic output-topic --bootstrap-server localhost:9092 --replication-factor 1 --partitions 1
```

With Kafka and the topics in place, you can now produce some test messages to the "input-topic" and consume the processed output from the "output-topic". Use the following commands to produce and consume messages via the Kafka console producer and consumer:

```
# Producing a message to input-topic
bin/kafka-console-producer.sh --broker-list localhost:9092 --topic input-topic
> hello world

# Consuming from output-topic
bin/kafka-console-consumer.sh --bootstrap-server localhost:9092 --topic output-topic --from-beginning
HELLO WORLD
```

This concludes the practical implementation of the "Hello World" example using Kafka Streams. The example demonstrated setting up the project, defining the stream processing topology, and executing the Kafka Streams application to process data.

Chapter 2

Setting Up Your Kafka Streams Environment

This chapter outlines the essential steps for setting up a Kafka Streams development environment. It begins with a discussion of system requirements and dependencies, followed by instructions for installing Apache Kafka and Zookeeper. The chapter details the installation of the Kafka Streams library, configuring Kafka brokers and topics, and running Kafka and Zookeeper services. It also covers configuring your development environment and provides guidance on setting up your first Kafka Streams application.

2.1 System Requirements and Dependencies

Setting up a Kafka Streams environment begins with ensuring that your system meets the necessary requirements and dependencies. These prerequisites are essential for smooth operation and development of Kafka Streams applications.

Hardware Requirements: To run Kafka Streams efficiently, your system should meet the following minimum hardware specifications:

- **CPU:** A multi-core processor is recommended. Dual-core processors may suffice for small-scale development and testing, but for production environments, a quad-core or higher processor is advisable.

- **Memory:** At least 8GB of RAM is recommended. For large-scale applications, 16GB or more is preferable to handle multiple streams and large datasets efficiently.
- **Disk Space:** A minimum of 100GB of disk space is suggested, as Kafka retains data on disk, and this space can be rapidly consumed by log files.
- **Network:** A reliable network connection is crucial, especially in a distributed setup where brokers communicate over the network.

Software Requirements: In addition to hardware, specific software components and dependencies must be installed and correctly configured:

- **Operating System:** Kafka Streams runs on various Unix-based systems including Linux and macOS. While it can run on Windows, it is generally recommended to use a Unix-based OS for production environments.
- **Java Development Kit (JDK):** Kafka Streams requires Java 8 or later. Ensure that JDK is installed by checking the version:

```
java -version
```

  The output should indicate a version of Java 1.8 or higher:

```
java version "1.8.0_221"
Java(TM) SE Runtime Environment (build 1.8.0_221-b11)
Java HotSpot(TM) 64-Bit Server VM (build 25.221-b11, mixed mode)
```

- **Apache Kafka:** Kafka Streams is built on top of Apache Kafka, so the Kafka binaries must be installed. The version of Kafka should be compatible with the Kafka Streams library you intend to use.
- **Zookeeper:** Kafka uses Zookeeper for coordination between brokers. It is necessary to install and configure Zookeeper before starting Kafka.

Dependencies: Several dependencies must be included in your project to use Kafka Streams. These dependencies are typically managed using build automation tools such as Maven or Gradle.

For Maven, include the Kafka Streams dependency in your pom.xml:

```
<dependency>
    <groupId>org.apache.kafka</groupId>
    <artifactId>kafka-streams</artifactId>
    <version>2.8.0</version>
</dependency>
```

For Gradle, add the dependency in your build.gradle file:

```
dependencies {
    implementation 'org.apache.kafka:kafka-streams:2.8.0'
}
```

Ensure these dependencies are compatible with your Kafka broker version to avoid runtime issues and incompatibilities.

Additional Libraries and Tools: Consider installing the following tools and libraries that can enhance development and debugging:

- **Kafka Command Line Tools:** These tools are part of the Kafka binaries and provide capabilities to create topics, produce and consume messages, and monitor your Kafka environment.
- **Confluent CLI:** A command-line interface provided by Confluent that simplifies interacting with Kafka clusters.
- **Monitoring Tools:** Tools such as Prometheus and Grafana can be invaluable for monitoring the health and performance of your Kafka Streams application.

Appropriate setup and verification of these requirements and dependencies are crucial steps in preparing your environment to run Kafka Streams applications. They ensure that all necessary components work harmoniously and help prevent issues during the development and deployment phases.

2.2 Installing Apache Kafka

Installing Apache Kafka involves several steps, starting with choosing an appropriate installation method and followed by configuring the necessary settings to ensure a smooth and functional setup. This section provides a step-by-step guide for installing Apache Kafka on a Linux-based system, which is the most common environment used for Kafka deployments.

Step 1: Downloading Apache Kafka

Begin by downloading the latest stable release of Apache Kafka from the official Apache Kafka website. Open a terminal and execute the following commands to download and extract Kafka:

```
wget https://downloads.apache.org/kafka/3.0.0/kafka_2.13-3.0.0.tgz
tar -xzf kafka_2.13-3.0.0.tgz
cd kafka_2.13-3.0.0
```

This code snippet downloads Kafka version 3.0.0 for Scala 2.13, extracts the contents of the downloaded file, and navigates into the extracted Kafka directory.

Step 2: Setting Up Kafka Environment Variables

To make it easier to run Kafka commands from any location, set up the environment variables by editing your .bashrc or .profile file:

```
# Open the .bashrc file in a text editor
nano ~/.bashrc

# Add the following lines at the end of the file
export KAFKA_HOME=/path/to/kafka_2.13-3.0.0
export PATH=$PATH:$KAFKA_HOME/bin

# Apply the changes
source ~/.bashrc
```

Replace /path/to/kafka_2.13-3.0.0 with the actual path where Kafka was extracted.

Step 3: Configuring Kafka

Before starting Kafka, ensure that the configuration files are set up correctly:

- server.properties: This file is located in the config directory and contains the configuration settings for the Kafka broker.
- zookeeper.properties: This file contains the settings for Zookeeper, a critical component that Kafka relies on.

To modify the server.properties file, use a text editor:

```
nano $KAFKA_HOME/config/server.properties
```

Ensure the following key settings are configured appropriately:

- broker.id: A unique identifier for the Kafka broker within the cluster.
- log.dirs: The directory where Kafka will store its logs.

- zookeeper.connect: The connection string for Zookeeper.

For a basic single-node setup, you might use the following configuration:

```
broker.id=0
log.dirs=/tmp/kafka-logs
zookeeper.connect=localhost:2181
```

Step 4: Starting Zookeeper and Kafka Servers

Kafka relies on Zookeeper for management and coordination. First, start the Zookeeper server:

```
# Start Zookeeper
$KAFKA_HOME/bin/zookeeper-server-start.sh $KAFKA_HOME/config/zookeeper.
    properties
```

In a separate terminal, start the Kafka broker:

```
# Start Kafka broker
$KAFKA_HOME/bin/kafka-server-start.sh $KAFKA_HOME/config/server.properties
```

The servers should now be running, with logs being output to the terminal. Open another terminal to interact with Kafka.

Step 5: Verifying the Installation

After starting both servers, verify the Kafka installation by creating a topic, producing, and consuming messages.

Create a sample topic named test:

```
$KAFKA_HOME/bin/kafka-topics.sh --create --topic test --bootstrap-server localhost
    :9092 --partitions 1 --replication-factor 1
```

Confirm that the topic was created:

```
$KAFKA_HOME/bin/kafka-topics.sh --list --bootstrap-server localhost:9092
```

Produce a message to the test topic:

```
$KAFKA_HOME/bin/kafka-console-producer.sh --topic test --bootstrap-server
    localhost:9092
> Hello, Kafka!
```

Consume the message from the test topic:

```
$KAFKA_HOME/bin/kafka-console-consumer.sh --topic test --from-beginning --
    bootstrap-server localhost:9092
```

The terminal should display the message:

```
Hello, Kafka!
```

This confirms that Apache Kafka has been successfully installed and is operational.

2.3 Setting Up Zookeeper

ZooKeeper is a centralized service for maintaining configuration information, naming, providing distributed synchronization, and providing group services. It is a crucial component in distributed systems, particularly in Kafka, where it is used for managing and coordinating Kafka brokers. To ensure a seamless setup of ZooKeeper, follow these detailed steps:

Download the ZooKeeper distribution from the Apache ZooKeeper website. Choose the stable release that is compatible with your operating system. In this guide, version 3.7.0 is used as an example. Extract the downloaded archive to a desired installation directory.

```
tar -zxf apache-zookeeper-3.7.0-bin.tar.gz -C /opt/
cd /opt/apache-zookeeper-3.7.0-bin
```

The next step involves configuring ZooKeeper. ZooKeeper uses a set of configuration files to define its operational parameters. The primary configuration file is zoo.cfg. Create a configuration directory within the extracted ZooKeeper directory, then create and edit the zoo.cfg file using a text editor of your choice.

```
mkdir -p /opt/apache-zookeeper-3.7.0-bin/conf
nano /opt/apache-zookeeper-3.7.0-bin/conf/zoo.cfg
```

The contents of the zoo.cfg file should resemble the following template:

```
# The number of milliseconds of each tick
tickTime=2000

# The number of ticks that the initial
# synchronization phase can take
initLimit=10

# The number of ticks that can pass between
# sending a request and getting an acknowledgement
syncLimit=5

# The directory where the snapshot is stored.
dataDir=/var/lib/zookeeper

# The port at which the clients will connect
clientPort=2181

# Increase the maximum client connections.
# This is particularly useful in systems
# with a large number of Kafka partitions
maxClientCnxns=60
```

- tickTime: Basic time unit in milliseconds used by ZooKeeper.
- initLimit: Number of ticks that the ZooKeeper servers in quorum have to connect and sync.
- syncLimit: Number of ticks that can pass between sending a request and getting an acknowledgment.
- dataDir: Directory to store the in-memory database snapshots.
- clientPort: Port to listen for client connections.
- maxClientCnxns: Limits the number of concurrent client connections.

Ensure that the dataDir specified in the zoo.cfg file exists and is writable by the ZooKeeper process.

```
mkdir -p /var/lib/zookeeper
chmod -R 755 /var/lib/zookeeper
```

After configuration, start ZooKeeper using the provided script. This script initiates the ZooKeeper service with the specified zoo.cfg file.

```
/opt/apache-zookeeper-3.7.0-bin/bin/zkServer.sh start /opt/apache-zookeeper-3.7.0-bin
    /conf/zoo.cfg
```

The console output should indicate that ZooKeeper has started successfully.

```
ZooKeeper JMX enabled by default
Using config: /opt/apache-zookeeper-3.7.0-bin/conf/zoo.cfg
Starting zookeeper ... STARTED
```

To verify that ZooKeeper is running, you can check the status of the ZooKeeper service using the following command:

```
/opt/apache-zookeeper-3.7.0-bin/bin/zkServer.sh status
```

The expected output should confirm that ZooKeeper is running:

```
ZooKeeper JMX enabled by default
Using config: /opt/apache-zookeeper-3.7.0-bin/conf/zoo.cfg
Mode: standalone
```

For production environments, consider deploying ZooKeeper in a replicated mode (ensemble) to ensure high availability and fault tolerance. Each ZooKeeper server in the ensemble must have a unique ID and additional settings in the zoo.cfg file to support the ensemble configuration. Each server's zoo.cfg should have entries like:

```
server.1=zookeeper1:2888:3888
server.2=zookeeper2:2888:3888
server.3=zookeeper3:2888:3888
```

Where 2888 is the port used for follower connections, and 3888 is for leader election.

Deployment and management of ZooKeeper in a production environment encompass further aspects such as monitoring, security configurations, and automated failover strategies, which should be explored to ensure operational robustness and resilience.

2.4 Installing Kafka Streams Library

The Kafka Streams library is an essential component for building applications and microservices that process data stored in Kafka topics. The installation process is straightforward, but it is crucial to adhere to the specific steps to ensure a smooth setup. This section elaborates on downloading, installing, and configuring the Kafka Streams library, focusing on Java since Kafka Streams is a part of the Kafka project and primarily supports Java applications.

Before proceeding with the installation, ensure that you have the following prerequisites configured:

- Apache Kafka: It is recommended to use the latest stable version.
- Java Development Kit (JDK): Ensure that the JDK version matches the version requirements specified by the Kafka Streams library.

- Integrated Development Environment (IDE): Any Java IDE that supports Maven or Gradle can be used. Examples are IntelliJ IDEA or Eclipse.
- Apache Maven or Gradle: These build automation tools are necessary for managing dependencies.

To install the Kafka Streams library, you need to configure your project's build tool to include the Kafka Streams dependency. This guide covers the configuration for both Maven and Gradle.

Using Maven:

- Open the pom.xml file in your project directory.
- Add the following dependency to the <dependencies> section:

```
<dependency>
    <groupId>org.apache.kafka</groupId>
    <artifactId>kafka-streams</artifactId>
    <version>3.3.1</version>
</dependency>
```

Ensure that the version number corresponds to the installed Kafka version. After saving the changes to pom.xml, Maven will automatically download and add the Kafka Streams library to your project.

Using Gradle:

- Open the build.gradle file in your project directory.
- Add the following line to the dependencies section:

```
implementation 'org.apache.kafka:kafka-streams:3.3.1'
```

Similarly to Maven, ensure the version number matches the installed Kafka version. Save the changes, and Gradle will manage the dependency download and inclusion.

Once the Kafka Streams library has been added to your project, it is necessary to verify the installation by running a simple Kafka Streams application. Create a new Java class named KafkaStreamsExample within your project and implement the following code:

```
import org.apache.kafka.streams.KafkaStreams;
import org.apache.kafka.streams.StreamsBuilder;
import org.apache.kafka.streams.StreamsConfig;
```

```
import org.apache.kafka.streams.Topology;

import java.util.Properties;

public class KafkaStreamsExample {
    public static void main(String[] args) {
        Properties props = new Properties();
        props.put(StreamsConfig.APPLICATION_ID_CONFIG, "streams-example");
        props.put(StreamsConfig.BOOTSTRAP_SERVERS_CONFIG, "localhost:9092"
            );
        props.put(StreamsConfig.DEFAULT_KEY_SERDE_CLASS_CONFIG, "org.
            apache.kafka.common.serialization.Serdes$StringSerde");
        props.put(StreamsConfig.DEFAULT_VALUE_SERDE_CLASS_CONFIG, "org.
            apache.kafka.common.serialization.Serdes$StringSerde");

        StreamsBuilder builder = new StreamsBuilder();
        builder.stream("input-topic").to("output-topic");

        Topology topology = builder.build();
        KafkaStreams streams = new KafkaStreams(topology, props);

        streams.start();

        Runtime.getRuntime().addShutdownHook(new Thread(streams::close));
    }
}
```

This example demonstrates basic usage of the Kafka Streams library by defining a simple topology that consumes messages from an input topic and produces them to an output topic. Ensure your Kafka cluster is up and running with the appropriate topics created. The key configuration properties include:

- StreamsConfig.APPLICATION_ID_CONFIG: Unique identifier for the application.
- StreamsConfig.BOOTSTRAP_SERVER_CONFIG: Kafka cluster address.
- StreamsConfig.DEFAULT_KEY_SERDE_CLASS_CONFIG and StreamsConfig.DEFAULT_VALUE_SERDE_CLASS_-CONFIG: Specify the serializers and deserializers for keys and values.

Compile and run your application using your IDE. If there are no errors and the application starts successfully, it indicates that the Kafka Streams library has been installed correctly.

By completing this setup, you are now prepared to develop more advanced stream processing applications utilizing Kafka Streams.

2.5 Configuring Kafka Brokers and Topics

The configuration of Kafka brokers and topics is a critical step in ensuring the proper functioning of your Kafka Streams applications. Proper configuration ensures that data flows smoothly between producers and consumers, while also providing the necessary reliability and scalability. Kafka brokers are the backbone of the message system, managing the storage and retrieval of message data. Topics are the categories or feed names to which messages are published. This section will detail the configuration process for both brokers and topics.

Start by configuring the Kafka broker settings. Kafka brokers are configured using a properties file, typically named server.properties. Key configuration parameters allow you to tailor the broker's behavior to suit your application's needs.

```
# A unique identifier for each broker in the cluster
broker.id=0

# The directory where Kafka data is stored
log.dirs=/var/lib/kafka/data

# The port on which the broker will accept client connections
port=9092

# Zookeeper connection string, containing the host:port pairs for ZooKeeper servers
zookeeper.connect=localhost:2181

# The number of partitions for default topics
num.partitions=3

# Logs retention time: the number of hours to keep a log file before it is discarded
log.retention.hours=168

# The maximum size of a log segment file
log.segment.bytes=1073741824

# The interval at which to check for log segment deletion
log.retention.check.interval.ms=300000
```

After configuring the server.properties file, there are essential aspects that require attention to optimize performance and security:

- **Broker Identification:** The broker.id should be unique across all brokers in the cluster. This allows each broker to be uniquely identified.
- **Storage Directories:** The log.dirs parameter specifies where the Kafka log data will be stored. This directory should be on a storage system optimized for high I/O operations.

- **Networking:** The port parameter sets the TCP port that the broker will use. Default is 9092. Ensure firewalls or other network devices allow traffic on this port.

- **ZooKeeper Connection:** The zookeeper.connect parameter lists the ZooKeeper instances used by the broker. For high availability, a list of comma-separated host:port pairs should be used.

- **Partitions and Segmentation:** num.partitions defines the default partition count per topic. Efficient partitioning can enhance performance and parallelism.

- **Log Management:** Log properties such as log.retention.hours, log.segment.bytes, and log.retention.check.interval.ms control how logs are managed, influencing both storage capacity and log performance.

Next, create and configure Kafka topics. Topics are distributed across partitions, and each partition can be hosted on various brokers, providing fault tolerance and parallel processing.

To create a topic, use the kafka-topics.sh script included in the Kafka distribution. Below is an example command to create a topic named test-topic with three partitions and a replication factor of one:

```
$ bin/kafka-topics.sh --create --topic test-topic --partitions 3 --replication-factor 1 --
    bootstrap-server localhost:9092
```

Here, –create indicates a new topic creation, –topic test-topic denotes the topic name, –partitions specifies the number of partitions, –replication-factor sets the replication factor, and –bootstrap-server localhost:9092 provides the broker's address.

After creating the topic, describe it to verify its configuration:

```
$ bin/kafka-topics.sh --describe --topic test-topic --bootstrap-server localhost:9092
```

Expected output:

```
Topic: test-topic       PartitionCount: 3       ReplicationFactor: 1    Configs:
        Topic: test-topic       Partition: 0    Leader: 0       Replicas: 0     Isr: 0
        Topic: test-topic       Partition: 1    Leader: 0       Replicas: 0     Isr: 0
        Topic: test-topic       Partition: 2    Leader: 0       Replicas: 0     Isr: 0
```

This output confirms that test-topic has been created with three partitions. The Leader field indicates the broker hosting the partition, Replicas lists the brokers replicating the partition, and Isr (In-Sync Replicas) shows the replicas currently in sync.

For efficient operation and scalability, fine-tuning topic-level configurations might be necessary:

```
$ bin/kafka-configs.sh --alter --entity-type topics --entity-name test-topic --add-config
    retention.ms=604800000
```

This command adjusts the retention.ms property to 7 days (604800000 milliseconds) for test-topic. Fine-tuning such parameters can improve performance and resource utilization.

Configuring Kafka brokers and topics precisely equips Kafka Streams applications with the reliability and efficiency required for production environments, laying the groundwork for advanced operations and optimizations in subsequent stages.

2.6 Running Kafka and Zookeeper

To initiate the Kafka Streams application development process, it is indispensable to ensure that both Kafka and Zookeeper services are up and running. These services are foundational to the operation of your Kafka Streams environment. This section elucidates the procedural syntax and semantics of starting Kafka and Zookeeper, providing an organized approach to execute these services.

Starting Zookeeper, a centralized service for maintaining configuration information, naming, providing distributed synchronization, and providing group services. Kafka leverages Zookeeper to manage and coordinate the brokers. Begin by navigating to the directory where Kafka is installed.

```
$ cd ~/kafka
$ bin/zookeeper-server-start.sh config/zookeeper.properties
```

Upon starting Zookeeper, the terminal will display logs indicating that the service is running. It is critical to verify that there are no errors in the output to ensure that Zookeeper has started successfully. Properly running logs should look similar to:

```
[2023-02-18 08:40:30,717] INFO Reading configuration from: config/zookeeper.properties
[2023-02-18 08:40:30,814] INFO Starting zookeeper (org.apache.zookeeper.server.ZooKeeperServerMain)
[2023-02-18 08:40:30,982] INFO binding to port 0.0.0.0/0.0.0.0:2181 (org.apache.zookeeper.server.nio.NIOServerCnxnFactory)
```

These log entries indicate that Zookeeper is running on port 2181. It will continue running in the foreground. You may wish to keep this terminal open to monitor the Zookeeper logs for any pertinent runtime information.

Next, launch the Kafka broker in a separate terminal window. The Kafka broker is responsible for receiving messages from producers, assigning offsets to messages, and committing the messages to disk. The default configuration is sufficient for many setups, but this can be customized if necessary.

```
$ cd ~/kafka
$ bin/kafka-server-start.sh config/server.properties
```

Once initiated, the terminal will output logs of the Kafka broker setup. It is crucial to monitor these logs initially to confirm successful startup. Typical log entries to expect are as follows:

```
[2023-02-18 08:41:15,132] INFO KafkaConfig values:...
[2023-02-18 08:41:16,219] INFO [KafkaServer id=0] started (kafka.server.KafkaServer)
[2023-02-18 08:41:16,375] INFO [SocketServer ioThread=2] Successfully accepted connection from /127.0.0.1:9092
```

The above log entries confirm that the Kafka broker has started, listening on port 9092, which is the default port. Ensure the logs do not display any error messages. Both services, Zookeeper and Kafka, need to be running to facilitate Kafka Streams operations.

After starting both services, it is prudent to verify their operation. This can be achieved by listing the topics in the Kafka broker, which should return an indication that the broker is operational and communicable.

```
$ bin/kafka-topics.sh --list --zookeeper localhost:2181
```

If the services are running correctly, available topics will be listed (which may show an empty list if no topics have been created yet). A response indicating that a connection was not possible would necessitate re-examining the configuration and logs to rectify any issues.

These steps ensure the fundamental components of the Kafka Streams environment are correctly configured and running. It is essential to keep the terminals open to monitor the logs, which provide real-time feedback and help identify potential issues swiftly. Following these procedures meticulously assures a robust foundation for developing applications using Kafka Streams.

2.7 Configuring Your Development Environment

Configuring your development environment for Kafka Streams involves several critical steps to ensure that your environment is optimized for both development and testing. This section provides detailed instructions on setting up your Integrated Development Environment (IDE), installing necessary plugins, configuring the build tools, and preparing the environment variables. For the purposes of this section, we will use IntelliJ IDEA as the IDE and Maven as the build automation tool, given their popularity and robust feature sets.

First, ensure that you have the latest version of IntelliJ IDEA installed. If you haven't installed it yet, you can download it from the JetBrains website. Choose the Ultimate edition if you're working on a commercial project; otherwise, the Community edition will suffice for most purposes.

Once IntelliJ IDEA is installed, open it and configure the necessary plugins. Plugins for working with Apache Kafka, Maven, and version control systems will be particularly useful.

- Navigate to File → Settings → Plugins.
- Search for the Apache Kafka plugin and install it.
- Search for the Maven plugin and ensure it is installed and enabled.
- Install any version control plugins you might need, such as Git or Subversion.

Next, create a new Maven project. This will involve specifying the project's GroupId, ArtifactId, and the version of the project. Additionally, we need to update the pom.xml file to include dependencies required for Kafka Streams development.

```
<dependency>
    <groupId>org.apache.kafka</groupId>
    <artifactId>kafka-streams</artifactId>
    <version>3.0.0</version>
</dependency>
<dependency>
    <groupId>org.apache.kafka</groupId>
    <artifactId>kafka-clients</artifactId>
    <version>3.0.0</version>
</dependency>
<dependency>
    <groupId>org.apache.kafka</groupId>
    <artifactId>kafka-streams-test-utils</artifactId>
    <version>3.0.0</version>
</dependency>
```

Ensure you have the Java Development Kit (JDK) installed. Kafka Streams requires JDK version 8 or higher. Set the JDK path in IntelliJ IDEA.

- Navigate to File → Project Structure → Project.
- Set the Project SDK to your installed JDK 8 or higher.

Configure the environment variables for Kafka and Zookeeper. This helps in seamless execution of Kafka-related commands from any terminal window.

```
export KAFKA_HOME=/path/to/kafka
export PATH=$PATH:$KAFKA_HOME/bin
export KAFKA_LOG4J_OPTS="-Dlog4j.configuration=file:/path/to/kafka/config/
    log4j.properties"
```

Within your project, create the following directory structure to organize your source code and resource files:

```
src/
|-- main/
|   |-- java/
|   |   `-- your/package/name/
|   |       `-- Application.java
|   |-- resources/
|       `-- application.properties
|-- test/
    |-- java/
        `-- your/package/name/
            `-- ApplicationTest.java
```

The application.properties file in the resources directory will be used to store your Kafka Streams configurations. Add the following sample properties to it:

```
application.id=my-kafka-streams-app
bootstrap.servers=localhost:9092
default.key.serde=org.apache.kafka.common.serialization.Serdes$StringSerde
default.value.serde=org.apache.kafka.common.serialization.Serdes$StringSerde
```

Now, let's create a simple Kafka Streams application. Open Application.java and add the following baseline code to initialize and start a Kafka Streams instance:

```
package your.package.name;

import org.apache.kafka.streams.KafkaStreams;
import org.apache.kafka.streams.StreamsBuilder;
import org.apache.kafka.streams.StreamsConfig;
import java.util.Properties;

public class Application {
    public static void main(String[] args) {
```

```
        Properties props = new Properties();
        props.put(StreamsConfig.APPLICATION_ID_CONFIG, "my-kafka-streams-
            app");
        props.put(StreamsConfig.BOOTSTRAP_SERVERS_CONFIG, "localhost:9092"
            );
        props.put(StreamsConfig.DEFAULT_KEY_SERDE_CLASS_CONFIG, "org.
            apache.kafka.common.serialization.Serdes$StringSerde");
        props.put(StreamsConfig.DEFAULT_VALUE_SERDE_CLASS_CONFIG, "org.
            apache.kafka.common.serialization.Serdes$StringSerde");

        StreamsBuilder builder = new StreamsBuilder();
        builder.stream("input-topic").to("output-topic");

        KafkaStreams streams = new KafkaStreams(builder.build(), props);
        streams.start();
    }
}
```

To verify that everything is set up correctly, you can write a simple test case in ApplicationTest.java using the Kafka Streams Test Utils.

```
package your.package.name;

import org.apache.kafka.common.serialization.Serdes;
import org.apache.kafka.streams.StreamsBuilder;
import org.apache.kafka.streams.Topology;
import org.apache.kafka.streams.TopologyTestDriver;
import org.apache.kafka.streams.test.ConsumerRecordFactory;
import org.apache.kafka.streams.test.OutputVerifier;
import org.apache.kafka.streams.test.TestRecord;
import org.junit.Test;

public class ApplicationTest {
    @Test
    public void testStreamProcessing() {
        StreamsBuilder builder = new StreamsBuilder();
        builder.stream("input-topic").to("output-topic");

        Topology topology = builder.build();
        TopologyTestDriver testDriver = new TopologyTestDriver(topology, new
            Properties());

        ConsumerRecordFactory<String, String> factory = new
            ConsumerRecordFactory<>(
              "input-topic", Serdes.String().serializer(), Serdes.String().serializer());

        testDriver.pipeInput(factory.create("input-topic", "key", "value"));

        OutputVerifier.compareKeyValue(testDriver.readOutput("output-topic", Serdes.
            String().deserializer(), Serdes.String().deserializer()),
              "key", "value");

        testDriver.close();
    }
}
```

Run the test cases to ensure that your Kafka Streams application is functioning as expected. If the test passes, your development environment is properly configured.

This meticulous setup guarantees that you have a robust foundation for developing, testing, and debugging Kafka Streams applications efficiently. Following these steps will ensure a smooth development experience free from common pitfalls related to environment configuration.

2.8 First Kafka Streams Application Setup

The correct setup of your first Kafka Streams application is crucial for seamless development and execution. This section will guide you through creating a basic Kafka Streams application, ensuring that you have all components and configurations in place for successful operation.

To begin with, we need to ensure that our project structure is correctly set up. Assuming that you are using Apache Maven as your build tool, your project's pom.xml must include the necessary dependencies for Kafka Streams. Below is an example snippet showing the necessary dependencies:

```
<dependency>
    <groupId>org.apache.kafka</groupId>
    <artifactId>kafka-streams</artifactId>
    <version>3.0.0</version>
</dependency>
<dependency>
    <groupId>org.apache.kafka</groupId>
    <artifactId>kafka-clients</artifactId>
    <version>3.0.0</version>
</dependency>
<dependency>
    <groupId>org.slf4j</groupId>
    <artifactId>slf4j-api</artifactId>
    <version>1.7.32</version>
</dependency>
<dependency>
    <groupId>org.slf4j</groupId>
    <artifactId>slf4j-log4j12</artifactId>
    <version>1.7.32</version>
</dependency>
```

Next, let's create the main application class. We'll start by configuring the basic properties needed by Kafka Streams, such as the application ID, Kafka brokers, and default key/value serdes (serializers/deserializers).

```
import org.apache.kafka.common.serialization.Serdes;
import org.apache.kafka.streams.StreamsConfig;
import org.apache.kafka.streams.kstream.KStreamBuilder;
import java.util.Properties;
```

```
public class KafkaStreamsApp {
    public static void main(String[] args) {
        Properties props = new Properties();
        props.put(StreamsConfig.APPLICATION_ID_CONFIG, "my-first-streams-app"
            );
        props.put(StreamsConfig.BOOTSTRAP_SERVERS_CONFIG, "localhost:9092"
            );
        props.put(StreamsConfig.DEFAULT_KEY_SERDE_CLASS_CONFIG, Serdes.
            String().getClass().getName());
        props.put(StreamsConfig.DEFAULT_VALUE_SERDE_CLASS_CONFIG,
            Serdes.String().getClass().getName());

        // Other configuration settings can be added here.
    }
}
```

With the properties configured, we now need to define our stream processing topology. For this introductory example, we'll create a simple stream from an input topic and write it to an output topic.

```
import org.apache.kafka.streams.StreamsBuilder;
import org.apache.kafka.streams.Topology;
import org.apache.kafka.streams.KafkaStreams;

public class KafkaStreamsApp {
    public static void main(String[] args) {
        Properties props = new Properties();
        props.put(StreamsConfig.APPLICATION_ID_CONFIG, "my-first-streams-app"
            );
        props.put(StreamsConfig.BOOTSTRAP_SERVERS_CONFIG, "localhost:9092"
            );
        props.put(StreamsConfig.DEFAULT_KEY_SERDE_CLASS_CONFIG, Serdes.
            String().getClass().getName());
        props.put(StreamsConfig.DEFAULT_VALUE_SERDE_CLASS_CONFIG,
            Serdes.String().getClass().getName());

        StreamsBuilder builder = new StreamsBuilder();

        // Create a stream from the input topic
        builder.stream("input-topic").to("output-topic");

        // Build the topology
        Topology topology = builder.build();

        // Create and start the Kafka Streams instance
        KafkaStreams streams = new KafkaStreams(topology, props);
        streams.start();

        // Add shutdown hook to respond to SIGTERM and gracefully close the stream
        Runtime.getRuntime().addShutdownHook(new Thread(streams::close));
    }
}
```

This basic example consists of the following steps:

- Creating the properties required to configure the Kafka Streams application.

- Setting up a StreamsBuilder instance used to construct the stream processing topology.
- Using the builder, streaming data from an "input-topic" to an "output-topic."
- Building the topology and starting the Kafka Streams instance.
- Adding a shutdown hook to ensure graceful shutdown on application termination.

Ensure you have Kafka running locally and the input topic ("input-topic") and output topic ("output-topic") created. You can create these topics manually using the Kafka CLI tools:

```
bin/kafka-topics.sh --create --topic input-topic --bootstrap-server localhost:9092 --
    partitions 1 --replication-factor 1
bin/kafka-topics.sh --create --topic output-topic --bootstrap-server localhost:9092 --
    partitions 1 --replication-factor 1
```

Finally, compile and run the Kafka Streams application. You should see data moved from the input topic to the output topic. To verify, produce some messages to the input topic and consume messages from the output topic using Kafka console producer and consumer tools:

For producing messages:

```
bin/kafka-console-producer.sh --topic input-topic --bootstrap-server localhost:9092
>{Sample message 1}
>{Sample message 2}
```

For consuming messages:

```
bin/kafka-console-consumer.sh --topic output-topic --from-beginning --bootstrap-server localhost:9092
{Sample message 1}
{Sample message 2}
```

This simple setup confirms your first Kafka Streams application is working as expected.

Chapter 3

Kafka Streams Architecture

This chapter delves into the architectural components of Kafka Streams, explaining the interaction between streams, state stores, and processors. It covers the concepts of topology and sub-topologies, partitioning and parallelism, and the roles of source and sink nodes. The chapter distinguishes between stateful and stateless processing, outlines the data flow within Kafka Streams applications, and explains stream partitions and tasks. Additionally, it discusses the Kafka Streams DSL and Processor API, providing a comprehensive understanding of the underlying architecture.

3.1 Introduction to Kafka Streams Architecture

Kafka Streams is a powerful stream processing library that is part of the Apache Kafka ecosystem. It enables the development of real-time applications that process or transform data streams. Unlike traditional batch processing systems, Kafka Streams provides low latency and is designed for fault-tolerant and scalable stream processing. Kafka Streams' architecture revolves around three fundamental components: streams, state stores, and processors, which collaborate to provide a comprehensive framework for real-time data processing.

- Streams are the core data abstraction in Kafka Streams. A stream represents an unbounded, continuously updating sequence of immutable records, and each record is a key-value pair. Streams can be transformed, filtered, aggregated, and joined to produce new streams. Kafka Streams provides built-in operators for common transformations, making it easy to build complex data processing pipelines.

- State stores are locally persisted key-value stores available to applications for maintaining stateful computations. They allow applications to retain intermediate results between processing steps and across application restarts. This is essential for implementing operations like aggregations and joins that require context beyond individual records. State stores can be queried and updated, and they can be persisted to disk or kept in-memory for quick access. In addition to local storage, state stores are backed up by Kafka changelogs for durability and fault tolerance.

- Processors, the fundamental building blocks of Kafka Streams architecture, are responsible for processing the records from input streams. Processors apply transformations and generate output records. Kafka Streams allows us to define custom processors or use predefined ones provided by the library. The communication between processors is facilitated by the processor topology, a directed acyclic graph that delineates the data flow and the relationships between processors.

The processor topology defines how data flows from source nodes, through processors, and ends up in sink nodes. Source nodes are where data streams enter the topology, usually from Kafka topics. Processors consume data from these nodes, perform transformations, and pass the results down the topology to sink nodes, where the processed data is typically written back to Kafka topics. This flexible architecture makes it possible to construct highly sophisticated data processing pipelines.

Partitioning and parallelism are fundamental aspects of Kafka Streams that allow for scalable data processing. Each stream is divided into partitions, enabling distributed processing. Kafka Streams leverages Kafka's partitioning mechanism to distribute workload across multiple instances of an application. Each instance processes a subset of partitions, which is crucial for ensuring that the applications can scale horizontally. Task parallelism within Kafka Streams further enhances the efficiency by dividing the workload within a partition.

A notable distinction in Kafka Streams architecture is between stateful and stateless processing. Stateless processes are those that do not rely on any stored state and simply operate on each record independently. Examples include filtering or simple transformations. On the other hand, stateful processing involves maintaining and updating state information across records. Aggregations, joins, and windowed operations are typical examples that require stateful processing, leveraging state stores to track and manage state.

Understanding the flow of data within Kafka Streams applications is integral to leveraging its capabilities effectively. The data flow begins with consuming records from Kafka topics, which are then transformed and processed as they traverse through the topology. Intermediate states are stored and updated in state stores as required. Finally, the output records are produced back to Kafka topics or other downstream systems.

Kafka Streams provides two main APIs: the Kafka Streams DSL and the Processor API. The Streams DSL (Domain Specific Language) is a functional programming style API that simplifies the development of streams processing applications by providing high-level abstractions for common operations, such as filtering, joining, and aggregating. It is recommended for most use cases due to its simplicity and expressive power. The Processor API offers finer control by allowing the development of custom processors, providing a mechanism to implement more complex and specialized logic.

As an integral part of Apache Kafka, Kafka Streams ensures strong fault tolerance through replication and persistence of both data and state. Changelogs and state stores are crucial elements that facilitate recovery from failures and maintain consistency across application instances.

Understanding the detailed architecture of Kafka Streams allows developers to harness its full capability to build robust, scalable, and real-time data processing applications. This section laid the foundation for exploring the distinct components and concepts that form the architecture of Kafka Streams, setting the stage for navigating through the deeper intricacies in subsequent sections.

3.2 Streams, State Stores, and Processors

In the Kafka Streams API, three fundamental components are essential for building stream processing applications: streams, state stores, and processors. Understanding these components is crucial for designing efficient and scalable stream processing systems.

A **stream** in Kafka Streams represents an unbounded, continuously updating dataset of records, where each record consists of a key, a value, and a timestamp. Streams are immutable and append-only; once a record is added to a stream, it cannot be modified or deleted. Streams can be processed in real-time, allowing the application to perform continuous computations over the incoming data. To illustrate a simple stream definition in Kafka Streams:

```
KStream<String, String> textLines = builder.stream("input-topic");
```

In this example, builder is an instance of StreamsBuilder, and textLines represents the stream obtained from the topic "input-topic".

State stores are used to maintain and manage the state within stream processing applications. State stores are crucial for stateful operations, as they allow applications to store intermediate computational results and perform stateful transformations such as aggregations, joins, and window operations. Kafka Streams provides different types of state stores, including persistent stores backed by RocksDB and in-memory stores. A state store can be integrated into processors, enabling them to read and write to the store during processing. An example of defining a persistent state store in Kafka Streams:

```
StoreBuilder<KeyValueStore<String, Long>> countStoreBuilder =
  Stores.keyValueStoreBuilder(
    Stores.persistentKeyValueStore("Counts"),
    Serdes.String(),
    Serdes.Long()
  );
builder.addStateStore(countStoreBuilder);
```

In this example, a persistent key-value store named "Counts" is created. The store uses default serializers and deserializers for String keys and Long values.

Processors form the core of the Kafka Streams processing topology. A processor is a node within a processing topology that applies a processing operation to records. Kafka Streams provides two ways to define processing logic: the Kafka Streams DSL (Domain Specific Language) and the Processor API. The DSL provides higher-level abstractions for common stream processing operations, while the Processor API offers fine-grained control over the processing steps.

A processor can both process the incoming records and interact with state stores to maintain and query state. Custom processors can be created by extending the AbstractProcessor class and overriding the process() method. Processors are connected in a directed acyclic graph (DAG), representing the flow of data through the application. An example of a custom processor interacting with a state store:

```
public class MyProcessor extends AbstractProcessor<String, Long> {
  private KeyValueStore<String, Long> stateStore;

  @Override
  public void init(ProcessorContext context) {
    super.init(context);
    this.stateStore = (KeyValueStore<String, Long>) context.getStateStore("Counts");
  }

  @Override
  public void process(String key, Long value) {
    Long currentValue = stateStore.get(key);
    if (currentValue == null) {
      currentValue = 0L;
    }
    stateStore.put(key, currentValue + value);
  }
}
```

In this custom processor, the init method initializes the processor by retrieving the state store named "Counts". The process method updates the state store with incoming records' values.

Integrating a custom processor into the processing topology is done using the Topology class:

```
Topology topology = new Topology();
topology.addSource("Source", "input-topic")
        .addProcessor("MyProcessor", MyProcessor::new, "Source")
        .addStateStore(countStoreBuilder, "MyProcessor")
        .addSink("Sink", "output-topic", "MyProcessor");
```

In this topology, records flow from the source "Source" to the processor "MyProcessor", which is connected to the state store. Processed results are then sent to the sink "Sink".

The interplay between streams, state stores, and processors is fundamental to Kafka Streams' capability to perform complex real-time processing. Streams provide the continuous flow of data, state stores ensure the persistence and management of state, and processors define the specific computations to be performed on the data.

Overall, the seamless integration of streams, state stores, and processors enables the construction of robust and fault-tolerant stream processing applications with Kafka Streams. By leveraging these components, developers can implement a wide range of real-time data processing use cases, from simple transformations to complex event-driven architectures.

3.3 Topology and Sub-topologies

In the Kafka Streams library, the abstraction of a topology is a crucial concept. A topology defines the data processing logic, representing a Directed Acyclic Graph (DAG) of stream processing nodes. Each node in the graph correlates to operations such as filtering, mapping, or aggregations, and edges represent the data flow between these operations.

When constructing a Kafka Streams application, a developer specifies the stream processing logic in terms of a topology. The topology itself can further be divided into smaller, logical components termed as sub-topologies.

Topologies

To illustrate, consider a simple Kafka Streams application where records from a source topic are transformed and written to a sink topic. The topology may look like this:

```
Kafka Source Topic -> [Process] -> Kafka Sink Topic
```

In the Kafka Streams DSL, this might be achieved with the following code:

```
StreamsBuilder builder = new StreamsBuilder();
KStream<String, String> sourceStream = builder.stream("source-topic");

sourceStream.mapValues(value -> value.toUpperCase())
            .to("sink-topic");

KafkaStreams streams = new KafkaStreams(builder.build(), properties);
streams.start();
```

Here, the topology consists of a single source node that reads from the "source-topic", a processor node that performs the mapValues operation, and a sink node that writes to the "sink-topic". The built topology is a linear chain in this example.

Sub-topologies

While small-scale applications like the one above have a straightforward topology, real-world applications often involve multiple sources, sinks, and intermediate processing operations that can be logically separated into sub-topologies. Each sub-topology represents an independent portion of the overall topology, typically isolating particular features of the stream processing logic.

A sub-topology is produced within a topology whenever there is no direct relationship between parts of the processing logic. For example, consider a scenario where there are two source topics processed independently, with their results eventually merged.

```
StreamsBuilder builder = new StreamsBuilder();
KStream<String, String> sourceStream1 = builder.stream("source-topic-1");
KStream<String, String> sourceStream2 = builder.stream("source-topic-2");

sourceStream1.mapValues(value -> value.toUpperCase())
        .to("intermediate-topic-1");

sourceStream2.mapValues(value -> value.toLowerCase())
        .to("intermediate-topic-2");

KStream<String, String> intermediateStream1 = builder.stream("intermediate-topic-1"
    );
KStream<String, String> intermediateStream2 = builder.stream("intermediate-topic-2"
    );

KStream<String, String> mergedStream = intermediateStream1.merge(
    intermediateStream2);

mergedStream.to("final-topic");

KafkaStreams streams = new KafkaStreams(builder.build(), properties);
streams.start();
```

This configuration generates at least three sub-topologies:

- Processing logic for "source-topic-1" leading to "intermediate-topic-1".
- Processing logic for "source-topic-2" leading to "intermediate-topic-2".
- Processing logic that consumes from "intermediate-topic-1" and "intermediate-topic-2" to produce records into "final-topic".

Each of these sub-topologies can be executed independently by Kafka Streams' task threads because there is no direct data dependency between them until they are merged.

Identifying Sub-topologies

Kafka Streams automatically identifies sub-topologies based on the processing logic defined by the developer. The segments of the processing graph that are connected by state stores, repartition topics, or other internal mechanisms are grouped into the same sub-topology. Conversely, segments without such connections are treated as distinct sub-topologies.

```
Topology topology = builder.build();
System.out.println(topology.describe());
```

The above example prints a description of the topology, detailing the individual sub-topologies and illustrating the nodes and edges within them. This feature helps developers visualize how Kafka Streams has divided the application into sub-topologies and verify the parallelism and task distribution.

Execution Implications

The formation of sub-topologies impacts the execution of the Kafka Streams application by defining the boundaries within which tasks can be parallelized. Each sub-topology runs in an isolated context, meaning that Kafka Streams can assign threads to process each sub-topology independently. This arrangement promotes high-throughput and concurrent data processing.

Furthermore, developers must understand how Kafka Streams handles the interactions between sub-topologies. For instance, sub-topologies that interact through intermediate topics introduce potential latencies due to inter-process communication. Consideration of such factors is vital when designing efficient, low-latency stream processing applications.

By comprehensively defining the topology and leveraging the concept of sub-topologies, developers can architect complex stream processing applications in Kafka Streams with enhanced modularity and maintainability. The logical segmentation provided by sub-topologies ultimately facilitates efficient scaling and resource allocation across distributed stream processing tasks.

3.4 Partitioning and Parallelism

In Kafka Streams, partitioning and parallelism are fundamental concepts that facilitate scalable and efficient stream processing. Leveraging Kafka's inherent distributed architecture, Kafka Streams achieves high throughput and fault-tolerance by partitioning data across multiple nodes. This section elaborates on how partitioning works in Kafka Streams and explains the mechanisms that enable parallel processing of stream data, ultimately leading to better utilization of resources and enhanced performance.

The basic unit of parallelism in Kafka Streams is the partition. Each stream is associated with one or more topics, and these topics are divided into partitions. The partitions allow Kafka Streams to split the data into smaller, manageable chunks, which can be processed independently. This framework inherently supports parallelism, as each partition can be assigned to different tasks or threads.

Consider a topic T with three partitions: P_0, P_1, and P_2. When a producer publishes messages to topic T, Kafka distributes these messages across the three partitions based on the partitioning strategy. By default, a partitioner assigns a message to a partition based on the message key, ensuring that all messages with the same key are directed to the same partition. This behavior is crucial for operations that require ordering guarantees or stateful processing.

```
Properties props = new Properties();
props.put(StreamsConfig.APPLICATION_ID_CONFIG, "partitioning-example");
props.put(StreamsConfig.BOOTSTRAP_SERVERS_CONFIG, "localhost:9092");
props.put(StreamsConfig.DEFAULT_KEY_SERDE_CLASS_CONFIG, Serdes.String()
      .getClass().getName());
props.put(StreamsConfig.DEFAULT_VALUE_SERDE_CLASS_CONFIG, Serdes.
      String().getClass().getName());

StreamsBuilder builder = new StreamsBuilder();
KStream<String, String> stream = builder.stream("input-topic");
KStream<String, String>[] branches = stream.branch(
    (key, value) -> key.startsWith("A"),
    (key, value) -> key.startsWith("B"),
    (key, value) -> true
);

branches[0].to("output-topic-0");
branches[1].to("output-topic-1");
branches[2].to("output-topic-2");

KafkaStreams streams = new KafkaStreams(builder.build(), props);
streams.start();
```

In this example, the stream is branched into three separate sub-streams based on key prefixes, and each sub-stream is written to a different output topic.

Parallelism in Kafka Streams is achieved through tasks. Each partition is processed by a task, and Kafka Streams creates a task for every partition in the input topics. Hence, if an application consumes data from a topic with five partitions, five tasks will be created. Each task is a self-contained unit that processes records from its assigned partition, maintains any local states, and performs the necessary computations defined in the processing topology.

$$\text{Tasks} = \sum_{i=1}^{n} \text{Partitions}(T_i)$$

Where n is the number of input topics (T) and Partitions(T_i) denotes the number of partitions in the i-th topic.

The distribution of tasks to threads is managed by the Kafka Streams framework. By default, the number of threads used by a Kafka Streams application is defined by the configuration property num.stream.threads. Increasing the number of threads allows the application to process multiple tasks concurrently, thus enhancing parallelism and throughput.

```
props.put(StreamsConfig.NUM_STREAM_THREADS_CONFIG, "4");
```

In a distributed deployment, the Kafka Streams application can run on multiple instances across different machines. Kafka Streams assigns the tasks to these instances, balancing the load based on the number of tasks and available instances. If the number of instances changes, Kafka Streams will automatically rebalance the tasks.

Consider three instances of a Kafka Streams application processing a topic with six partitions. Initially, each instance might be assigned two tasks. If another instance is added, Kafka Streams will redistribute the tasks to ensure an even load across the four instances. This dynamic rebalance capability is critical for maintaining performance as the cluster size changes.

```
Instance 1: Task 0, Task 1
Instance 2: Task 2, Task 3
Instance 3: Task 4, Task 5
```

After adding a fourth instance:

```
Instance 1: Task 0
Instance 2: Task 1
Instance 3: Task 2, Task 3
Instance 4: Task 4, Task 5
```

- **Data Locality**: For stateful operations, such as aggregations or joins, data locality is essential. The chosen partitioning key should ensure that related records are directed to the same partition. This locality minimizes the overhead of state shuffling across partitions and maintains the integrity of the computations.

- **Load Distribution**: An even distribution of load across partitions ensures optimal resource utilization. Uneven partitioning can lead to hotspots, where some partitions receive a disproportionately high amount of data, resulting in a bottleneck. Custom partitioners can be implemented to adopt strategies that account for load distribution.

```
public class CustomPartitioner implements Partitioner {
    @Override
    public void configure(Map<String, ?> configs) { }

    @Override
    public int partition(String topic, Object key, byte[] keyBytes, Object value, byte[]
        valueBytes, Cluster cluster) {
        int numPartitions = cluster.partitionsForTopic(topic).size();
        if (keyBytes == null) {
            return 0;
        }
        return Utils.toPositive(Utils.murmur2(keyBytes)) % numPartitions;
    }

    @Override
    public void close() { }
}

props.put(StreamsConfig.PARTITIONER_CLASS_CONFIG, CustomPartitioner.class.
    getName());
```

For stateless operations, partitioning decisions have less impact on the correctness of the output but can still affect performance and throughput.

The assignment of streams to tasks follows a deterministic strategy based on the partition numbers. Tasks are uniquely identified by the input topics and the respective partition numbers they handle. This identification ensures that each task aligns with its partition's data processing responsibilities. Kafka Streams serializes the state of each task in local state stores, which can be persisted and restored during failovers, playing a pivotal role in ensuring resilience and consistency.

In summary, understanding and correctly implementing partitioning and parallelism in Kafka Streams is essential for building robust and scalable streaming applications. Partitioning divides the data into consumable segments, while parallelism leverages distributed computing resources to process these partitions simultaneously, significantly boosting processing efficiency and resilience.

3.5 Source and Sink Nodes

In Kafka Streams, the fundamental building blocks of any processing topology are nodes, specifically source and sink nodes. These nodes define the entry and exit points within a Kafka Streams topology, determining how data flows through the system. Understanding the operational mechanics and functional roles of source and sink nodes is crucial for designing efficient data processing applications.

Source nodes act as the initiation points of a topology, consuming data from Kafka topics. When a source node is defined, it subscribes to the specified Kafka topic(s). This enables the application to read messages from the partitions of these topics and forward them to downstream processors. Source nodes are implemented using the StreamsBuilder class and the .stream or .table methods.

Consider the following example where a source node is defined to consume data from a Kafka topic named "input-topic":

```
StreamsBuilder builder = new StreamsBuilder();
KStream<String, String> sourceStream = builder.stream("input-topic");
```

Here, the StreamsBuilder instance builder creates a stream from the "input-topic" Kafka topic. The sourceStream variable now represents the stream of records consumed by this source node.

Sink nodes, conversely, serve as the termination points in a topology. They are responsible for writing the processed data back into Kafka topics. Sink nodes allow data that has undergone transformations and aggregations to be stored back in Kafka for further processing or consumption by other applications or systems. The to method on a KStream or KTable can be used to direct data to a sink node.

An example of defining a sink node to produce data to a Kafka topic named "output-topic" is shown below:

```
sourceStream.to("output-topic");
```

This code snippet ensures that the data in sourceStream, after any specified transformations, is written to the "output-topic" Kafka topic.

To elucidate the interaction between source and sink nodes further, consider a simple topology where data from an input Kafka topic undergoes a transformation before being written to an output Kafka topic. The following code demonstrates this process:

```
public class SimpleTopology {
```

```
  public static void main(String[] args) {
    Properties props = new Properties();
    props.put(StreamsConfig.APPLICATION_ID_CONFIG, "simple-topology");
    props.put(StreamsConfig.BOOTSTRAP_SERVERS_CONFIG, "localhost:9092");

    StreamsBuilder builder = new StreamsBuilder();
    KStream<String, String> sourceStream = builder.stream("input-topic");

    KStream<String, String> transformedStream = sourceStream.mapValues(value ->
        value.toUpperCase());

    transformedStream.to("output-topic");

    KafkaStreams streams = new KafkaStreams(builder.build(), props);
    streams.start();
  }
}
```

In this example, a source node reads data from "input-topic". The stream undergoes a transformation, converting each message value to uppercase. Finally, the transformed data is sent to an output Kafka topic "output-topic" through a sink node.

The source and sink nodes, therefore, play crucial roles in the data ingestion and output phases of a Kafka Streams application. They enable seamless integration with Kafka topics, allowing for the ingestion of raw data and expulsion of processed information back into the Kafka ecosystem, thus forming a continuous and efficient data pipeline.

Additionally, connection points between source and sink nodes permit the creation of complex topologies. Within these intricate structures, various data processing units can collaborate and execute numerous operations, yielding comprehensive and enriched data streams. The efficient utilization and clear understanding of these nodes facilitate the construction of robust and scalable data processing applications using Kafka Streams.

3.6 Stateful vs Stateless Processing

Stateful and stateless processing constitute fundamental paradigms in Kafka Streams applications, influencing how data is managed and processed throughout the stream processing workflow. A clear understanding of the distinction between these two types is essential for effectively architecting and deploying Kafka Streams solutions.

Stateless processing refers to transformations that operate on each record independently of any other records. These operations do not require any additional context or memory beyond the data in the current record being processed. Examples of stateless operations include filtering records, mapping data to a new form, and simple aggregations where no historical data is maintained.

Stateless transformations in Kafka Streams are typically implemented using methods such as filter, map, flatMap, and foreach. These operations can efficiently handle high-throughput data streams due to their limited resource requirements.

```
KStream<String, String> sourceStream = builder.stream("source-topic");
KStream<String, String> filteredStream = sourceStream.filter(
    (key, value) -> value.contains("filter-criteria")
);
filteredStream.to("filtered-topic");
```

In the above example, the filter method processes each record independently, filtering out records that do not meet the specified criteria. This operation does not require storing any state information.

Conversely, stateful processing involves operations that depend on state, which is often derived from previous records. These types of transformations maintain data across multiple events and enable functionalities such as aggregations, joins, and windowed operations. Stateful operations necessitate the management of state stores to retain the intermediate processing state.

Stateful transformations in Kafka Streams are facilitated by methods like aggregate, reduce, count, and join. These operations inherently require maintaining context over the data stream, which is often achieved utilizing state stores.

```
KTable<String, Long> wordCounts = sourceStream
    .flatMapValues(value -> Arrays.asList(value.toLowerCase().split("\\W+")))
    .groupBy((key, word) -> word)
    .count(Materialized.as("word-counts-store"));
```

In this example, a stateful transformation is demonstrated where the word counts are maintained for each word encountered in the stream. The count method is used to keep a running tally of the occurrences of each word, necessitating a state store named "word-counts-store" to manage this state.

The Kafka Streams API provides robust mechanisms for managing state through the use of state stores, which are embedded in the processing topology. State stores are local to the stream processing application instance and can be either in-memory or persisted to disk. Kafka Streams allows configuring these stores based on the requirements for throughput, latency, and durability.

Stateful operations introduce complexities such as state management, fault tolerance, and scalability. Kafka Streams handles fault tolerance by changelogging all state store updates to a Kafka topic. In the event of a failure, the state can be reconstructed by replaying the changelog. This ensures that the state remains consistent and recoverable.

To maximize application scalability, Kafka Streams partitions the state store by the key of the record, aligning with Kafka topic partitions. Each partition is handled by a separate stream task, allowing parallel processing across multiple instances of the application. This partitioning mechanism is crucial for distributing the workload and managing state efficiently in large-scale stream processing scenarios.

Stateful processing unlocks powerful capabilities but demands careful consideration of state store configuration, application design, and resource management. Developers must ensure that the stateful application is scalable, fault-tolerant, and optimized for performance, leveraging Kafka Streams' inherent mechanisms and best practices.

3.7 Data Flow in Kafka Streams

In the Kafka Streams library, the concept of data flow is central to understanding how data is processed and traverses through different components of a Kafka Streams application. Data flow is the journey of records through the source nodes to processors, intermediate state stores, and finally to sink nodes. The correct design and management of data flow are essential in achieving desired performance and reliability in a stream processing application.

Data flow begins at the source nodes, where records are ingested into the Kafka Streams topology. A source node in Kafka Streams subscribes to one or more Kafka topics. When new messages are produced on these topics, they are fetched by the source node. The task of the source node is to convert the Kafka ConsumerRecords into a stream-processing internal representation, typically a stream of key-value pairs.

```
KStream<String, String> sourceStream = builder.stream("source-topic");
```

The provided code snippet demonstrates how a Kafka Streams application can create a source stream by subscribing to a Kafka topic named "source-topic". This stream forms a directed acyclic graph (DAG), where the nodes represent computational operations, and the edges represent the data flow between these operations.

The next component in the data flow is the processor node. Processor nodes perform the core processing logic on the incoming data. They can range from simple stateless operations like map, filter, and flatMap, to more complex stateful operations like aggregations and joins. Processor nodes can be implemented using the Kafka Streams DSL for simpler use cases or the Processor API for more advanced custom processing.

An example of a simple stateless processor operation is filtering out records based on a specific condition:

```
KStream<String, String> filteredStream = sourceStream.filter(
  (key, value) -> value.contains("important")
);
```

In stateful processing, processor nodes utilize state stores to maintain and manipulate state information. A state store is a durable storage integrated into a processor that preserves state across reboots and failures. When a stateful operation such as aggregation or a windowed join is performed, the results are stored in these state stores and can be accessed for future computations or queries.

```
KTable<String, Long> aggregatedTable = sourceStream.groupByKey()
    .aggregate(
        () -> 0L,
        (key, value, aggregate) -> aggregate + 1,
        Materialized.<String, Long, KeyValueStore<Bytes, byte[]>>as("counts-store")
    );
```

The aggregated data is stored in a state store named "counts-store", which Kafka Streams maintains automatically. This ensures fault-tolerance and recovery capabilities by continually backing up the state store's data to a special Kafka topic.

Upon completion of the processing logic, the results are sent to sink nodes. Sink nodes are responsible for writing the processed data to Kafka topics. This ensures that the processed data is available for further downstream processing or for consumption by other applications.

```
resultStream.to("sink-topic");
```

The code snippet above showcases how a Kafka Streams application can direct the final processed stream, 'resultStream', to a Kafka topic named "sink-topic", thus completing the data flow cycle.

Data flow in Kafka Streams is inherently parallel and distributed due to the partitioning of Kafka topics. Each topic is split into partitions, which allows for concurrent processing of data. Each partition in a Kafka topic is processed by a single task within a Kafka Streams application. This enables scalability by leveraging multiple processors in a distributed manner.

Task distribution plays a significant role in balancing the data processing load across the available resources. Each task within a Kafka Streams application corresponds to a partition of the Kafka topic. Tasks operate independently of each other, consuming records from their assigned partitions, processing the records according to the defined topology, and producing the results back to Kafka topics through sink nodes.

Understanding and leveraging the strengths of Kafka Streams' data flow architecture allows developers to build robust, scalable, and fault-tolerant stream processing applications.

3.8 Stream Partitions and Tasks

In Kafka Streams, the concepts of stream partitions and tasks form the backbone of application scalability and parallelism. By understanding how data is divided and processed across these components, users can effectively design and optimize their stream processing applications.

Stream Partitions are fundamental units of scalability within Kafka. Each stream is composed of multiple partitions, which are essentially subsets of the overall data set. The number of partitions is determined at the time of topic creation and remains fixed unless explicitly modified. Each partition is an ordered, immutable sequence of records that allows for parallel processing and data distribution across multiple instances.

To demonstrate the concept of stream partitions, consider the following Kafka topic creation command:

```
kafka-topics --create --topic my_topic --partitions 4 --replication-factor 1 --bootstrap-
    server localhost:9092
```

This command creates a topic named my_topic with four partitions. Each partition can be processed independently, enabling concurrent processing and load distribution across multiple nodes or threads within a Kafka Streams application.

Tasks are the operational entities that perform the actual processing in Kafka Streams. Each task is responsible for processing one or more partitions. The relationship between partitions and tasks is many-to-one; a single task can handle multiple partitions, but each partition is assigned to only one task. This assignment ensures that records within a partition are processed in order.

The Kafka Streams runtime orchestrates the distribution of tasks across the available processing instances, known as stream threads. This distribution aims to achieve load balancing and fault tolerance. Whenever a new instance joins the application or an existing instance fails, the runtime dynamically redistributes tasks to maintain an even workload.

Consider the following example of a Kafka Streams application configuration:

```
Properties props = new Properties();
props.put(StreamsConfig.APPLICATION_ID_CONFIG, "partition-task-example");
props.put(StreamsConfig.BOOTSTRAP_SERVERS_CONFIG, "localhost:9092");
props.put(StreamsConfig.NUM_STREAM_THREADS_CONFIG, 2); // Two stream
     threads

KafkaStreams streams = new KafkaStreams(builder.build(), props);
streams.start();
```

In this example, the application is configured with two stream threads. Given four partitions, the runtime may assign two partitions to each thread, resulting in two tasks, each handling two partitions.

The efficiency of processing depends on a balanced allocation of tasks to stream threads. If the number of partitions does not evenly divide by the number of stream threads, some threads may handle more tasks than others. This imbalance can be mitigated by adjusting the number of partitions or stream threads.

The following code demonstrates how to retrieve metadata about the assignment of tasks and partitions within a running Kafka Streams application:

```
for (ThreadMetadata threadMetadata : streams.metadataForLocalThreads()) {
    System.out.println("Thread ID: " + threadMetadata.threadName());
    for (TaskMetadata taskMetadata : threadMetadata.activeTasks()) {
        System.out.println("Task ID: " + taskMetadata.taskId());
        System.out.println("Partitions: " + taskMetadata.topicPartitions());
    }
}
```

This code provides insight into the current state of task assignment, showing which stream thread is responsible for which task, and the partitions assigned to each task.

The rebalance process facilitates dynamic adjustment of task assignments in response to changes in the application's environment. When a new instance starts, or an existing one shuts down, Kafka Streams triggers a rebalance to redistribute tasks evenly. During this process, the state of the tasks that include state stores may need to be restored from changelog topics, ensuring that all instances have the necessary data to resume processing without data loss.

An example rebalance listener implementation can be seen below:

```
streams.setStateListener((newState, oldState) -> {
    if (newState == KafkaStreams.State.REBALANCING) {
        System.out.println("Rebalancing in progress...");
    } else if (newState == KafkaStreams.State.RUNNING) {
        System.out.println("Rebalance complete. Streams running.");
    }
});
```

This listener logs status messages during the rebalance process, providing visibility into the state transitions of the Kafka Streams application.

Combining the concepts of stream partitions and tasks, along with their dynamic allocation and rebalancing, enables Kafka Streams to scale effectively and maintain high availability. By thoroughly understanding these mechanisms, developers can build robust streaming applications capable of handling large-scale data processing challenges.

3.9 Kafka Streams DSL and Processor API

The Kafka Streams API is designed to simplify the development of real-time data processing applications. Two prominent approaches can be employed in Kafka Streams: the Kafka Streams Domain Specific Language (DSL) and the Processor API. These two approaches serve different needs, offering varying levels of abstraction and control.

The Kafka Streams DSL provides a high-level, fluent API that simplifies the common data stream processing tasks. It allows developers to apply transformations, aggregations, joins, and window operations on the streams using familiar functional programming constructs such as map, filter, and reduce. Below is an example of a Kafka Streams DSL application that reads from an input topic, applies some transformations, and writes to an output topic.

```
Properties props = new Properties();
props.put(StreamsConfig.APPLICATION_ID_CONFIG, "streams-example");
```

```
props.put(StreamsConfig.BOOTSTRAP_SERVERS_CONFIG, "localhost:9092");
props.put(StreamsConfig.DEFAULT_KEY_SERDE_CLASS_CONFIG, Serdes.String()
    .getClass());
props.put(StreamsConfig.DEFAULT_VALUE_SERDE_CLASS_CONFIG, Serdes.
    String().getClass());

StreamsBuilder builder = new StreamsBuilder();
KStream<String, String> source = builder.stream("input-topic");

KStream<String, String> transformed = source
    .filter((key, value) -> value.length() > 4)
    .mapValues(String::toUpperCase);

transformed.to("output-topic");

KafkaStreams streams = new KafkaStreams(builder.build(), props);
streams.start();
```

In the code above, the example initializes properties for the stream processing application, sets up the topology using the StreamsBuilder, and defines the stream transformations using methods such as filter and mapValues. The DSL thus provides a concise and expressive way to define stream processing logic.

For developers requiring finer control over the processing logic or needing to implement custom processing logic, the Processor API is appropriate. The Processor API allows the definition of custom processors and state stores, providing comprehensive control over the data processing stages. Below is a basic example outlining the implementation of a custom processor.

```
public class CustomProcessor implements Processor<String, String> {
    private ProcessorContext context;

    @Override
    public void init(ProcessorContext context) {
        this.context = context;
    }

    @Override
    public void process(String key, String value) {
        if (value.length() > 4) {
            context.forward(key, value.toUpperCase());
        }
        context.commit();
    }

    @Override
    public void close() {
        // Any necessary cleanup
    }
}
```

This custom processor filters and converts messages to uppercase if the message length is greater than four. To integrate this processor into a topology, the following setup can be utilized:

```
Topology topology = new Topology();
topology.addSource("Source", "input-topic")
        .addProcessor("Process", CustomProcessor::new, "Source")
        .addSink("Sink", "output-topic", "Process");

KafkaStreams streams = new KafkaStreams(topology, props);
streams.start();
```

In this example, the topology is explicitly defined, adding a source node, a processor node, and a sink node. This structure provides clear control over the data flow and makes it easier to employ custom logic that may be cumbersome with the DSL.

Moreover, state stores in Kafka Streams enhance the capabilities of both the DSL and Processor API. State stores keep local copies of specified data, allowing for stateful operations like windowed aggregations and joins. The DSL provides built-in support for stateful operations; for example:

```
KStream<String, String> source = builder.stream("input-topic");
KGroupedStream<String, String> groupedStream = source.groupByKey();
KTable<String, Long> aggregatedTable = groupedStream.count(Materialized.as("
      count-store"));
```

The Materialized.as method specifies the underlying state store required for the aggregation, facilitating stateful stream processing. Similarly, the Processor API allows manual creation and management of state stores, offering robust state management capabilities.

For instance, managing state within a custom processor involves initializing a state store and using it within the processing logic:

```
public class StatefulProcessor implements Processor<String, String> {
    private ProcessorContext context;
    private KeyValueStore<String, Long> stateStore;

    @Override
    public void init(ProcessorContext context) {
        this.context = context;
        this.stateStore = (KeyValueStore<String, Long>) context.getStateStore("counts
              -store");
    }

    @Override
    public void process(String key, String value) {
        Long count = stateStore.get(key);
        if (count == null) {
            count = 0L;
        }
        stateStore.put(key, count + 1);
        context.commit();
    }
```

```
    @Override
    public void close() {
        // Any necessary cleanup
    }
}
```

The initialization of the state store is done through the `init` method, ensuring it is accessible during processing. To integrate this stateful processor into the topology:

```
Topology topology = new Topology();
topology.addSource("Source", "input-topic")
        .addProcessor("StatefulProcessor", StatefulProcessor::new, "Source")
        .addStateStore(Stores.keyValueStoreBuilder(
            Stores.persistentKeyValueStore("counts-store"),
            Serdes.String(),
            Serdes.Long()), "StatefulProcessor")
        .addSink("Sink", "output-topic", "StatefulProcessor");

KafkaStreams streams = new KafkaStreams(topology, props);
streams.start();
```

This setup illustrates the explicit addition of the state store to the topology and its association with the processor. The added control and granularity provided by the Processor API make it a powerful tool for complex stream processing scenarios.

By leveraging the Kafka Streams DSL for rapid development and the Processor API for advanced control, developers can efficiently harness the full capabilities of Kafka Streams to build robust, scalable real-time data processing applications.

Chapter 4

Streams and Tables in Kafka Streams

This chapter explores the data models of Kafka Streams, focusing on streams and tables. It explains the creation and use of streams and tables, including global tables and the concept of stream-table duality. The chapter also covers stream-table and table-table joins, providing practical examples of how to implement these operations. Additionally, it addresses handling schema changes, ensuring that your Kafka Streams applications remain flexible and adaptable.

4.1 Introduction to Streams and Tables

In Kafka Streams, comprehending the fundamental concepts of streams and tables is pivotal in leveraging the full potential of this powerful stream-processing library. Streams and tables represent the foundational data models in Kafka Streams, each embodying distinct characteristics and use cases. This section delineates these concepts, laying the groundwork for understanding more advanced operations and structures.

A **stream** in Kafka Streams is an unbounded, continuously updating sequence of records. Each record in the stream is an immutable key-value pair, potentially accompanied by a timestamp. Streams are inherently dynamic; they evolve as new data arrives. This trait makes streams an ideal choice for real-time processing scenarios where prompt reactions to incoming data are required.

On the contrary, a **table** in Kafka Streams signifies a collection of key-value pairs where the latest value for each key is maintained. Tables are mutable by nature – they can be updated by incoming data, enabling an accurate reflection of the most recent state. This characteristic renders tables highly suitable for applications where current state representation is crucial, such as in aggregations or stateful transformations.

The interaction between streams and tables is embodied in the concept known as *stream-table duality*. This duality emphasizes that every stream can be viewed as a continually updated table, where the stream's aggregate state at any point in time corresponds to the table. Conversely, every table can be perceived as a snapshot of a stream's state at a given time, representing the latest known values for its keys.

Here's an example to elucidate these concepts further. Suppose we have a stream of user activity events, each represented by a key (user ID) and a value (activity), with a corresponding timestamp. As new activities occur, events continuously stream into the system. If we consider this stream as a table, each user ID will map to their latest activity, updating whenever a new activity for that user is received.

To provide a more concrete understanding, let us examine a simple Kafka Streams application that prints out the contents of a stream and a table. The code snippet below captures the essence of processing a stream and a table within Kafka Streams.

```
import org.apache.kafka.common.serialization.Serdes;
import org.apache.kafka.streams.KafkaStreams;
import org.apache.kafka.streams.StreamsBuilder;
import org.apache.kafka.streams.kstream.KStream;
import org.apache.kafka.streams.kstream.KTable;

public class StreamTableExample {
    public static void main(String[] args) {
        StreamsBuilder builder = new StreamsBuilder();

        // Define a stream
        KStream<String, String> stream = builder.stream("input-stream-topic");
        stream.foreach((key, value) -> System.out.println("Stream record - key: " + key
                + " value: " + value));

        // Define a table
        KTable<String, String> table = builder.table("input-table-topic");
        table.toStream().foreach((key, value) -> System.out.println("Table record - key:
                " + key + " value: " + value));

        KafkaStreams streams = new KafkaStreams(builder.build(),
```

```
            getStreamProperties());
        streams.start();

        // Add shutdown hook to gracefully close the Kafka Streams application
        Runtime.getRuntime().addShutdownHook(new Thread(streams::close));
    }

    private static Properties getStreamProperties() {
        Properties props = new Properties();
        props.put(StreamsConfig.APPLICATION_ID_CONFIG, "stream-table-example
            ");
        props.put(StreamsConfig.BOOTSTRAP_SERVERS_CONFIG, "localhost:9092"
            );
        props.put(StreamsConfig.DEFAULT_KEY_SERDE_CLASS_CONFIG, Serdes.
            String().getClass());
        props.put(StreamsConfig.DEFAULT_VALUE_SERDE_CLASS_CONFIG,
            Serdes.String().getClass());
        return props;
    }
}
```

In this example:

- A *KStream* is created from a Kafka topic named input-stream-topic. The *foreach* method processes each record in the stream, printing its key and value.

- A *KTable* is formed from another Kafka topic called input-table-topic. Since *KTables* inherently store only the latest value for each key, we convert the table to a stream using the *toStream()* method to print out its records similarly.

The output of this application would look like the following in the console:

```
Stream record - key: user1 value: login
Stream record - key: user2 value: view
Table record - key: user1 value: login
Table record - key: user2 value: view
```

Resolutely grasping the underlying differences between streams and tables is crucial before embarking on more intricate Kafka Streams operations. Streams and tables underpin the core data infrastructure in Kafka Streams, setting the stage for various transformative capabilities. Subsequent sections will build upon this knowledge, delving into more complex constructs and operations, including how to create, manipulate, and harness streams and tables effectively in your applications.

4.2 Kafka Streams Data Model: Streams

Kafka Streams represents a conceptual model built upon streams of data. A stream in Kafka Streams is an unbounded, continuously updating sequence of immutable records. Each record in the stream consists of a key, a value, and a timestamp. These components are fundamental to processing and manipulating data within Kafka Streams applications.

- **Key:** The key in a Kafka Streams record functions as the unique identifier for the record within its stream. Keys are used to partition data across multiple instances for parallel processing. Effective keying is crucial as it ensures balanced data distribution and efficient processing.
- **Value:** The value in a Kafka Streams record contains the actual data payload. This can be any object, from simple data types to more complex structures, serialized according to the chosen format like Avro, JSON, or Protobuf.
- **Timestamp:** The timestamp marks the moment a record is produced. Kafka Streams leverages timestamps to order records within a stream, which is particularly important for time-based operations such as windowing and temporal joins.

Streams in Kafka Streams are inherently append-only, reflecting a core principle of immutable data flows. Records are never updated or removed; instead, new records that contain updated data or corrections are appended to the stream.

```
KStream<String, Long> inputStream = builder.stream("input-topic");
```

In this example, an input stream is created from a Kafka topic named "input-topic". The stream processes records with keys of type String and values of type Long. The ‘KStream‘ interface in Kafka Streams provides various methods to process and transform streams, retaining the immutability characteristic.

- **Basic Stream Operations**

The fundamental operations on streams are filtering, mapping, and flatMapping, which are akin to operations in functional programming.

- **Filter:** The filter operation allows the selection of records that satisfy a given predicate. For example:

```
KStream<String, Long> filteredStream = inputStream.filter(
    (key, value) -> value > 100
);
```

This code filters the input stream, retaining only records with values greater than 100.

- **Map:** The map operation transforms each record in the stream into a new record, allowing changes to both key and value. An example is changing the value type:

```
KStream<String, String> mappedStream = inputStream.map(
    (key, value) -> new KeyValue<>(key, value.toString())
);
```

Here, the values in the stream are converted from Long to String.

- **FlatMap:** The flatMap operation produces zero or more records for each input record, which is useful for splitting records or producing multiple related records.

```
KStream<String, String> flatMappedStream = inputStream.flatMap(
    (key, value) -> {
        List<KeyValue<String, String>> result = new ArrayList<>();
        result.add(new KeyValue<>(key, "prefix_" + value));
        result.add(new KeyValue<>(key, "suffix_" + value));
        return result;
    }
);
```

In this example, two new records are produced for each input record, one with a prefixed value and another with a suffixed value.

- **Windowing and Time-based Operations**

Windowing is essential when working with infinite data streams to group records into finite chunks based on time.

- **Tumbling Windows:** Fixed-size non-overlapping windows.

```
KTable<Windowed<String>, Long> tumblingWindowCounts = inputStream
    .groupByKey()
    .windowedBy(TimeWindows.of(Duration.ofMinutes(5)))
    .count();
```

This example counts the number of records within five-minute tumbling windows.

- **Hopping Windows:** Overlapping windows that allow records to belong to multiple windows.

```
KTable<Windowed<String>, Long> hoppingWindowCounts = inputStream
    .groupByKey()
    .windowedBy(TimeWindows.of(Duration.ofMinutes(5))
                        .advanceBy(Duration.ofMinutes(1)))
    .count();
```

Here, a five-minute window advances every minute, creating overlapping windows.

- **Session Windows:** Dynamically sized windows based on gaps of inactivity.

```
KTable<Windowed<String>, Long> sessionWindowCounts = inputStream
    .groupByKey()
    .windowedBy(SessionWindows.with(Duration.ofMinutes(5)))
    .count();
```

Records are grouped into sessions that timeout after five minutes of inactivity.

- **Stateless and Stateful Transformations**

Stream processing in Kafka Streams encompasses both stateless and stateful transformations. Stateless transformations compute the output based solely on the current input record, exemplified by operations discussed previously (e.g., filter, map).

Stateful transformations require maintaining state across multiple records. Examples include aggregations, joins, and windowed operations.

- **Aggregation:** Aggregates records by key.

```
KTable<String, Long> aggregatedStream = inputStream
    .groupByKey()
    .aggregate(
        () -> 0L,
        (aggKey, newValue, aggValue) -> aggValue + newValue,
        Materialized.<String, Long, KeyValueStore<Bytes, byte[]>>as("aggregated-
            store")
            .withValueSerde(Serdes.Long())
    );
```

This code snippet aggregates the values by key, summing the values in the stream.

In Kafka Streams, transformations and operations on streams are designed to be composable, enabling powerful and expressive stream processing topologies. Understanding and correctly implementing these stream operations is paramount for constructing efficient and effective Kafka Streams applications.

4.3 Kafka Streams Data Model: Tables

Kafka Streams provides a versatile data model that includes tables in addition to streams. A table in Kafka Streams represents a collection of key-value pairs where each key is unique. Unlike streams that capture the immutable series of events over time, tables embody the current state of data. In this context, tables are mutable, allowing updates and deletions, which makes them a powerful construct for stateful processing.

Key-Value Store Semantics

Tables in Kafka Streams embody the key-value store semantics. Each table can be visualized as a map (or dictionary) containing unique keys associated with values. Notably, any operation affecting a table involves updates to this key-value map. When new records with a particular key arrive, the existing value for that key is updated, or a new key-value pair is added if the key does not already exist. This mutable nature of tables aligns well with use cases involving stateful transformations, querying for current states, and materialized views.

The underlying topics in Kafka serve as the storage layer, while the tables represent a distributed, fault-tolerant state store that Kafka Streams manages. The application state is backed by Kafka topics, ensuring durability and scalability.

Creating and Using Tables in Kafka Streams

To create a table in Kafka Streams, the KTable interface is used. The following code demonstrates how to build a KTable instance from an existing Kafka topic:

```
StreamsBuilder builder = new StreamsBuilder();
KTable<String, Long> wordCounts = builder.table("word-count-topic",
    Consumed.with(Serdes.String(), Serdes.Long()));
```

In this example, builder.table is used to create a KTable from the topic word-count-topic, with the keys and values deserialized using the specified SerDes.

Stateful Processing with KTable

Tables are particularly powerful for stateful processing scenarios. For instance, maintaining counts, aggregating values, or managing the state of a process fits well with the capabilities of KTable. Operations such as filter, mapValues, and groupBy are supported.

The example below illustrates how to perform a filter operation on a KTable:

```
KTable<String, Long> filteredCounts = wordCounts.filter(
    (key, value) -> value > 100);
```

This code filters the wordCounts table to retain only those entries where the value exceeds 100.

Table Joins

Tables can participate in different types of joins, enhancing their utility in aggregating and correlating data across multiple sources. Kafka Streams supports various joins between tables, including inner joins, left joins, and outer joins. Here is an example of an inner join between two KTable instances:

```
KTable<String, Long> anotherTable = builder.table("another-topic",
    Consumed.with(Serdes.String(), Serdes.Long()));
KTable<String, Long> joinResult = wordCounts.join(anotherTable,
    (count, anotherCount) -> count + anotherCount);
```

In this example, the join operation combines wordCounts and anotherTable by adding their respective values for matching keys.

Materialized Views

Table transformations can also result in materialized views. Materialized views are updated in real-time as the input data evolves, providing a continuously up-to-date snapshot of aggregated or processed data. Kafka Streams allows these materialized views to be queried reliably, offering an interactive querying capability.

```
KTable<String, Long> materializedView = wordCounts.groupBy(
    (key, value) -> KeyValue.pair(value.toString(), key),
    Grouped.with(Serdes.String(), Serdes.String()))
    .count(Materialized.as("counts-store"));
```

This code snippet demonstrates grouping the wordCounts by values and counting the occurrences, resulting in a materialized view stored in a state store named counts-store.

Handling Updates and Deletes

Tables inherently handle updates, where an arriving record with an existing key will update the current value. Deletes are managed through special tombstone messages, which nullify the value for a specific key. Here's how to handle deletes explicitly:

```
wordCounts.send("some-key", null);
```

This operation sends a null value for the key some-key, effectively deleting the entry from the table.

Tables in Kafka Streams serve as a powerful abstraction for stateful processing, enabling a variety of real-time interactive applications and state management capabilities. They offer a mutable data model that harmonizes with Kafka's robust, distributed architecture, ensuring scalability, fault tolerance, and seamless integration with stream processing constructs.

4.4 Global Tables

In Kafka Streams, a global table is a special type of table that presents a unique way to handle state. Unlike regular tables, which partition data and distribute it across multiple instances, a global table ensures that all instances of a Kafka Streams application have a complete copy of the underlying data. This is particularly useful in scenarios requiring all nodes to have instant access to the full dataset without querying other nodes.

The primary use case for global tables is to manage lookup tables, reference data, or other stateful information that must be accessible entirely by all instances. Global tables are helpful in use cases such as authorization rules, configuration settings, or any other small-to-medium datasets that must be instantly available.

When creating a global table, Kafka Streams performs a full replication of the underlying topic to each instance. This replication ensures each instance has an identical copy of the data, allowing fast local access.

To illustrate the creation and usage of a global table, consider the following example. Suppose we have a Kafka topic named user_permissions that stores user ID and their corresponding permission levels. We want to create a global table from this topic.

First, we define a stream configuration and initialize the Kafka Streams application:

```
Properties props = new Properties();
props.put(StreamsConfig.APPLICATION_ID_CONFIG, "global-table-app");
props.put(StreamsConfig.BOOTSTRAP_SERVERS_CONFIG, "localhost:9092");
props.put(StreamsConfig.DEFAULT_KEY_SERDE_CLASS_CONFIG, Serdes.String()
    .getClass());
props.put(StreamsConfig.DEFAULT_VALUE_SERDE_CLASS_CONFIG, Serdes.
    String().getClass());
KafkaStreams streams = new KafkaStreams(builder.build(), props);
```

Next, we create a global table by defining its schema and specifying the topic from which it will read the data. We use the StreamsBuilder to build the topology:

```
StreamsBuilder builder = new StreamsBuilder();
GlobalKTable<String, String> globalUserPermissions = builder.globalTable(
    "user_permissions",
    Consumed.with(Serdes.String(), Serdes.String())
);
```

Here, user_permissions is the topic name, and Serdes.String() indicates that both the key and value of the records in this topic are strings.

With the global table created, we can perform lookups in this table when processing other streams. For example, suppose we have another stream, user_actions, that logs user actions and includes user ID as its key. We can join the user actions stream with the global table to enrich each action with the user's permission level:

```
KStream<String, String> userActions = builder.stream("user_actions", Consumed.
    with(Serdes.String(), Serdes.String()));

KStream<String, String> enrichedActions = userActions.join(
    globalUserPermissions,
    (key, value) -> key, // User ID is the joining key
    (action, permission) -> action + " (permission level: " + permission + ")" //
        Enriching the action with permission
);
```

This code snippet joins the user_actions stream with the globalUserPermissions global table, using user ID as the joining key. The result is a new stream, enrichedActions, which contains enriched records that include both the original action and the associated permission level.

The advantages of using global tables include:

- Instant Access: Local access to the complete table for swift lookups without network latency.

- Simplified Development: Eliminates the need for partition-key-based design when quick access to full data is required.
- Accuracy: Ensures data replication consistency as managed by Kafka.

It is important to handle certain considerations when using global tables:

- Scalability: Since all instances receive the entire data set, the topic must contain a manageable amount of data that fits within the memory or storage constraints of each instance.
- Latency: Changes propagated to the global table distribute to all instances, potentially incurring additional network overhead depending on the topic's update frequency.

Global tables can be a powerful construct in Kafka Streams, allowing for stateful stream processing where complete data replication across instances is essential.

4.5 Stream-Table Duality

The concept of stream-table duality is fundamental to understanding the Kafka Streams API. It draws from the deep-seated relationship between distributed logs, continuous data streams, and materialized views. This section delves into the theoretical underpinnings of this duality and explains its practical applications within Kafka Streams.

Streams and Tables: Definitions

A *stream* is an unbounded, continuously updating sequence of records or events. Each record in a stream represents a solitary, immutable fact that occurred at a particular point in time. The inherent nature of a stream is that it has no beginning or end, thereby reflecting an infinite sequence of events.

Conversely, a *table* represents a collection of evolving facts. Each record in a table signifies the latest value or state for a given key at any point in time. Unlike a stream, a table captures the culmination of a data state rather than individual data events. Essentially, a table maps keys to values, where the value for each key is subject to change as new records related to that key arrive.

The Duality Principle

The duality between streams and tables manifests from the recognition that every stream can be viewed as changes to an implicit table, and every table can be seen as the result of applying a continuously updating stream of changes. This duality is crucial for designing and reasoning about Kafka Streams applications because it allows developers to employ the most suitable data model according to their use-case requirements.

The stream-table duality can be summarized by two central points:

1. **Stream as a Table**: Any stream can be treated as a table that represents the latest value for each key. Conceptually, this table is derived from the stream by applying all historical records and retaining only the most recent value for each key. The derived table is referred to as a KTable in Kafka Streams, which exhibits stateful properties by keeping track of the latest state for every key.

```
KStream<String, Long> inputStream = builder.stream("input-topic");
KTable<String, Long> tableFromStream = inputStream.toTable(Materialized.as("
    state-store"));
```

2. **Table as a Stream**: Any table can be viewed as a stream of data changes. For instance, insertions, updates, and deletions within a table can be interpreted as a stream of change events, often referred to as a KStream in Kafka Streams. This perspective allows us to process the changes occurring in a table in real-time.

```
KTable<String, Long> existingTable = builder.table("input-table-topic");
KStream<String, Long> streamFromTable = existingTable.toStream();
```

Practical Implications

The stream-table duality introduces significant flexibility in Kafka Streams applications. Developers can switch perspectives between streams and tables to leverage the strengths of both models:

- **Stateful Processing**: For stateful operations, such as windowed aggregations or joins, the table model (e.g., KTable) is often more appropriate because it inherently maintains the state.
- **Event Processing**: For operations focusing on each discrete event (e.g., filtering, mapping), the stream model (e.g., KStream) is preferred due to its event-oriented nature.

Consider a scenario where a developer needs to maintain a running word count from a stream of documents:

```
KStream<String, String> documentStream = builder.stream("documents-topic");
KTable<String, Long> wordCounts = documentStream
    .flatMapValues(value -> Arrays.asList(value.toLowerCase().split(" ")))
    .groupBy((key, word) -> word)
    .count(Materialized.as("counts-store"));
```

This example demonstrates the application of stream-table duality: the document stream is initially processed as a KStream, but the resulting word counts are stored and maintained as a KTable, providing an evolving snapshot of word frequencies.

Stream-Table Joins

The duality also enables powerful join operations. Integrating a stream with a table (stream-table join) or joining two tables (table-table join) becomes straightforward due to the seamless transitions between streams and tables. These joins allow for complex data enrichment and real-time analytics.

```
KStream<String, String> userClicks = builder.stream("user-clicks");
KTable<String, String> userProfiles = builder.table("user-profiles");
KStream<String, UserClickEnriched> enrichedClicks = userClicks
    .leftJoin(userProfiles, (click, profile) -> new UserClickEnriched(click, profile));
```

Here, the user clicks stream is joined with the user profiles table to enrich each click event with user profile information, illustrating the practical application of stream-table duality.

By leveraging both stream and table abstractions, developers can build robust, stateful, and scalable stream processing applications that can handle complex real-time data scenarios with Kafka Streams.

4.6 Creating and Using Streams

Kafka Streams provides an abstraction for reading and processing real-time stream data. To create and utilize streams effectively, understanding the essential components and methods is crucial. This section delves into the creation of streams, operations on these streams, and practical usage, ensuring a comprehensive grasp of their functional aspects.

To create a stream, you typically start by defining a Kafka Streams configuration and then specify the input topic from which the stream will read data. The following example illustrates the basic setup for a Kafka

Streams application, including the configuration and stream definition.

```
// Import necessary Kafka Streams classes
import org.apache.kafka.streams.KafkaStreams;
import org.apache.kafka.streams.StreamsBuilder;
import org.apache.kafka.streams.StreamsConfig;
import org.apache.kafka.streams.kstream.KStream;
import org.apache.kafka.common.serialization.Serdes;

import java.util.Properties;

// Define the Kafka Streams configuration
Properties props = new Properties();
props.put(StreamsConfig.APPLICATION_ID_CONFIG, "stream-app");
props.put(StreamsConfig.BOOTSTRAP_SERVERS_CONFIG, "localhost:9092");
props.put(StreamsConfig.DEFAULT_KEY_SERDE_CLASS_CONFIG, Serdes.String()
    .getClass().getName());
props.put(StreamsConfig.DEFAULT_VALUE_SERDE_CLASS_CONFIG, Serdes.
    String().getClass().getName());

// Create a StreamsBuilder instance
StreamsBuilder builder = new StreamsBuilder();

// Define the input stream from a Kafka topic
KStream<String, String> inputStream = builder.stream("input-topic");

// Perform operations on the input stream
KStream<String, String> outputStream = inputStream.mapValues(value -> value.
    toUpperCase());

// Define the output stream to a Kafka topic
outputStream.to("output-topic");

// Build and start the Kafka Streams application
KafkaStreams streams = new KafkaStreams(builder.build(), props);
streams.start();
```

In this example, a ‘StreamsBuilder‘ object is used to define the processing topology. The ‘stream‘ method is utilized to create a ‘KStream‘ instance, representing the data stream from the input topic "input-topic". The ‘mapValues‘ operation demonstrates a simple transformation by converting the stream's values to uppercase. Finally, the ‘to‘ method assigns the modified stream to the output topic "output-topic".

Several key stream operations can be performed on a ‘KStream‘, such as filtering, transforming, aggregating, and joining. Below are a few examples demonstrating these operations.

- **Filtering:**

You can filter records in a stream based on a specific condition using the ‘filter‘ method.

```
KStream<String, String> filteredStream = inputStream.filter((key, value) -> value.
    length() > 5);
```

This line creates a new ‘KStream‘ containing only records where the value’s length exceeds 5.

- **Transforming:**

Transformations manipulate the records in a stream. The ‘map‘ method allows both the key and value to be transformed.

```
KStream<String, String> transformedStream = inputStream.map((key, value) -> new
    KeyValue<>(key, value.toUpperCase()));
```

Here, both the key and value are left unchanged, but in practice, this method can be used to modify both.

- **Aggregating:**

Aggregation operations combine multiple records into a single result, such as counting the number of records. This typically involves converting a stream to a table (a ‘KTable‘).

```
KTable<String, Long> wordCounts = inputStream
    .flatMapValues(value -> Arrays.asList(value.split("\\W+")))
    .groupBy((key, word) -> word)
    .count(Materialized.as("word-counts-store"));
```

In this example, the ‘flatMapValues‘ method is used to split each record’s value into words, the ‘groupBy‘ method groups by each word, and ‘count‘ computes the number of occurrences of each word.

- **Joining:**

Stream joins combine records from two streams based on a shared key. A common join operation is the inner join, which pairs records with matching keys in both streams.

```
KStream<String, String> otherStream = builder.stream("other-topic");

KStream<String, String> joinedStream = inputStream.join(
    otherStream,
    (value1, value2) -> value1 + " joined with " + value2,
    JoinWindows.of(Duration.ofMinutes(5))
);
```

Here, ‘inputStream‘ joins with ‘otherStream‘ within a 5-minute window, concatenating the values of matching records.

The examples above illustrate fundamental stream operations in Kafka Streams, providing a robust foundation for creating and manipulating

'KStream' instances. Properly defining and transforming streams are pivotal steps in building robust Kafka Streams applications. The next section will build on this by introducing the creation and usage of tables within Kafka Streams, further enhancing your stream processing capabilities.

4.7 Creating and Using Tables

In Kafka Streams, tables represent the stateful counterparts of stateless streams. They provide a persistent, interactive view of the data, usually derived from a stream. This section delves into the creation and utilization of tables in Kafka Streams, demonstrating how they can be employed in various scenarios to enhance data processing tasks.

Tables in Kafka Streams are implemented using the KTable interface. A KTable allows one to store the latest value for each key and enables updates to be retrieved instantaneously. The key-value storage paradigm ensures efficient lookups and modifications, which is critical for applications demanding quick access to stateful data.

- **Creating Tables**

Creating a KTable generally involves reading from a Kafka topic, akin to how one creates a KStream. The following example demonstrates the creation of a KTable from a Kafka topic named users-table:

```
KTable<String, User> usersTable = builder.table("users-table",
    Consumed.with(Serdes.String(), userSerde));
```

Here, the builder.table method ingests data from the Kafka topic users-table. The Consumed.with method specifies the deserializers for the key and value, ensuring the data is appropriately parsed into a String key and a User value, respectively.

- **Using Tables for Data Retrieval and Updates**

Once created, a KTable allows querying for the value associated with a specific key. This capability is invaluable for applications requiring the most recent data state for a key. The following example demonstrates how to perform a lookup:

```
KTable<String, User> usersTable = builder.table("users-table",
```

```
    Consumed.with(Serdes.String(), userSerde));

User user = usersTable.get("user123");
if (user != null) {
    // Process the user details
}
```

In the example above, the get method retrieves the current value associated with "user123". This synchronous query mechanism is a staple for implementing interactive data operations.

- **Materializing Tables**

It is possible to materialize the state of a KTable into a local storage for efficient access. Materialization is particularly useful when dealing with large datasets that need frequent updates and fast access. To materialize a KTable, we use a state store, as shown below:

```
Materialized<String, User, KeyValueStore<Bytes, byte[]>> materializedStore =
    Materialized.<String, User, KeyValueStore<Bytes, byte[]>>as("users-store")
        .withKeySerde(Serdes.String())
        .withValueSerde(userSerde);

KTable<String, User> usersTable = builder.table("users-table",
    Consumed.with(Serdes.String(), userSerde), materializedStore);
```

Here, the Materialized.as method names the state store "users-store" and specifies the key and value serdes. This configuration ensures that the KTable is materialized locally, enhancing read and write performance.

- **Transforming Tables**

Like KStreams, KTables can undergo transformation operations. A common transformation is to map each record to a new key-value pair. The following example transforms a KTable by mapping the user data to include only user IDs and their emails:

```
KTable<String, String> userEmails = usersTable.mapValues(user -> user.getEmail());
```

In this transformation, the mapValues method creates a new KTable containing only the email addresses of users, indexed by their user ID.

- **Aggregating Table Data**

Aggregation is a powerful feature of KTables, allowing us to perform computations like sums, counts, and averages over grouped data. Aggregations are defined using the groupBy and aggregate methods. The following example counts the number of users registered for each city:

```
KTable<String, Long> userCountsByCity = usersTable
    .groupBy((userId, user) -> KeyValue.pair(user.getCity(), userId))
    .count(Materialized.as("user-counts-by-city"));
```

Here, groupBy re-keys the table by the city name, and count creates a new KTable that counts the number of users per city. The results are materialized into a state store named "user-counts-by-city".

- **Joining Tables**

Joining tables is another common operation that combines data from two or more tables based on their keys. Kafka Streams supports various types of joins, including inner joins, left joins, and outer joins. The following example demonstrates an inner join between two tables, usersTable and ordersTable, to combine user details with their corresponding orders:

```
KTable<String, OrderDetails> ordersTable = builder.table("orders-table",
    Consumed.with(Serdes.String(), orderSerde));

KTable<String, UserOrderDetails> userOrderDetailsTable = usersTable.join(
    ordersTable,
    (user, order) -> new UserOrderDetails(user, order),
    Materialized.<String, UserOrderDetails, KeyValueStore<Bytes, byte[]>>as("user-
        order-details-store")
        .withKeySerde(Serdes.String())
        .withValueSerde(userOrderDetailsSerde)
);
```

In this example, the join method merges the usersTable and ordersTable based on the key, resulting in a new KTable that stores UserOrderDetails objects.

The subsequent sections will cover stream-table joins and table-table joins in more detail, providing comprehensive insights into these advanced operations.

Knowing how to create and use tables effectively is foundational for any robust Kafka Streams application. Tables represent stateful streams and allow powerful operations such as materializations, transformations, aggregations, and joins, paving the way for more complex real-time data processing scenarios.

4.8 Stream-Table Joins

Stream-table joins are a powerful feature of Kafka Streams that enable the combination of real-time streaming data with static or slowly changing data stored in tables. This operation is analogous to the SQL join operation where two data sets are merged based on a common key. Understanding and effectively utilizing stream-table joins are crucial for performing complex event processing and enriching streaming data with contextual information.

To perform a stream-table join, we begin with a Kafka topic containing the stream data and a topic containing the table data. The table data is typically materialized into a state store, over which the join operation is performed. Below, we will explore the intricacies of stream-table joins, providing theoretical explanations and practical code examples to illustrate their usage.

When joining a stream with a table, the stream elements are continuously produced and the table elements are periodically updated. Each stream record is joined with the latest corresponding table value using the specified key. This results in an output stream where each record is enriched with additional information from the table.

Suppose we have a stream of customer transactions and a table of customer information. We want to combine these two data sets to produce a stream that includes transaction details along with customer metadata.

First, let us define the stream and the table in our Kafka Streams application.

```
StreamsBuilder builder = new StreamsBuilder();
KStream<String, Transaction> transactionsStream = builder.stream("transactions-
    topic");
KTable<String, Customer> customersTable = builder.table("customers-topic");
```

In this example, transactionsStream is a KStream representing the stream of transactions, and customersTable is a KTable representing the table of customer information. The key for both the stream and the table is the customer ID, which allows us to join the records on this common attribute.

The join operation can be performed using the join method on the KStream interface:

```
KStream<String, EnrichedTransaction> enrichedTransactionsStream =
    transactionsStream.join(
```

```
    customersTable,
    (transaction, customer) -> new EnrichedTransaction(transaction, customer),
    Joined.with(Serdes.String(), SpecificAvroSerde<Transaction>(), SpecificAvroSerde<
        Customer>())
);
```

Here, transactionsStream.join takes three parameters:

- The customersTable to join with.
- A ValueJoiner lambda expression that defines how to merge a Transaction and a Customer into an EnrichedTransaction.
- An optional Joined parameter that specifies SerDes (Serializer/Deserializer) for the key, stream value, and table value.

The ValueJoiner lambda expression combines the transaction and customer records into a new EnrichedTransaction object, which contains information from both the transaction and the customer record.

Here is a simplified version of the EnrichedTransaction class:

```
public class EnrichedTransaction {
    private final Transaction transaction;
    private final Customer customer;

    public EnrichedTransaction(Transaction transaction, Customer customer) {
        this.transaction = transaction;
        this.customer = customer;
    }

    // Getters and other methods
}
```

After joining the stream with the table, the enrichedTransactionsStream KStream now contains enriched transaction records.

The stream-table join operation ensures that the stream records are joined with the latest available value in the table. If a stream record's key does not find a match in the table, the join result for that particular record will not produce output until a matching key is found in the table. Handling missing keys gracefully is essential to prevent data loss.

Kafka Streams also offers an option for left joins, where each stream record is always included in the output stream, even if there is no corresponding record in the table. This is achievable using the leftJoin method:

```
KStream<String, EnrichedTransaction> enrichedTransactionsStream =
        transactionsStream.leftJoin(
    customersTable,
```

```
    (transaction, customer) -> customer != null ? new EnrichedTransaction(transaction,
        customer) : new EnrichedTransaction(transaction, new Customer("Unknown",
        "Unknown")),
    Joined.with(Serdes.String(), SpecificAvroSerde<Transaction>(), SpecificAvroSerde<
        Customer>())
);
```

This left join ensures that every transaction is present in the enrichedTransactionsStream, even if the customer information is missing (in which case, placeholder values are used).

Stream-table joins are fundamental in applications requiring the combination of real-time and static data, such as enriching event data, fraud detection, and real-time analytics. By leveraging these joins, developers can create more contextual and insightful data streams, enhancing the capabilities of their Kafka Streams applications.

4.9 Table-Table Joins

Table-table joins in Kafka Streams facilitate combining records from two different KTables based on a common key, producing a new KTable with the results. This operation is crucial when there is a need to correlate data between two discrete datasets, enriching the data model and enabling more complex analytics and data processing tasks.

When performing a table-table join, the process adheres to the following general pattern: matching records with the same key from two tables, merging their values according to a join function, and updating the target table whenever there are changes in the source tables. This mechanism ensures that the resulting KTable stays consistent with the latest state of the source tables.

The following block of code exemplifies a table-table join:

```
KTable<String, User> usersTable = builder.table("users-topic", Consumed.with(Serdes.
    String(), userSerde));
KTable<String, Region> regionsTable = builder.table("regions-topic", Consumed.with(
    Serdes.String(), regionSerde));

KTable<String, UserRegion> userRegionsTable = usersTable.join(
    regionsTable,
    (user, region) -> new UserRegion(user.getName(), user.getAge(), region.getName())
);
```

In this example, two source tables, 'usersTable' and 'regionsTable', are joined. The 'join' function specifies how the values from these tables should be combined. The resulting 'userRegionsTable' includes a value containing both user and region information.

Key points to consider for table-table joins:

- **Primary Keys and Data Locality**: The join operation hinges on matching primary keys. Both KTables should share the same key type, and Kafka Streams automatically ensures the correct partitioning and data locality to perform the join efficiently.
- **Value Semantics and Null Handling**: In table-table joins, handling null values is vital. In practice, the join functions are designed to manage possible nulls due to non-matching keys or updates resulting in null values in one of the tables.
- **Stream Operations Internal Mechanics**: Kafka Streams maintains an internal changelog topic for each KTable, which records every update to the table. This log is replayed to materialize the joined KTable, ensuring resilience and fault-tolerance of the state.

To provide a more comprehensive understanding, consider the following example where we join a KTable of product information with another KTable of product sales data:

```
KTable<String, Product> productsTable = builder.table("products-topic", Consumed.
    with(Serdes.String(), productSerde));
KTable<String, Sales> salesTable = builder.table("sales-topic", Consumed.with(Serdes.
    String(), salesSerde));

KTable<String, ProductSales> productSalesTable = productsTable.join(
   salesTable,
   (product, sales) -> new ProductSales(product.getName(), product.getCategory(),
        sales.getAmount())
);
```

In this scenario, 'productsTable' contains data about products, identified by their product ID, while 'salesTable' holds the sales figures for products, keyed by the same product ID. The resulting 'productSalesTable' emerges by merging these records, producing an enriched dataset that includes product details and associated sales figures.

The construction 'productsTable.join(...)' illustrates a succinct way to merge data, but also calls for attention to:

- **Schema Design**: Ensure schemas of the joining tables are well-defined and compatible. Schema evolution strategies are employed to handle changes progressively, preserving the table's compatibility.

- **Performance Considerations**: Table-table joins involve state stores for maintaining the KTable states. Efficient state management, thus, directly impacts performance. Compression of internal topics and optimization strategies in Kafka Streams play a significant role in managing large datasets.

By implementing table-table joins efficiently, Kafka Streams applications achieve enriched datasets enabling advanced querying capabilities. The join operations are scalable, benefiting from Kafka's inherent horizontal scalability and the robust stream processing capabilities of Kafka Streams. Thus, the seamless integration of such operations ensures high performance and accuracy in data-driven applications.

4.10 Handling Schema Changes in Streams and Tables

Schema evolution is a critical aspect of managing data streams and tables in Apache Kafka Streams. Schema changes may arise from new requirements, feature enhancements, or backend system modifications. Handling these changes seamlessly ensures that your Kafka Streams applications remain robust and adaptable. In this section, we delve into techniques and best practices for managing schema evolution in streams and tables within Kafka Streams.

Schema compatibility in Kafka Streams primarily revolves around evolving the data model without breaking existing consumers or producers. This necessitates a careful approach to schema design and evolution. Here, we explore various strategies and tools that facilitate this process.

One of the effective ways to manage schemas is through the use of Confluent Schema Registry, which provides a centralized repository for schema management and versioning. It allows schemas to evolve while ensuring compatibility between producers and consumers.

```
{
  "type": "record",
  "name": "User",
  "namespace": "com.example",
  "fields": [
    {"name": "user_id", "type": "string"},
    {"name": "user_name", "type": "string"}
  ]
}
```

As shown in Listing **??**, an example schema for a User record is defined using Avro format. The schema contains two fields: user_id and user_name. When modifying this schema, it is crucial to follow strict compatibility rules.

Kafka Streams relies on Avro's schema evolution capabilities to handle changes. Avro facilitates three types of compatibility: backward, forward, and full.

- **Backward Compatibility:** New schema can read data written by the old schema.
- **Forward Compatibility:** Old schema can read data written by the new schema.
- **Full Compatibility:** Both backward and forward compatibility are maintained.

Consider extending the User schema by adding a new field:

```
{
  "type": "record",
  "name": "User",
  "namespace": "com.example",
  "fields": [
    {"name": "user_id", "type": "string"},
    {"name": "user_name", "type": "string"},
    {"name": "email", "type": ["null", "string"], "default": "null"}
  ]
}
```

Listing **??** depicts the extended schema where an email field has been added. By specifying a default value, compatibility is maintained. Old consumers unaware of the new field can still process the data.

Kafka Streams applications need to recognize and react to schema changes. To ensure that the stream processing logic remains consistent, the schema registry can enforce these compatibility rules. When setting up Schema Registry, you can specify the compatibility mode:

```
curl -X PUT \
  -H "Content-Type: application/vnd.schemaregistry.v1+json" \
  --data '{"compatibility": "BACKWARD"}' \
  http://localhost:8081/config/com.example.User
```

In Listing **??**, we set the schema compatibility mode to BACKWARD for the User schema. This command ensures that any new schemas registered under com.example.User must be backward compatible with existing schemas.

When it comes to applying schema changes in Kafka Streams, careful handling is required in both the serialization and deserialization processes. Here is how you can configure a stream to use a schema registry for Avro serialization:

```
Properties config = new Properties();
config.put(StreamsConfig.APPLICATION_ID_CONFIG, "user-app");
config.put(StreamsConfig.BOOTSTRAP_SERVERS_CONFIG, "localhost:9092");
config.put(AbstractKafkaAvroSerDeConfig.SCHEMA_REGISTRY_URL_CONFIG, "
     http://localhost:8081");

StreamsBuilder builder = new StreamsBuilder();
KStream<String, GenericRecord> userStream = builder.stream("users",
  Consumed.with(Serdes.String(), new SpecificAvroSerde<>()));

userStream.mapValues(value -> {
  value.put("email", ""); // Handle new field gracefully
  return value;
});
```

In Listing **??**, the schema registry configuration is set up with the required properties. The SpecificAvroSerde class is used to deserialize the Avro messages, ensuring that the schema registry is consulted for the schema versions.

Changes in table schemas can be managed similarly. When the schema of a Kafka topic backing a table changes, the table needs to reflect this update to maintain data integrity. Here's an example where the table schema is evolved:

```
KTable<String, GenericRecord> userTable = builder.table("user-table",
  Consumed.with(Serdes.String(), new SpecificAvroSerde<>()));

userTable.toStream().foreach((key, value) -> {
  if (value != null && value.get("email") == null) {
    value.put("email", ""); // Ensure the new field is handled
  }
});
```

Listing **??** demonstrates the handling of schema changes in a KTable. By checking and updating new fields, you can ensure that your application's processing logic remains consistent even as schemas evolve.

Maintaining schema evolution in Kafka Streams is crucial for the continued operation of data pipelines. By leveraging the capabilities of Avro and Confluent Schema Registry, alongside meticulous planning and implementation of schema changes, developers can ensure seamless schema transitions without interrupting the data flow.

Chapter 5

Stateless Transformations

This chapter focuses on stateless transformations in Kafka Streams, detailing various operations such as filter, map, and mapValues. It covers advanced transformations like flatMap and flatMapValues, as well as how to use selectKey, peek, branch, and merge functions. Additionally, the chapter explains groupBy and groupByKey operations, providing practical examples and best practices for implementing stateless transformations in your Kafka Streams applications.

5.1 Introduction to Stateless Transformations

Stateless transformations in Kafka Streams are operations that process each record independently of any other records. These transformations do not require any state to be maintained between records, meaning that the processing of one record does not affect the processing of another record. This independence makes stateless transformations simpler to implement and reason about compared to stateful transformations, which require maintaining information across multiple records.

One of the key benefits of stateless transformations is their inherent scalability. Since each record can be processed independently, these operations can be parallelized easily. In a distributed system like Kafka Streams, this means that stateless transformations can be spread across multiple instances, making efficient use of available processing resources.

The fundamental stateless transformations available in Kafka Streams include filter, map, mapValues, flatMap, and flatMapValues. Additional operations like selectKey, peek, branch, and merge further enrich the capabilities of stateless transformations by allowing for key selection, side-effect operations, conditional branching, and stream merging, respectively. These transformations form the building blocks for more complex stream processing pipelines.

- filter: The filter operation allows you to retain only those records that satisfy a given predicate. The predicate is a boolean function applied to each record, and only records for which the predicate returns true are included in the output stream.

```
KStream<String, String> filteredStream = inputStream.filter(
    (key, value) -> value.contains("important")
);
```

In this example, the inputStream is filtered to include only those records where the value contains the substring "important".

- map and mapValues: The map operation transforms each record in the input stream into a new record, potentially altering both the key and the value. The mapValues operation, on the other hand, only transforms the value, leaving the key unchanged.

```
KStream<String, Integer> mappedStream = inputStream.map(
    (key, value) -> KeyValue.pair(key.toUpperCase(), value.length())
);

KStream<String, Integer> valueMappedStream = inputStream.mapValues(
    value -> value.length()
);
```

In the map example, each key is converted to uppercase, and each value is replaced by its length. In the mapValues example, only the values are transformed to their lengths while keeping the keys unchanged.

- flatMap and flatMapValues: These operations are similar to map and mapValues, but they allow each input record to be transformed into zero, one, or many output records. This is useful for cases where an input record might naturally expand into multiple records.

```
KStream<String, String> flatMappedStream = inputStream.flatMap(
    (key, value) -> {
        List<KeyValue<String, String>> result = new ArrayList<>();
        for (String word : value.split("\\s+")) {
            result.add(new KeyValue<>(key, word));
        }
        return result;
    }
);

KStream<String, String> valueFlatMappedStream = inputStream.flatMapValues(
    value -> Arrays.asList(value.split("\\s+"))
);
```

In the flatMap example, each value is split into words, and each word generates a new record with the same key. The flatMapValues example achieves the same effect but only transforms the values.

- selectKey: This operation allows the key of each record to be recomputed, which can be crucial for grouping and partitioning records differently. The new key is determined by a user-provided function.

```
KStream<String, String> rekeyedStream = inputStream.selectKey((key, value) ->
      value.split("\\s+")[0]);
```

Here, the key of each record is set to the first word of the value.

- peek: The peek operation is used for performing side effects on each record, such as logging, without altering the records themselves. It is useful for debugging and monitoring purposes.

```
inputStream.peek((key, value) -> System.out.println("Processing record: key=" + key
      + ", value=" + value));
```

The peek method prints each record to the console as it is processed.

- branch: This operation allows a stream to be split into multiple streams based on a set of predicates. Each predicate defines a branch, and records are routed to the first branch whose predicate evaluates to true.

```
KStream<String, String>[] branches = inputStream.branch(
    (key, value) -> value.contains("error"),
    (key, value) -> value.contains("warning"),
    (key, value) -> true // default branch
);
```

In this example, the input stream is branched into three streams: one for error messages, one for warning messages, and a default branch for all other messages.

- merge: The merge operation combines two or more streams into a single stream. This is useful when records from different sources need to be processed together.

```
KStream<String, String> mergedStream = stream1.merge(stream2).merge(stream3);
```

Here, stream1, stream2, and stream3 are merged into a single stream.

Stateless transformations serve as a foundational concept in Kafka Streams, enabling the creation of flexible and efficient stream processing pipelines. By employing these transformations, developers can perform a wide array of operations on streaming data, all while leveraging the distributed nature of Kafka Streams to ensure scalability and fault tolerance.

5.2 Filter

The filter operation is fundamental in stream processing using Kafka Streams. This operation allows for the selection of key-value pairs from a stream that meet a specified predicate. A predicate is a function that takes a key-value pair and returns a boolean value, indicating whether the pair should be included in the resulting stream.

The filter method in Kafka Streams is defined as follows:

```
KStream<K, V> filter(Predicate<? super K, ? super V> predicate);
```

The predicate parameter is a functional interface provided by the java.util.function package. It requires implementation of a single method:

```
boolean test(K key, V value);
```

When the test method returns true, the key-value pair is included in the output stream. If it returns false, the pair is excluded.

Consider the following example where we have a stream of user events with keys representing user IDs and values representing event types. Suppose we are interested in filtering the stream to include only login events. The implementation would look as follows:

```
KStream<String, String> events = builder.stream("user-events");
KStream<String, String> loginEvents = events.filter(
    (userId, eventType) -> eventType.equals("login")
);
```

In this example:

- events is a stream of key-value pairs where the key is a String representing the user ID and the value is a String representing the event type.
- The filter operation applies the predicate eventType.equals("login"), which tests whether the value of the event type is equal to "login".
- The result, loginEvents, is a new stream containing only the key-value pairs where the event type is "login".

The filter operation is useful in numerous scenarios, such as filtering out unnecessary data, preprocessing data for downstream operations, and enforcing data quality constraints. Notably, filter operations in Kafka Streams are stateless, meaning each key-value pair is evaluated independently without relying on prior state or context.

Another example demonstrates filtering numeric values. Suppose we have a stream of temperature readings, with keys representing sensor IDs and values representing temperature. The following snippet filters temperatures below freezing point (32°F):

```
KStream<String, Integer> temperatures = builder.stream("temperature-readings");
KStream<String, Integer> aboveFreezing = temperatures.filter(
    (sensorId, temperature) -> temperature > 32
);
```

In this case:

- temperatures stream contains key-value pairs with sensor IDs as keys and temperature readings as values.

- The filter operation uses the predicate temperature > 32 to include only those readings where the temperature is above freezing.
- The result, aboveFreezing, is a stream of key-value pairs where the temperature exceeds 32°F.

When applying the filter operation, it is essential to consider the performance implications. The computational complexity hinges on the frequency and cost of evaluating the predicate. Complex predicates, or those that involve external data access, may degrade performance. Optimization strategies include simplifying predicates, minimizing external dependencies, and leveraging efficient data structures.

Moreover, memory usage remains relatively constant for filter operations, as they do not accumulate state across records. Each key-value pair is processed independently, making filter highly scalable, even for high-velocity streams. This stateless nature of filter underpins its broad applicability in diverse streaming scenarios within Kafka Streams.

Practical use cases may combine filter with other stateless transformations such as map or flatMap. An example of a combined transformation pipeline is shown below, where we filter and then transform the stream:

```
KStream<String, Integer> temperatures = builder.stream("temperature-readings");
KStream<String, Integer> filteredAndMapped = temperatures
    .filter((sensorId, temperature) -> temperature > 32)
    .map((sensorId, temperature) -> KeyValue.pair(sensorId, (temperature - 32) * 5 /
        9));
```

Here, the stream is first filtered for temperatures above the freezing point, and then the remaining temperatures are converted from Fahrenheit to Celsius. Using this combination of filter and map, we efficiently preprocess data for further analysis or downstream processing.

The filter operation in Kafka Streams is a vital tool for stream processing, enabling selective data inclusion based on custom predicates. Its versatility and stateless nature make it an indispensable technique for building robust, high-performance streaming applications.

5.3 Map and MapValues

The map and mapValues operations are foundational transformations in Kafka Streams that allow for the modification of data flowing through the stream. These transformations are essential when the objective is to change the structure or content of the key-value pairs. Understanding these operations and their appropriate usage is crucial for effective stream processing.

map is a general-purpose transformation that can modify both the key and the value of each record in the stream. It involves applying a KeyValueMapper function to each key-value pair, resulting in an output stream with potentially different key-value pairs. The function should be user-defined to meet specific transformation requirements. The signature of the map method is as follows:

```
<KR, VR> KStream<KR, VR> map(KeyValueMapper<? super K, ? super V, ?
    extends KeyValue<? extends KR, ? extends VR>> mapper);
```

In this context, K and V represent the types of keys and values in the input stream, while KR and VR represent the types of keys and values in the output stream. The KeyValueMapper is a functional interface that requires implementing a apply method, which processes each key-value pair and returns a new KeyValue pair.

Here is an example demonstrating how to use map to transform a stream of records where the keys are user IDs and the values are user names. We aim to concatenate the user ID with the user name to create a new key and convert the user name to uppercase.

```
KStream<String, String> userStream = builder.stream("user-topic");
KStream<String, String> transformedStream = userStream.map(
    (key, value) -> KeyValue.pair(key + "-" + value.toUpperCase(), value.toUpperCase
        ())
);
transformedStream.to("transformed-user-topic");
```

In the above example, the input stream userStream consists of key-value pairs where the key is a user ID and the value is a user name. The map function transforms each record by concatenating the key with the uppercase value, resulting in a new stream where both the key and the value are transformed.

On the other hand, mapValues is a more specialized operation that only modifies the value component of each record while keeping the key unchanged. This transformation is useful when the key is intended to remain constant, and only the value requires modification. The method signature for mapValues is:

```
<VR> KStream<K, VR> mapValues(ValueMapper<? super V, ? extends VR>
    mapper);
```

In this case, K represents the type of the key, and V and VR represent the types of the input and output values, respectively. The ValueMapper is a functional interface that implements an apply method to transform the value.

Consider an example where we want to convert the user names in the same stream to uppercase without changing the keys:

```
KStream<String, String> upperCaseNamesStream = userStream.mapValues(value ->
    value.toUpperCase());
upperCaseNamesStream.to("uppercase-user-topic");
```

Here, mapValues is utilized to convert the value (user name) to uppercase while preserving the original key (user ID).

It is also possible to chain multiple transformations for more complex processing. For instance, if there is a requirement to prepend a prefix to the key and convert the value to uppercase, one can combine map and mapValues as follows:

```
KStream<String, String> complexTransformedStream = userStream
    .map((key, value) -> KeyValue.pair("prefix-" + key, value))
    .mapValues(value -> value.toUpperCase());
complexTransformedStream.to("complex-transformed-topic");
```

This chaining ensures that the key transformation occurs first, followed by the value transformation, producing a stream with modified keys and values.

map and mapValues are powerful operators that provide flexibility in transforming streams within Kafka Streams. Utilizing these transformations appropriately can significantly enhance data processing capabilities, allowing developers to tailor the stream content to meet specific application requirements.

5.4 FlatMap and FlatMapValues

The flatMap and flatMapValues operations in Kafka Streams provide powerful functionality to transform the stream by producing zero, one, or more key-value pairs or values from an input key-value pair. This distinction allows these methods to be particularly useful when the transformation logic involves generating an arbitrary number of outputs for each input, which is not possible with the basic map and mapValues methods.

The flatMap method takes a KeyValueMapper<K, V, Iter-

able<KeyValue<KR, VR»> as a parameter. This mapper is applied to each input key-value pair, producing an iterable of new key-value pairs.

```
KStream<String, String> inputStream = builder.stream(”input-topic”);
KStream<String, String> transformedStream = inputStream.flatMap(
    (key, value) -> {
        List<KeyValue<String, String>> result = new ArrayList<>();
        for (String word : value.split(” ”)) {
            result.add(new KeyValue<>(key, word));
        }
        return result;
    }
);
transformedStream.to(”output-topic”);
```

In this example, the flatMap operator splits each input value by spaces and emits each word as a new key-value pair, retaining the original key. If the input stream contains records with values "hello world" and "kafka streams," the output stream will contain the records "hello" and "world" for the first input and "kafka" and "streams" for the second input, maintaining the same key for all new pairs.

Similarly, flatMapValues transforms the value part of each key-value pair but leaves the key unchanged. The function provided to flatMapValues returns an iterable of new values. This is particularly useful when multiple derived values should be emitted for a single input value while keeping the input key intact.

```
KStream<String, String> inputStream = builder.stream(”input-topic”);
KStream<String, String> transformedStream = inputStream.flatMapValues(
    value -> Arrays.asList(value.split(” ”))
);
transformedStream.to(”output-topic”);
```

In this example, the flatMapValues splits each input value by spaces, similar to the flatMap example, but here only the values are changed, with the keys remaining the same. The output stream will contain records with each word from the input values while retaining the original key.

When compared to map and mapValues, where each input key-value pair generates exactly one output key-value pair, flatMap and flatMapValues provide much more flexibility, with each input potentially resulting in zero or many output records. This allows for more complex and varied transformations which are vital in processing pipelines where fan-out is necessary.

To understand the practical applications of flatMap and flatMapValues, consider a real-world example where an e-commerce application receives orders which contain multiple items. Each order is represented as a key-value pair in a Kafka stream, where the key is the order ID and the value is a string listing the items.

```
KStream<String, String> ordersStream = builder.stream("orders");
KStream<String, String> itemsStream = ordersStream.flatMap(
    (orderId, items) -> {
        List<KeyValue<String, String>> itemPairs = new ArrayList<>();
        for (String item : items.split(",")) {
            itemPairs.add(new KeyValue<>(orderId, item));
        }
        return itemPairs;
    }
);
itemsStream.to("items-topic");
```

In this scenario, each input order results in multiple output records, one for each item in the order, all sharing the same order ID as the key.

Overall, utilizing flatMap and flatMapValues correctly allows for sophisticated stream transformations enabling advanced use cases where multiple outputs from a single input are required. These functions enhance the versatility of Kafka Streams by facilitating complex event processing pipelines and enriching the capabilities of stream processing applications.

5.5 SelectKey

The selectKey function in Kafka Streams is a crucial operation that allows transforming the key of a key-value pair within a data stream. This transformation does not alter the value associated with the key and is particularly useful when you need to reorganize the stream based on different key partitions for further processing steps.

To understand selectKey, consider the following method signature from the Kafka Streams API:

```
<K1> KStream<K1, V> selectKey(KeyValueMapper<? super K, ? super V, ? extends
    K1> mapper);
```

Here, K1 is the new key type, and V is the type of the value which remains unchanged. The mapper parameter is a function that takes the current key and value as inputs and returns the new key.

Example Usage:

Suppose you have a stream of user activities where the key is the user ID and the value consists of various user action details. If you need to re-key the stream based on the region of the user instead of their ID, selectKey can be utilized as follows:

```
KStream<String, UserActivity> userActivityStream = ...;

KStream<String, UserActivity> regionKeyedStream = userActivityStream.selectKey(
    (key, value) -> value.getRegion()
);
```

In this example, userActivityStream is the original stream keyed by user ID, and regionKeyedStream is the resulting stream keyed by the user's region. The lambda function (key, value) -> value.getRegion() extracts the region information from the UserActivity value to use as the new key, thus changing the key based on the region attribute while keeping the value, i.e., UserActivity, unchanged.

Internal Working:

When selectKey is invoked, Kafka Streams creates a new stream where each key-value pair is processed through the provided KeyValueMapper. Internally, for each key-value pair (K, V), the pair is transformed to $(K1, V)$, where the new key $K1$ is derived from the mapping function.

Here is a detailed step-by-step breakdown of what happens internally:

- **Key-Value Pair Processing:** Each key-value pair from the original stream is processed.
- **Key Transformation:** The mapper function is applied to each pair, deriving the new key $K1$.
- **Re-Keying the Pair:** The transformed key-value pair $(K1, V)$ is emitted to the resulting stream.

```
Original Stream: (userId1 -> UserActivity1), (userId2 -> UserActivity2), ...
                |
                v
Mapped Stream: (region1 -> UserActivity1), (region2 -> UserActivity2), ...
```

This transformation is stateless, meaning each key-value pair is re-keyed independently of others, aligning with Kafka Streams' approach to parallel processing.

Key Considerations:

- **Idempotency:** Ensure that the transformation function is idempotent, meaning applying it multiple times yields the same result. This is critical for ensuring consistency in stream processing.

- **Key Uniqueness:** After re-keying, multiple original keys might map to the same new key, potentially leading to collisions. Downstream operations should be designed to handle such cases appropriately.
- **Partitioning:** Kafka Streams relies on keys to distribute records across partitions. Re-keying will alter how records are partitioned, which can impact the parallelism and order of record processing. Choose the new key carefully to balance load across partitions.
- **State Management:** Since selectKey is stateless, it does not retain any history of keys and values. Ensure that the logic dependent on stateful operations is applied downstream.

Advanced Example:

Consider a scenario where you are processing transactions and you need to re-key based on transaction types for aggregated processing:

```
KStream<String, Transaction> transactionStream = ...;

KStream<String, Transaction> transactionTypeKeyedStream = transactionStream.
        selectKey(
    (key, value) -> value.getTransactionType()
);
```

This example keys the transactions based on their type, facilitating subsequent operations like aggregations or joins according to transaction types. The lambda function (key, value) -> value.getTransactionType() maps each transaction to its type.

This function integrates seamlessly with other Kafka Streams operations like filtering, mapping, and windowing, forming a cohesive pipeline for stream processing tasks. Effective use of selectKey can optimize stream processing strategies, making it a powerful tool in the Kafka Streams API for achieving flexible and efficient data pipeline designs.

5.6 Peek

The peek function in Kafka Streams is a powerful tool that allows for side effects during the processing of a stream without altering the original stream. This operator provides a mechanism to inspect, log, or interact with each record in the stream pipeline, facilitating debugging and monitoring tasks.

peek is best understood within the context of a stream processing pipeline where visibility into each individual record at various stages of the pipeline is beneficial. The peek function accepts a ForeachAction, which is a BiConsumer that processes each record without modifying the stream's data flow.

Syntax:

```
KStream<K, V> peek(ForeachAction<? super K, ? super V> action);
```

The ForeachAction is defined as follows:

```
@FunctionalInterface
public interface ForeachAction<K, V> {
    void apply(K key, V value);
}
```

Consider a scenario where you need to log the key-value pairs of a stream for debugging purposes. Using peek, you can achieve this elegantly:

```
KStream<String, String> stream = builder.stream("input-topic");
stream.peek((key, value) -> System.out.println("Key: " + key + ", Value: " + value))
      .mapValues(value -> value.toUpperCase())
      .to("output-topic");
```

In this example, the peek function logs each record's key and value before the mapValues transformation is applied. Notably, the original stream remains unmodified, and the continuation of the stream processing pipeline is unaffected by the side-effect operations performed within peek.

The peek function is particularly advantageous when dealing with complex transformations and enrichments within the stream. For instance, when performing multiple transformations, inserting peek at intermediate steps allows for verification of intermediate states, thus simplifying troubleshooting.

```
KStream<String, String> dataStream = builder.stream("sensor-data");
dataStream.mapValues(value -> value.split(",")[1])
          .peek((key, value) -> System.out.println("Intermediate value: " + value))
          .mapValues(Integer::parseInt)
          .filter((key, value) -> value > 50)
          .to("filtered-data");
```

In this context, peek helps confirm that the values have been correctly parsed and split before subsequent transformations and filters are applied.

Implementations involving peek should be used judiciously, particularly in production environments, as indiscriminate logging or side effects could lead to performance impacts and increased resource utilization. Ensuring that the operations within peek are lightweight and efficient mitigates these risks.

Given the stateless nature of peek, it interacts seamlessly with other stateless transformations like map and filter. It does not affect the state stores or the materialized views within Kafka Streams, preserving the integrity of the stream processing while offering a window into the streaming data.

When dealing with nested streams or joining multiple streams, peek can be peppered across different stages to provide granular visibility:

```
KStream<String, String> leftStream = builder.stream("left-topic");
KStream<String, String> rightStream = builder.stream("right-topic");

leftStream.peek((key, value) -> System.out.println("Left stream: " + key + " -> " +
    value))
        .join(rightStream,
              (leftValue, rightValue) -> leftValue + "|" + rightValue,
              JoinWindows.of(Duration.ofMinutes(5)))
        .peek((key, value) -> System.out.println("Joined stream: Key: " + key + ",
              Value: " + value))
        .to("joined-output");
```

Here, peek provides visibility into both the left stream and the result of the join operation, thereby enabling the validation of the join logic and its outcome.

In summary, peek is a non-intrusive, debugging-friendly function that empowers developers to monitor stream contents and transformations effectively during the stream processing lifecycle. Properly leveraged, it facilitates robust and maintainable Kafka Streams applications.

5.7 Branch

The branch method in Kafka Streams provides a mechanism for splitting a single KStream into multiple KStream branches based on specified predicates. This is particularly useful when you want to process different data records differently depending on certain conditions.

The branch method takes a variable number of predicates and evaluates them in the order they are provided. Each predicate is a Predicate<K, V> functional interface which takes a key and value as parameters and returns a boolean. When a record matches a predicate, it is redirected to the corresponding branch. If a record does not match any of the predicates, it gets routed to a default branch or is discarded.

Here is a typical usage of the branch method:

```
KStream<String, String> sourceStream = builder.stream("source-topic");

KStream<String, String>[] branches = sourceStream.branch(
    (key, value) -> value.contains("error"),
    (key, value) -> value.contains("info")
);

KStream<String, String> errorStream = branches[0];
KStream<String, String> infoStream = branches[1];
```

In this example, the sourceStream is branched into two streams based on whether the value contains the substring "error" or "info". The first predicate checks for "error" and directs matching records to errorStream. The second predicate checks for "info" and directs matching records to infoStream.

- **Order of Predicates**

The order of predicates is crucial because each record is evaluated sequentially against each predicate. Once a record matches a predicate, it will not be evaluated against subsequent predicates. The following example illustrates this:

```
KStream<String, String>[] branches = sourceStream.branch(
    (key, value) -> value.length() > 10,
    (key, value) -> value.contains("short"),
    (key, value) -> value.length() <= 10
);
```

In this setup, if a record has a length greater than 10, it will be directed to the first branch and will not be evaluated for "short" or length less than or equal to 10. Careful consideration should be given to the order of predicates to ensure correct branching behavior.

- **Default Branch Handling**

If there is a possibility that some records do not match any of the provided predicates, you can add a final predicate that always returns true to serve as a default branch:

```
KStream<String, String>[] branches = sourceStream.branch(
    (key, value) -> value.contains("error"),
    (key, value) -> value.contains("info"),
    (key, value) -> true // catch-all branch
);

KStream<String, String> otherStream = branches[2];
```

Records that do not satisfy the first two predicates get directed to otherStream.

- **Real-World Application**

To demonstrate the practical application of the branch method, consider a scenario where a company processes various types of notifications: errors, warnings, and informational messages. Each type of message requires a different processing pipeline.

```
KStream<String, String> notificationStream = builder.stream("notifications");

KStream<String, String>[] notificationBranches = notificationStream.branch(
    (key, value) -> value.contains("ERROR"),
    (key, value) -> value.contains("WARN"),
    (key, value) -> value.contains("INFO")
);

KStream<String, String> errorStream = notificationBranches[0];
KStream<String, String> warningStream = notificationBranches[1];
KStream<String, String> infoStream = notificationBranches[2];

errorStream.to("error-topic");
warningStream.to("warning-topic");
infoStream.to("info-topic");
```

In this real-world example, the notificationStream is branched into three separate streams, each processed and redirected to its respective Kafka topic.

- **Performance Considerations**

While using the branch method, it's important to balance the complexity of predicates and performance. Evaluating simple conditions in predicates ensures low overhead. Complex predicates, especially those involving external resources or computationally expensive operations, should be optimized or handled differently to maintain efficient stream processing.

Testing and profiling should be conducted to ensure that the branching logic meets performance requirements under varying loads.

- **Combining Branches**

In practice, you might need to combine multiple branched streams back into a single stream for consolidated processing. The merge method is used to combine multiple KStream instances into one. Consider the following example:

```
KStream<String, String> unifiedStream = errorStream.merge(warningStream).merge(
    infoStream);
unifiedStream.to("all-notifications");
```

This combines all branches into a single stream, which is then redirected to the "all-notifications" topic. Stream compositions like this showcase powerful ways to segment and unify data flows according to specific application requirements without compromising performance.

By understanding and correctly utilizing the branch method, one can create sophisticated data processing pipelines that cater to diversified handling of streaming data. The above directives and examples present a foundation for implementing and leveraging the branch method effectively within Kafka Streams applications.

5.8 Merge

The merge function in Kafka Streams is utilized to combine two or more streams into a single stream. This operation is particularly useful when handling data from multiple Kafka topics that need to be processed together or when combining transformations from different streams. Unlike joins in Kafka Streams which match records based on keys, the merge function simply unifies multiple streams without considering key-value pair relationships.

The merge function can be applied to any KStream. Its syntax is straightforward and user-friendly. To demonstrate the usage of merge, consider the following practical example:

```
KStream<String, Long> stream1 = builder.stream("topic1");
KStream<String, Long> stream2 = builder.stream("topic2");

KStream<String, Long> mergedStream = stream1.merge(stream2);
```

In the above example, two streams, stream1 and stream2, are created from two different topics, "topic1" and "topic2", respectively. By applying the merge function, a new stream, mergedStream, is created that combines the data from stream1 and stream2.

The merged stream retains all the records from both input streams. It's important to note that the order of data in the merged stream is not guaranteed to follow the order of the original streams. Kafka Streams processes records based on the internal logic of its task assignment and partitioning.

- **Advantages of Using merge**

Using the merge function offers several advantages:

- Combining related data: It allows combining multiple related data streams into a single stream for unified processing.
- Simplifies topology: By merging streams, we can simplify the Kafka Streams topology, making it easier to manage and understand.
- Scalable processing: The merged stream can benefit from Kafka's parallel processing capabilities, enabling scalable data processing.

- **Example Scenario**

Consider a scenario where we have two topics, one containing user click events and another containing user purchase events. Each event type is processed in its stream, but we want to analyze user behavior by combining these two streams into one.

We start by defining the streams for clicks and purchases:

```
KStream<String, UserEvent> clickStream = builder.stream("user-clicks");
KStream<String, UserEvent> purchaseStream = builder.stream("user-purchases");
```

Next, we merge these two streams into a single stream:

```
KStream<String, UserEvent> userEventsStream = clickStream.merge(purchaseStream);
```

Once merged, we can perform further transformations on the unified stream to derive meaningful insights:

```
userEventsStream.peek((key, event) -> System.out.println("User Event: " + event))
                .filter((key, event) -> event.isAnomalous())
                .to("anomalous-user-events");
```

In this example, we print each event to the console using the peek function. We then filter the events to identify any anomalous user behavior and write those events to a new topic named "anomalous-user-events".

- **Error Handling and Stream Recovery**

Merging streams might introduce challenges such as handling incompatible data formats and recovering from stream failures. It is crucial to implement robust error handling mechanisms when working with merged streams.

Incompatible data formats can lead to serialization/deserialization errors. Ensure all streams have compatible key-value types before merging. If data format discrepancies are unavoidable, consider using custom serializers and deserializers to convert data to a compatible format.

For example, if one stream has keys as Strings and another has keys as Longs, you must convert them to a common type:

```
KStream<String, Long> stream1 = builder.<String, Long>stream("topic1").selectKey
    ((key, value) -> key.toString());
KStream<String, Long> stream2 = builder.<String, Long>stream("topic2").selectKey
    ((key, value) -> key.toString());

KStream<String, Long> mergedStream = stream1.merge(stream2);
```

Stream recovery involves handling stream failures gracefully. Implementing a retry mechanism or a dead-letter queue can ensure the system is resilient and the data flow is not interrupted.

- **Best Practices**

- Keep streams homogeneous: Merge streams with similar data structures and processing logic to avoid complications.
- Monitor and log: Implement monitoring and logging to track stream behavior and detect anomalies early.
- Testing: Ensure thorough testing of merged streams, especially edge cases like empty streams and heterogeneous data formats.

Merging streams in Kafka Streams provides a powerful tool for combining and processing data from multiple sources. By understanding its capabilities and potential pitfalls, developers can efficiently build complex stream-processing topologies.

5.9 GroupBy and GroupByKey

The groupBy and groupByKey operations in Kafka Streams are essential for organizing records by a new key for subsequent processing steps like aggregations, joins, and windowing operations. These transformations allow for the restructuring of the stream such that records are regrouped based on their keys.

groupByKey is the simpler of the two methods, used directly on KStreams or KTables where the key of each record remains unchanged. It returns a KGroupedStream<K, V> or KGroupedTable<K, V>.

groupBy is more versatile and allows for transforming the key. It is typically used when the grouping criteria differ from the current key, thereby enabling dynamic re-keying based on the record's value or some other transformation logic. This method returns a KGroupedStream<K1, V> or KGroupedTable<K1, V>.

```
import org.apache.kafka.common.serialization.Serdes;
import org.apache.kafka.streams.KafkaStreams;
import org.apache.kafka.streams.StreamsBuilder;
import org.apache.kafka.streams.kstream.KStream;
import org.apache.kafka.streams.kstream.KTable;
import org.apache.kafka.streams.kstream.Materialized;

StreamsBuilder builder = new StreamsBuilder();

// Create an initial KStream
KStream<String, String> initialStream = builder.stream("input-topic");

// Example of groupBy
KTable<String, Long> groupedByNewKey = initialStream
    .groupBy((key, value) -> value.substring(0, 5))
    .count(Materialized.with(Serdes.String(), Serdes.Long()));

// Example of groupByKey
KTable<String, Long> groupedByKey = initialStream
    .groupByKey()
    .count(Materialized.with(Serdes.String(), Serdes.Long()));

// Building and starting the Kafka Streams application
KafkaStreams streams = new KafkaStreams(builder.build(), props);
streams.start();
```

In the example above, the initialStream is first created from the input-topic. For the groupBy example, records are re-keyed to the first five characters of their values before being counted. For the groupByKey example, records are grouped and counted directly by their existing keys.

The core idea behind grouping is to enable downstream operations that depend on the keyed grouping, such as aggregations. It's essential to materialize the grouped results properly, as shown with the Materialized.with method in the example. This ensures that Kafka Streams manages the state stores required to maintain the intermediate aggregation results.

Considerations for Using groupBy and groupByKey:

- Cardinality: Grouping generates a state store for the new keys, and the cardinality of keys directly affects the memory and storage requirements. High cardinality may lead to increased resource consumption.

- Serialization: Custom serializers may be necessary if the new keys after a groupBy operation are of a different type from the original keys.
- State Store Management: Proper configuration of state store settings, such as retention period and changelog settings, is crucial for efficient resource management.

A typical use case for groupBy is when the grouping criterion requires a more complex computation than the current key, thereby necessitating the transformation of the key itself. For example, if records represent user actions, one might group based on a derived user segment rather than the user ID.

```
KStream<String, String> userActions = builder.stream("user-actions");

// Example of complex key transformation using groupBy
KTable<String, Long> userSegmentCounts = userActions
    .groupBy((key, value) -> {
        // Hypothetical method to determine user segment from the value
        String userSegment = getUserSegment(value);
        return userSegment;
    })
    .count(Materialized.with(Serdes.String(), Serdes.Long()));

// Hypothetical method to determine user segment
private static String getUserSegment(String value) {
    // Example transformation logic for user segment
    if (value.contains("premium")) {
        return "premium";
    } else {
        return "standard";
    }
}
```

In this example, the stream userActions is grouped by a derived user segment, which could be determined by examining the value. This method demonstrates the flexibility and power of groupBy to facilitate dynamic re-keying based on more complex business logic.

groupByKey is straightforward and appropriate when the existing key is sufficient for further processing. It doesn't require any transformation of the key, making it simpler and more efficient.

The selection between groupBy and groupByKey ultimately hinges on whether the existing key structure fulfills the requirements for downstream processing. Proper understanding and application of these methods enable efficient key-based stream processing, crucial for real-time analytics and stateful operations in Kafka Streams applications.

Chapter 6

Stateful Transformations

This chapter delves into stateful transformations in Kafka Streams, beginning with an understanding of state management and state stores. It explores key operations such as aggregate and reduce functions, alongside practical applications for counting and summarizing data. The chapter also covers the intricacies of joining streams, windowed joins, and creating materialized views. Detailed guidance on persisting state ensures that applications maintain consistency and reliability during stateful processing.

6.1 Introduction to Stateful Transformations

Stateful transformations in Kafka Streams extend the functional capabilities of stream processing by integrating the concept of state. In contrast to stateless transformations—where operations are applied independently to each incoming record—stateful transformations maintain and modify state across multiple records. This enables more complex data processing tasks like aggregations, joins, and windowing operations.

Kafka Streams API introduces stateful transformations through the use of state stores. A state store is a storage mechanism where the state needed for transformations can be held. State stores can be local or distributed, with local state stores residing on the same instance of the processing application, and distributed state stores spanning across multiple instances.

When configuring stateful transformations, it is critical to manage the state efficiently to ensure fault tolerance and scalability. Kafka Streams provides built-in mechanisms for persistent state storage and recovery. For instance, RocksDB is often employed as the default state store due to its high performance and compact storage format.

The implementation of stateful transformations involves defining operations that modify the state in response to new data. Key operations in this category include aggregations such as sum, count, average, and more complex composites. By maintaining state, these operations can compute running totals, averages, or other metrics that evolve over time.

Consider the aggregate operation. Aggregations can be implemented by defining a state store that keeps track of cumulative results up to the current point in the stream. When a new record arrives, the state store is queried, the record is incorporated into the current state, and the updated state is written back to the store. This process ensures that the state is always synchronized with the processed stream.

```
KStream<String, Long> stream = builder.stream("input-topic");

KTable<String, Long> aggregatedTable = stream
    .groupByKey()
    .aggregate(
        () -> 0L,
        (aggKey, newValue, aggValue) -> aggValue + newValue,
        Materialized.<String, Long, KeyValueStore<Bytes, byte[]>>as("aggregated-
            store")
            .withValueSerde(Serdes.Long())
    );

aggregatedTable.toStream().to("output-topic", Produced.with(Serdes.String(), Serdes.
    Long()));
```

In this example, the stateful aggregation maintains a cumulative count of values in the stream under each key. The groupByKey() method re-partitions the stream by key, which is necessary for correct distribution of records across the instances. The aggregate() function specifies the initial value (0L), the aggregator function that updates state with each new value, and the state store configuration (Materialized.as("aggregated-store")).

The state store, named "aggregated-store", is explicitly defined to provide durability and recoverability. Kafka Streams ensures this store is maintained across application reboots by periodically persisting the state to disk and integrating it with Kafka's built-in fault-tolerance guarantees.

Another fundamental stateful operation is the reduce function, which similarly maintains and updates state in response to incoming records. The reduce function merges records into a single cumulative result, often used when applying associative and commutative operations.

Beyond individual stateful operations, Kafka Streams allows the composition of multiple transformations. One can combine aggregations with joins or windowed operations to achieve comprehensive, stateful stream processing pipelines.

Efficient state management necessitates careful consideration of the state store's lifecycle, including initialization, access patterns, and cleanup. Kafka Streams handles many of these concerns internally, but understanding state store configuration and management can optimize performance and resilience.

Stateful transformations thus empower Kafka Streams applications to perform sophisticated analyses of streaming data, enabling enriched insights and real-time data processing capabilities. Integrating state into stream processing unlocks new possibilities, crucial for applications requiring real-time analytics, dynamic joins, or continuously updated materialized views.

6.2 Understanding State in Kafka Streams

In Kafka Streams, understanding state management is crucial for implementing sophisticated stream processing tasks. State refers to the intermediate data that is remembered between processing steps. This is necessary for various transformations and operations such as aggregations, joins, and windowing functions, which inherently rely on keeping track of past data to produce accurate outputs.

Kafka Streams State Management

In Kafka Streams, state management is accomplished using state stores. State stores are local databases that reside within each instance (or task) of a Kafka Streams application. State stores enable Kafka Streams to retain the state associated with stream processing operations. Thus, the processing state is not stateless and is kept consistent, even in the face of failures.

State stores in Kafka Streams can be categorized into two main types:

persistent and in-memory.

- **Persistent stores** are backed by durable storage like disk using technologies such as RocksDB. Persistent stores ensure that state information is durable and can survive application restarts. This makes them suitable for use cases where fault tolerance and recovery are important.
- **In-memory stores** are maintained entirely in RAM. These stores provide faster access times compared to persistent stores but do not offer durability guarantees. They are typically used for transient state needs where speed is critical and data persistence is not necessary.

The interface for a state store in Kafka Streams is provided through the StateStore interface. Kafka Streams also provides a variety of built-in state stores like KeyValueStore, WindowStore, and SessionStore for different use cases.

Creating State Stores

Creating a state store involves defining its properties including name, type, and durability. In Kafka Streams, state stores can be added to the topology using the StoreBuilder API. Below is an example of creating a key-value store:

```
StoreBuilder<KeyValueStore<String, Long>> keyValueStoreBuilder =
    Stores.keyValueStoreBuilder(
        Stores.persistentKeyValueStore("my-state-store"),
        Serdes.String(),
        Serdes.Long()
    );
```

In this example, a persistent key-value store named "my-state-store" is created with String keys and Long values.

Accessing State Stores

State stores are accessible from within stateful operations such as transformers and processors. Access to a state store is typically done in the init method of a processor. The following example illustrates how to access a key-value store within a transformer:

```
public class StatefulTransformer implements Transformer<String, Long, KeyValue<
    String, Long>> {

    private KeyValueStore<String, Long> stateStore;

    @Override
```

```
    public void init(ProcessorContext context) {
        this.stateStore = (KeyValueStore<String, Long>) context.getStateStore("my-
            state-store");
    }

    @Override
    public KeyValue<String, Long> transform(String key, Long value) {
        Long oldValue = stateStore.get(key);
        Long newValue = (oldValue == null) ? value : oldValue + value;
        stateStore.put(key, newValue);
        return KeyValue.pair(key, newValue);
    }

    @Override
    public void close() {
        // No-op
    }
}
```

In this transformer, the state's store is retrieved using the context.getStateStore method during initialization. The state store is then used to maintain and update state information as records are processed.

Fault Tolerance and Recovery

Kafka Streams ensures fault tolerance and state recovery through a combination of changelogs and repartition topics.

- **Changelogs** are Kafka topics that receive updates (changes) to the state store. Every time the state store is updated in a task, the change is also written to its corresponding change log. This log can later be replayed to reconstruct the state store during recovery.
- **Repartition topics** are used when the data distribution needs to change, such as after a key-based repartitioning. This ensures that state stores remain consistent across tasks.

These techniques ensure that state information is reliably maintained and can be recovered after failures, achieving Exactly-Once semantics (EOS) in stream processing.

Example of State Store Recovery

Consider a scenario where a persistent state store is being used with a Kafka Streams application. If the application instance crashes, upon restart, the state store will be restored from its last committed state using the changelog topic:

```
Properties props = new Properties();
```

```
props.put(StreamsConfig.APPLICATION_ID_CONFIG, "example-app");
props.put(StreamsConfig.BOOTSTRAP_SERVERS_CONFIG, "localhost:9092");
props.put(StreamsConfig.REPLICATION_FACTOR_CONFIG, 3); // Changelog
    replication
```

In this example configuration, the changelog for the state store will have a replication factor of 3, ensuring resiliency against broker failures.

Understanding how state is managed in Kafka Streams enables developers to build robust, fault-tolerant applications that can accurately process and maintain stateful information across distributed systems. By leveraging state stores, changelogs, and proper configuration, Kafka Streams applications can achieve efficient stateful stream processing.

6.3 Managing State Stores

Kafka Streams provides robust mechanisms for managing state, allowing applications to maintain and query state information efficiently. State stores are pivotal in this context, enabling the persistence of data between streaming operations. This section explores the structure and functionality of state stores, methods for their management, and practical implementations.

A state store in Kafka Streams is a durable storage mechanism that holds stateful information necessary for stream processing tasks. These state stores can be queried and used by streaming operations such as aggregations, joins, and windowing. Kafka Streams supports various types of state stores, including persistent (backed by disk storage) and in-memory stores.

To initialize and manage state stores, Kafka Streams leverages the org.apache.kafka.streams.state.Stores factory. This factory provides methods to create and configure state stores according to the application's requirements. Below is an example of creating an in-memory state store using the Stores factory:

```
import org.apache.kafka.streams.state.Stores;
import org.apache.kafka.streams.state.KeyValueStore;

KeyValueStore<String, Long> stateStore = Stores
    .keyValueStoreBuilder(
        Stores.inMemoryKeyValueStore("in-memory-store"),
        Serdes.String(),
        Serdes.Long()
    )
    .withLoggingDisabled() // Disable changelog for this store.
    .build();
```

The keyValueStoreBuilder method constructs a key-value store builder, with the inMemoryKeyValueStore specifying the type of state store. The arguments include serdes for the key and value, defining how the data is serialized and deserialized.

State stores can also be persistent, which is crucial when applications need to recover from failures or need to maintain state across restarts. Consider the following example, which creates a persistent state store with a changelog:

```
import org.apache.kafka.streams.state.Stores;
import org.apache.kafka.streams.state.KeyValueStore;

KeyValueStore<String, Long> stateStore = Stores
    .keyValueStoreBuilder(
        Stores.persistentKeyValueStore("persistent-store"),
        Serdes.String(),
        Serdes.Long()
    )
    .withLoggingEnabled() // Enable changelog for reliability.
    .build();
```

Persistent state stores use a changelog topic managed by Kafka to ensure durability. The withLoggingEnabled method enables Kafka Streams to persist state changes to this changelog, thereby making the store fault-tolerant.

State stores are commonly used with the Processor API, which allows developers to directly interact with the data in these stores. When creating topology, processors and state stores are linked using a topology builder. Below is an example illustrating this integration:

```
import org.apache.kafka.streams.StreamsBuilder;
import org.apache.kafka.streams.Topology;
import org.apache.kafka.streams.processor.api.ProcessorSupplier;
import org.apache.kafka.streams.processor.api.Processor;
import org.apache.kafka.streams.processor.api.ProcessorContext;

public class StateStoreExample {

    public static void main(String[] args) {
        StreamsBuilder builder = new StreamsBuilder();
        builder.addStateStore(stateStore);

        builder.stream("input-topic")
                .process(new MyProcessorSupplier(), "persistent-store");

        Topology topology = builder.build();
    }

    private static class MyProcessorSupplier implements ProcessorSupplier<String,
          String, Void, Void> {
        @Override
        public Processor<String, String, Void, Void> get() {
            return new MyProcessor();
```

```
        }
    }

    private static class MyProcessor implements Processor<String, String, Void, Void>
        {
        private KeyValueStore<String, Long> stateStore;

        @Override
        public void init(ProcessorContext<Void, Void> context) {
            stateStore = (KeyValueStore<String, Long>) context.getStateStore("
                persistent-store");
        }

        @Override
        public void process(String key, String value) {
            Long count = stateStore.get(key);
            if (count == null) {
                stateStore.put(key, 1L);
            } else {
                stateStore.put(key, count + 1);
            }
        }

        @Override
        public void close() {}
    }
}
```

This example demonstrates how to integrate a state store with a Kafka Streams application. The processor reads and updates the state store based on the incoming stream data, enabling stateful operations that count occurrences of keys.

Embedded queries within stateful applications provide a powerful mechanism to interact with state stores. Kafka Streams enables querying of state stores through the Interactive Queries API. Here is an example of exposing a state store via a simple REST API using InteractiveQueryService:

```
import org.apache.kafka.streams.KafkaStreams;
import org.apache.kafka.streams.state.QueryableStoreTypes;
import org.apache.kafka.streams.state.ReadOnlyKeyValueStore;

@Path("/state")
public class StateQueryService {

    private KafkaStreams streams;

    public StateQueryService(KafkaStreams streams) {
        this.streams = streams;
    }

    @GET
    @Path("/{storeName}/{key}")
    @Produces(MediaType.APPLICATION_JSON)
    public String getValue(@PathParam("storeName") String storeName,
                           @PathParam("key") String key) {
        ReadOnlyKeyValueStore<String, Long> keyValueStore =
```

```
            streams.store(storeName, QueryableStoreTypes.keyValueStore());

        Long value = keyValueStore.get(key);
        if (value != null) {
            return String.valueOf(value);
        } else {
            return "Key not found";
        }
    }
}
```

This RESTful endpoint enables querying the state store to get the value associated with a key. The use of QueryableStoreTypes.keyValueStore() ensures that the correct store type is used when accessing the state store.

Managing state stores effectively is integral to designing resilient and scalable stream processing applications. Combining state store management with Kafka's fault-tolerant mechanisms allows stateful operations to be performed reliably, even in the face of system failures.

6.4 The Aggregate Function

The aggregate function in Kafka Streams serves as a cornerstone of stateful transformations, allowing for the computation of a cumulative result based on incoming records. It is a powerful mechanism that supports the aggregation of data over time, providing users with the ability to compute complex stateful derivations from streaming data.

When utilizing the aggregate function, users define an initial value, an aggregator, and an optional materialized state store. The initial value acts as a starting point for the aggregation. The aggregator function processes each input record, updating the cumulative result accordingly. If a state store is specified, Kafka Streams will persist the aggregation state, aiding in fault tolerance and providing access to the computed state.

```
KGroupedStream<String, Long> groupedStream = stream
    .groupByKey();

KTable<String, Long> aggregatedTable = groupedStream
    .aggregate(
        () -> 0L,
        (key, value, aggregate) -> aggregate + value,
        Materialized.<String, Long, KeyValueStore<Bytes, byte[]>>as("aggregated-
            store")
          .withKeySerde(Serdes.String())
          .withValueSerde(Serdes.Long()));
```

The above code snippet demonstrates the use of the aggregate function in Kafka Streams. Here, a KGroupedStream is produced by grouping the original KStream by key. Subsequently, the aggregate method initializes the aggregation with a value of 0L. The aggregator function, expressed as a lambda expression, sums the value of each incoming record with the current aggregate. The results are materialized in a state store named "aggregated-store".

Key aspects to note:

- The initial value () -> 0L is defined using a supplier function.
- The aggregator $(key, value, aggregate) \rightarrow aggregate + value$ updates the cumulative result.
- The materialized state store Materialized.<String, Long, KeyValueStore<Bytes, byte[]»as("aggregated-store") ensures the persistence of the aggregation result.

Materializing state stores is crucial for maintaining consistency during stateful stream processing. These stores can be queried and recovered in the event of application restarts or failures, providing resilience and stability to the stream processing pipeline.

Kafka Streams supports multiple types for the aggregated result. Common types include numerical summaries, such as sums and averages, as well as complex structures like lists or sets. The flexibility of the aggregation function facilitates a wide array of analytic and operational use cases.

Consider a more complex scenario where a custom object Purchase is aggregated. The aggregator function can include transformations on individual fields within the custom object.

```
KGroupedStream<String, Purchase> groupedPurchases = purchasesStream
    .groupByKey();

KTable<String, PurchaseSummary> purchaseSummaryTable = groupedPurchases
    .aggregate(
        PurchaseSummary::new,
        (key, purchase, summary) -> summary.addPurchase(purchase),
        Materialized.<String, PurchaseSummary, KeyValueStore<Bytes, byte[]>>as("
            purchase-summary-store")
          .withKeySerde(Serdes.String())
          .withValueSerde(purchaseSummarySerde));
```

In this example, PurchaseSummary::new initializes the aggregation with a new PurchaseSummary object. The aggregator function $(key, purchase, summary) \rightarrow summary.addPurchase(purchase)$

updates the PurchaseSummary object with each incoming Purchase. The aggregation result is stored in "purchase-summary-store" using a custom serializer/deserializer (serde) for PurchaseSummary.

Aggregating data significantly enhances the analytical capabilities of stream processing applications. Implementations can tailor the aggregation logic to specific requirements, ensuring that the derived insights are both accurate and actionable.

Furthermore, combining the aggregate function with windowing operations unlocks additional analytical power. By applying time-windowed aggregations, developers can compute results over fixed intervals, sliding windows, or session-based windows. This approach allows for temporal segmentation of data, capturing trends and patterns over time.

```
TimeWindows windows = TimeWindows.of(Duration.ofMinutes(1)).grace(Duration.
    ofSeconds(10));

KTable<Windowed<String>, Long> windowedAggregatedTable = groupedStream
    .windowedBy(windows)
    .aggregate(
        () -> 0L,
        (key, value, aggregate) -> aggregate + value,
        Materialized.<String, Long, WindowStore<Bytes, byte[]>>as("windowed-
            aggregated-store")
          .withKeySerde(Serdes.String())
          .withValueSerde(Serdes.Long()));
```

The above example demonstrates the use of time-windowed aggregation. Here, a TimeWindows object is defined with a window size of one minute and a grace period of ten seconds. The windowedBy method applies the windowing specifications to the KGroupedStream, enabling the computation of time-windowed aggregations. The aggregated result is stored in a windowed state store named "windowed-aggregated-store".

Understanding and utilizing the aggregate function is fundamental for stream processing. It empowers developers to build sophisticated real-time applications capable of deriving meaningful insights from continuous data streams. By leveraging Kafka Streams' stateful transformations, organizations can effectively analyze and act on their streaming data, driving timely and informed business decisions.

6.5 The Reduce Function

In Kafka Streams, the reduce function plays a fundamental role in condensing and aggregating data within a stream. This function is particularly vital when there is a need to combine values that arrive at the same key in the stream. Unlike some other transformation operations, reduce operates by applying an associative reduction operation to the values of each key in a KTable.

The reduce function in Kafka Streams takes two primary arguments: a reducer function and a materialized view. The reducer function defines how two values associated with the same key are combined into a single value. The materialized view specifies how the results of this reduction will be stored and made accessible for future operations.

```
KTable<String, Integer> reducedTable = sourceStream
    .groupByKey()
    .reduce(
        (aggValue, newValue) -> aggValue + newValue,
        Materialized.<String, Integer, KeyValueStore<Bytes, byte[]>>as("reduced-store
            ")
            .withKeySerde(Serdes.String())
            .withValueSerde(Serdes.Integer())
    );
```

In the above example, the reduce function is used to sum integer values associated with the same key. The groupByKey() method is first called on the source stream, creating a KGroupedStream from the KStream. The reduce function then takes two arguments:

- A lambda function (aggValue, newValue) -> aggValue + newValue that specifies the reduction logic.
- A Materialized instance that configures the state store where the reduced results are stored.

The reducer function (aggValue, newValue) -> aggValue + newValue takes two arguments: the current aggregated value (or a newly initialized value when there is no prior value) and the new value to be added. It returns the updated aggregated value.

Key Considerations

- **Associativity**: The reduction function must be associative to ensure consistent results, regardless of the order in which records are processed.

- **Initial Value**: The first value in the reduction process represents the initial value. If no value exists prior, the new value effectively becomes the initial value.

Implementation Details

The reduce operation is internally backed by a state store that Kafka Streams manages. This state store ensures that the intermediate aggregation results are stored and made retrievable for further operations or fault recovery. The configuration parameter Materialized.as("reduced-store") names this state store "reduced-store."

State Store Configuration

Careful configuration of the state store's serdes (serializers and deserializers) ensures that the keys and values are correctly serialized and deserialized when stored and retrieved. This avoids data corruption and ensures operational correctness.

```
Materialized.<String, Integer, KeyValueStore<Bytes, byte[]>>as("reduced-store")
    .withKeySerde(Serdes.String())
    .withValueSerde(Serdes.Integer());
```

In this example, Serdes.String() and Serdes.Integer() are used to specify that the keys are strings and the values are integers. This configuration is integral when dealing with a potentially diverse data schema, ensuring that all transformations and reductions are valid for the given data types.

Handling Complex Reductions

When dealing with more complex data types or reduction logic, the reducer function will expand accordingly. For example, aggregating more complex objects (e.g., custom classes) requires a more sophisticated reducer function and potentially custom serdes.

Here is an example where we are aggregating custom objects:

```
KTable<String, CustomObject> reducedTable = sourceStream
    .groupByKey()
    .reduce(
        (aggValue, newValue) -> {
            aggValue.updateWith(newValue);
            return aggValue;
        },
        Materialized.<String, CustomObject, KeyValueStore<Bytes, byte[]>>as("
            custom-reduced-store")
            .withKeySerde(Serdes.String())
            .withValueSerde(new CustomObjectSerde())
    );
```

In this excerpt, CustomObject is a user-defined class with an updateWith method that merges the new value into the existing aggregate. CustomObjectSerde is a custom serializer/deserializer necessary to handle the custom serialization logic.

Operational Efficiency

Effective use of the reduce function improves operational efficiency by minimizing the amount of data sent across the network and reducing the storage footprint. The reduction takes place at each step where the values are grouped by key, ensuring that only the combined, reduced values are transmitted and stored.

The reduce function is a critical component for situations requiring the aggregation of values over time, such as summing sales transactions, counting occurrences, or merging records. Configuring and applying it correctly allows for powerful stream processing that can handle vast amounts of data efficiently while maintaining state integrity.

6.6 Counting and Summarizing

In practical streaming applications, counting and summarizing operations are essential for extracting meaningful insights from data. Kafka Streams provides several mechanisms to perform these operations efficiently. This section discusses the approaches and techniques for implementing counting and summarizing functions in Kafka Streams, with an emphasis on the nuances involved in handling real-time data. We will utilize state stores to maintain and update these summaries to ensure data reliability and consistency.

The count() operation in Kafka Streams is used to count the number of records in a stream. It is particularly useful for tasks such as monitoring the frequency of events, tracking user activities, or maintaining counts of items like product sales. The following example demonstrates how to create a stream that counts the occurrences of each key:

```
KStream<String, String> inputStream = builder.stream("input-topic");

KTable<String, Long> counts = inputStream
    .groupByKey()
    .count(Materialized.as("counts-store"));

counts.toStream().to("output-topic", Produced.with(Serdes.String(), Serdes.Long()));
```

In this example, the input stream is grouped by key using the group-

ByKey() method, followed by the count() operation. The counts are stored in a state store named "counts-store". Finally, the results are written to an output topic.

When performing summarizations, one might use the aggregate() function to compute custom aggregations over the stream. The aggregate() function allows for the implementation of more complex summarization logic beyond simple counting. Consider the following example, which calculates the total sales amount by product:

```
KStream<String, Sale> salesStream = builder.stream("sales-topic");

KTable<String, Double> totalSales = salesStream
    .groupBy((key, sale) -> sale.getProduct())
    .aggregate(
        () -> 0.0,
        (key, sale, aggregate) -> aggregate + sale.getAmount(),
        Materialized.<String, Double, KeyValueStore<Bytes, byte[]>>as("total-sales-
            store")
            .withKeySerde(Serdes.String())
            .withValueSerde(Serdes.Double())
    );

totalSales.toStream().to("total-sales-topic", Produced.with(Serdes.String(), Serdes.
    Double()));
```

In this example, a Sale object contains information about the product and the amount for each sale. The stream is grouped by the product key, and the aggregate() function is used to compute the total sales amount by summing up the amounts. The results are stored in a state store called "total-sales-store" and written to an output topic.

Another commonly used operation for summarizing data is the reduce() function. Similar to aggregate(), reduce() is used for combining multiple records into a single result, but it requires the reduction logic to be associative and commutative. Here's an example of reducing multiple reviews per product into a single concatenated string:

```
KStream<String, String> reviewsStream = builder.stream("reviews-topic");

KTable<String, String> productReviews = reviewsStream
    .groupBy((key, review) -> review.getProduct())
    .reduce(
        (review1, review2) -> review1 + "; " + review2,
        Materialized.as("reviews-store")
    );

productReviews.toStream().to("product-reviews-topic", Produced.with(Serdes.String(),
    Serdes.String()));
```

Here, the stream of reviews is grouped by product, and the reduce() function concatenates reviews for the same product separated by a semicolon. The combined reviews are stored and emitted to a topic.

Handling state and ensuring the consistency of counts and summaries are crucial aspects. Kafka Streams automatically manages the backing state stores, which are essential for maintaining state. When an application is restarted or rebalanced, these state stores ensure that the stateful transformations such as count(), aggregate(), and reduce() are preserved correctly. The following principles help maintain consistency and reliability:

- **Transactional Processing**: Leveraging exactly-once semantics (EOS) to ensure that records are processed exactly once and the state is consistently updated.
- **State Store Backup**: Regularly creating backups of state stores to prevent data loss during failures.
- **Changelog Topics**: Utilizing changelog topics to log state changes, allowing state recovery during application restarts or rebalances.

Synchronizing the views maintained by these state stores with downstream systems can be achieved by writing updates to Kafka topics, as shown in the examples. By doing so, both the stateful Kafka Streams application and other consumers of these topics have a consistent view of the data.

Applying these techniques enables efficient and reliable counting and summarizing in Kafka Streams, making it possible to derive actionable insights from real-time data streams.

6.7 Joining Streams

Joining streams in Kafka Streams involves the combination of two or more streams of data based on a common key. This operation is pivotal when there is a need to correlate or integrate data from different sources streaming in real-time. Stream joins are crucial in scenarios such as enriching event data with reference information, correlating metrics, or creating complex analytical pipelines. Kafka Streams supports several types of joins, including stream-stream joins, stream-table joins, and table-table joins. In this section, we will focus on the technical intricacies and practical applications of stream-stream joins and stream-table joins.

Stream joins in Kafka Streams are performed using the join operators:

```
join
leftJoin
outerJoin
```

These operators allow for various joining semantics:

- join: An inner join that outputs records with keys that exist in both joining streams.
- leftJoin: A left outer join that outputs all records from the left stream, and when matching records exist in the right stream, combines them; otherwise, includes null values for the right stream's fields.
- outerJoin: A full outer join that outputs records with keys present in either stream, combining records when possible, and filling null values when no counterpart exists.

Stream-Stream Joins

In a stream-stream join, two Kafka streams are joined based on their keys within a specified window. This ensures that late-arriving records can be joined correctly within the defined time bounds. Let us consider an example where we have two streams: one stream of orders and another stream of shipments. The goal is to join orders with shipments based on the order ID within a 5-minute window.

Assuming the following stream definitions:

```
KStream<String, Order> ordersStream = builder.stream("orders");
KStream<String, Shipment> shipmentsStream = builder.stream("shipments");
```

To join these streams, we define a join window and use the join operator:

```
Duration joinWindow = Duration.ofMinutes(5);
KStream<String, OrderShipment> joinedStream = ordersStream.join(
    shipmentsStream,
    (order, shipment) -> new OrderShipment(order, shipment),
    JoinWindows.of(joinWindow),
    StreamJoined.with(Serdes.String(), orderSerde, shipmentSerde)
);
```

Here, JoinWindows.of specifies the window within which records from the two streams should be joined. The StreamJoined.with method specifies the serialization format for the keys and values of the joining streams. The join operation produces a new stream where the records are of type OrderShipment, combining the order and shipment details.

Stream-Table Joins

Stream-table joins involve joining a Kafka stream with a Kafka table, where the table represents a materialized and continuously updated view of data. This is useful when you want to enrich a stream of events with static or slowly changing data in a table.

Let us examine an example where we have a stream of user activity events and a table of user profiles. The goal is to enrich each user activity with the corresponding user's profile information. Assuming the following stream and table definitions:

```
KStream<String, UserActivity> userActivityStream = builder.stream("user_activity");
KTable<String, UserProfile> userProfilesTable = builder.table("user_profiles");
```

We can perform a left join to enrich user activities with user profiles:

```
KStream<String, EnrichedUserActivity> enrichedStream = userActivityStream.leftJoin
    (
    userProfilesTable,
    (userActivity, userProfile) -> new EnrichedUserActivity(userActivity, userProfile),
    Joined.with(Serdes.String(), userActivitySerde, userProfileSerde)
);
```

In this case, the leftJoin operator ensures that all user activities are included in the enriched stream, and the corresponding user profiles are added where available. If a user profile is missing, the fields from the UserProfile class will be null in the resulting EnrichedUserActivity class.

Handling Late Arriving Data

When dealing with joins, particularly stream-stream joins, it is essential to handle late-arriving data gracefully. Kafka Streams provides configuration options and methods to manage out-of-order and delayed records. The gracePeriod API allows specifying an additional grace period during which late records are still accepted for joining. For example:

```
JoinWindows joinWindows = JoinWindows.of(Duration.ofMinutes(5)).grace(Duration.
    ofMinutes(1));
KStream<String, OrderShipment> joinedStreamWithGrace = ordersStream.join(
    shipmentsStream,
    (order, shipment) -> new OrderShipment(order, shipment),
    joinWindows,
    StreamJoined.with(Serdes.String(), orderSerde, shipmentSerde)
);
```

This configuration ensures that records arriving up to one minute after the end of the 5-minute join window are still eligible for joining, thereby improving the robustness of the join operation.

Optimizations and Performance Considerations

Stream joins can be resource-intensive operations. Several techniques can optimize performance and resource usage:

- **State Store Configuration**: Each join operation maintains a state store for managing the windowed state of the incoming streams. Fine-tuning the retention period and the size of these stores can significantly impact performance.
- **Serdes Efficiency**: Efficient serialization and deserialization configurations (Serdes) can reduce overhead and improve throughput.
- **Parallel Processing**: Leveraging parallelism by adjusting the number of Kafka Streams threads can enhance processing efficiency, especially in high-throughput environments.

In practice, carefully considering the nature of the data, join window configurations, and the underlying infrastructure will help in achieving optimal performance for streaming join operations.

6.8 Windowed Joins

Windowed joins are a sophisticated mechanism in Kafka Streams that allow for joining two streams within specified time windows. They provide a way to correlate records from two streams based on their timestamps, ensuring that only records falling within the same window are considered for the join operation. Windowed joins are essential for scenarios where time-bound relationships between events need to be captured.

The key concept here is the *window*, a logical partitioning of the time continuum. Windows can be fixed duration, sliding, or session-based, each serving different analytical purposes and use cases.

Windows in Kafka Streams are defined using the TimeWindows, SlidingWindows, or SessionWindows classes. The most commonly used is TimeWindows, which defines windows of a fixed size. Here's an example of how to define a time window of 5 minutes:

```
// Create a time window of 5 minutes
TimeWindows timeWindows = TimeWindows.of(Duration.ofMinutes(5));
```

When defining windows, it is also possible to specify a grace period using the grace method. The grace period allows late-arriving data to be included in the window. For instance:

```
// Create a time window of 5 minutes with a grace period of 1 minute
TimeWindows timeWindows = TimeWindows.of(Duration.ofMinutes(5)).grace(
    Duration.ofMinutes(1));
```

Windowed joins in Kafka Streams are performed using the join method on KStream objects. The join method requires the specification of the window, a ValueJoiner to combine values from the left and right streams, and a Joined parameter to define serdes and other join configurations.

For example, consider two streams: a stream of user clicks and a stream of user purchases. The following snippet demonstrates how to perform a windowed join over a 5-minute window:

```
KStream<String, Click> clicks = builder.stream("user-clicks");
KStream<String, Purchase> purchases = builder.stream("user-purchases");

KStream<String, UserActivity> userActivities = clicks.join(
    purchases,
    (click, purchase) -> new UserActivity(click, purchase),
    JoinWindows.of(Duration.ofMinutes(5)),
    Joined.with(Serdes.String(), clickSerde, purchaseSerde)
);
```

In this example, the resulting stream userActivities contains records that are created by joining click events with purchase events that occurred within the same 5-minute window.

The JoinWindows class provides methods to fine-tune the window specifications for a join. By default, the join window has symmetric boundaries (i.e., the window starts and ends at the same distance relative to the event timestamp). However, the before and after methods can be used to create asymmetric windows. For example:

```
// Create an asymmetric window: 3 minutes before and 2 minutes after the event
    timestamp
JoinWindows asymmetricWindow = JoinWindows.ofTimeDifferenceAndGrace(Duration.
    ofMinutes(3), Duration.ofMinutes(2), Duration.ofSeconds(90));
```

Asymmetric windows are useful when the timing relationship between events is not uniform in both directions.

Consider an e-commerce application where we want to analyze user behavior by correlating clickstream data with transaction records.

Specifically, we are interested in identifying users who viewed a product and made a purchase within 10 minutes. We define a 10-minute join window as follows:

```
KStream<String, ViewEvent> views = builder.stream("user-views");
KStream<String, PurchaseEvent> purchases = builder.stream("user-purchases");

KStream<String, UserBehavior> userBehaviorStream = views.join(
    purchases,
    (view, purchase) -> new UserBehavior(view, purchase),
    JoinWindows.of(Duration.ofMinutes(10)),
    Joined.with(Serdes.String(), viewSerde, purchaseSerde)
);
```

The UserBehavior object captures the combined information from both the view event and the purchase event. The JoinWindows.of method ensures that only purchase events that occur within 10 minutes of a view event are considered for the join.

Windowed joins come with certain nuances and considerations:

- **State Stores:** Windowed joins are inherently stateful operations. Kafka Streams maintains state stores to keep track of the records in each window. This ensures that records can be joined even if they arrive out of order.

- **Late Arrivals:** The grace period allows for late-arriving records to be included in the window. Records that arrive after the grace period are discarded.

- **Data Skew:** When defining window durations and grace periods, it is essential to consider the characteristics of your data. High data skew can lead to imbalanced state stores and increased latency.

- **Memory Usage:** Since windowed joins maintain state for each window, they can be memory-intensive. Proper sizing of state stores and the use of retention policies are crucial for efficient resource management.

Understanding the underlying mechanics and considerations of windowed joins empowers developers to design robust stream processing applications that effectively handle time-based event correlations.

6.9 Materialized Views

Materialized views in Kafka Streams serve as precomputed views of data that encapsulate the results of processing operations. These views are stored and continuously updated, reflecting the latest data available in the stream. Materialized views allow applications to efficiently access the results of transformations without the need for recomputation, which is beneficial for performance and resource utilization.

In Kafka Streams, materialized views are typically represented by state stores that capture the results of aggregations, joins, or other stateful transformations. These state stores are updated in real-time as new records are processed, ensuring that the materialized view remains current. The concept of materialized views is crucial for scenarios where the same query might need to be executed repeatedly, and the overhead of recalculating the results each time would be prohibitive.

To create a materialized view, one would use the 'Materialized' class provided by the Kafka Streams API. This class allows us to specify the underlying storage mechanism, serialization format, and other configurations for the state store that will hold the view.

Here is an example of how to create a simple materialized view for counting occurrences of keys in a stream:

```
KStream<String, Long> inputStream = builder.stream("input-topic");

KTable<String, Long> materializedView = inputStream
    .groupByKey()
    .count(Materialized.<String, Long, KeyValueStore<Bytes, byte[]>>as("counts-store
        "));
```

In this example, the 'count' operation is used to aggregate the input stream by key, and the results are stored in a state store named 'counts-store'. The 'Materialized' class allows us to configure this state store, specifying that it should be a key-value store. The materialized view 'materializedView' is a 'KTable' that holds the counts for each key and is continuously updated as new records arrive in the stream.

The materialized view can be queried in real-time to obtain the latest count for any given key. To do this, we need to expose the state store through an interactive query.

```
KafkaStreams streams = new KafkaStreams(builder.build(), properties);

// Start the streams application
streams.start();
```

```
// Query the state store
ReadOnlyKeyValueStore<String, Long> keyValueStore =
    streams.store("counts-store", QueryableStoreTypes.keyValueStore());

Long count = keyValueStore.get("some-key");
System.out.println("Count for 'some-key': " + count);
```

In the above snippet, we start the Kafka Streams application using the 'streams.start()' method. Once the application is running, we query the state store 'counts-store' to retrieve the count for a specific key, 'some-key'. The 'QueryableStoreTypes.keyValueStore()' method is used to indicate that we want a read-only view of the key-value store.

Materialized views are not limited to simple aggregations. They can also be created from more complex transformations, such as joins and windowed operations. For example, we can create a materialized view that holds the results of a join between two streams.

```
KStream<String, Long> streamA = builder.stream("stream-a");
KStream<String, Long> streamB = builder.stream("stream-b");

KTable<String, String> joinedStream = streamA
    .join(streamB,
          (valueA, valueB) -> valueA + "-" + valueB,
          JoinWindows.of(Duration.ofMinutes(5)),
          Materialized.<String, String, KeyValueStore<Bytes, byte[]>>as("joined-store"
              ));

ReadOnlyKeyValueStore<String, String> joinedStore =
    streams.store("joined-store", QueryableStoreTypes.keyValueStore());

String result = joinedStore.get("some-key");
System.out.println("Joined result for 'some-key': " + result);
```

In this example, 'streamA' and 'streamB' are joined with a window of 5 minutes, and the results of the join are stored in a state store named 'joined-store'. The join operation concatenates the values from both streams using a hyphen as a separator. The resulting joined data is stored in the materialized view 'joinedStore', which can be queried to obtain the joined result for any given key.

Such materialized views enable efficient data retrieval and significantly reduce the computational load on the system, as the precomputed results can be accessed directly from the state store. This is particularly important in applications that require real-time data access and high throughput.

An important consideration when working with materialized views is the configuration of the state store. Kafka Streams provides various options for customizing the storage backend, including in-memory stores, RocksDB stores, and others. The choice of storage can have significant implications for performance and durability. Properly configuring the state store involves selecting an appropriate storage format, tuning buffer sizes, and configuring logging and compaction settings.

Creating materialized views with Kafka Streams requires careful planning and an understanding of the data processing requirements. The state stores must be managed efficiently to ensure that they do not become a bottleneck. Regular monitoring and tuning are essential to maintain the performance and reliability of the system.

Efficient use of materialized views enables Kafka Streams applications to deliver high-performance stateful processing, providing immediate access to precomputed results and ensuring consistent and accurate data across the application. This makes materialized views a powerful tool in the Kafka Streams toolkit for building real-time data processing applications.

6.10 Persisting State

Persisting state in Kafka Streams is fundamental to ensure both fault tolerance and scalability in stateful stream processing applications. State in Kafka Streams refers to any data that needs to be stored between processing steps, such as intermediate computations, aggregations, or other transformations. This state must be reliably managed, particularly because Kafka Streams applications are distributed and can be restarted or rebalanced.

Kafka Streams provides state stores to maintain state data, and these state stores can be backed by durable storage to preserve state across application restarts or failures. There are two primary backing stores for persisting state: RocksDB and in-memory stores. RocksDB is the default and recommended for most use cases due to its balance between performance and durability.

$$\text{State Persistence} \rightarrow \text{State Stores} \rightarrow \begin{cases} \text{RocksDB Store} \\ \text{In-Memory Store} \end{cases}$$

The crucial aspects to consider when persisting state are state store configuration, state retention, changelog topics, and fault tolerance mechanisms.

- **State Store Configuration**

State stores need to be correctly configured to ensure efficient persistence and retrieval of state data. When initializing a state store, the developer needs to define several key parameters such as the store name, type, and retention policy.

```
StoreBuilder<KeyValueStore<String, Long>> storeBuilder =
  Stores.keyValueStoreBuilder(
    Stores.persistentKeyValueStore("persistent-store"),
    Serdes.String(),
    Serdes.Long())
  .withLoggingEnabled(configs)
  .withCachingEnabled();
```

In the code snippet above, we create a persistent key-value store named "persistent-store" with specific Serdes for serialization and deserialization of keys and values. Logging and caching features are enabled to improve fault tolerance and performance.

- **State Retention**

State retention policies dictate how long state information is kept in the state store before being purged. Retention settings impact the application's memory footprint and the timeliness of state information.

$$\text{Retention} = \begin{cases} \text{Windowed State} & \text{Time-based retention} \\ \text{Non-windowed State} & \text{Remove outdated entries} \end{cases}$$

- **Changelog Topics**

For durability, state stores in Kafka Streams leverage changelog topics. These topics capture every update made to the state stores, allowing the state to be reconstructed in the event of a failure. When a state store is created with logging enabled, Kafka Streams automatically creates a changelog topic that corresponds to the state store's data. Each update to the state store is asynchronously written to this topic.

```
.withLoggingEnabled(Collections.singletonMap("retention.ms", "172800000"))
```

The above configuration sets the retention period for the changelog topic to 48 hours (172800000 milliseconds), ensuring that the topic keeps updates for a specified duration before age-based deletion occurs.

- **Fault Tolerance Mechanisms**

Ensuring fault tolerance involves enabling state recovery processes, which utilize the changelog topics to restore state after a crash or restart. Kafka Streams replays the changelog to rebuild the state store to its last known state.

The state recovery process works as follows:

1. Upon restart, Kafka Streams initializes the state store.
2. The processor reads from the changelog topic.
3. Updates from the changelog are applied to the state store iteratively until the state represents the last known committed state.

```
State Restoration:
  - Replay changelog: topic___store-changelog
  - Apply updates to: persistent-store
```

- **Practical Guidelines for State Persistence**

1. Choose the right backing store: Use RocksDB for most use cases due to its durability and performance. Consider in-memory stores for ephemeral or low-latency requirements where persistence isn't essential.
2. Configure retention appropriately: Align retention policies with the application's data retention requirements to balance memory usage and data freshness.
3. Monitor changelog topics: Ensure that changelog topics are appropriately configured with sufficient retention to avoid data loss. Monitor and manage these topics to prevent issues.
4. Leverage caching: Enable caching to reduce state store read costs, benefiting from faster access times and reduced load on the underlying store.

Integrating these considerations into your Kafka Streams applications ensures robust and reliable state management, enhancing the system's overall resilience and performance.

Chapter 7

Windowed Operations

This chapter explores windowed operations in Kafka Streams, focusing on various window types including time-based, session, tumbling, and hopping windows. It details the implementation of windowed joins and windowed aggregations, as well as customizing windows to meet specific requirements. The chapter also addresses handling late-arriving data and managing window retention and expiration, ensuring accurate and efficient processing of time-sensitive data.

7.1 Introduction to Windowed Operations

Windowed operations in Kafka Streams are powerful constructs that allow for the processing of data streams within finite time intervals. Unlike unbounded streams, which can extend indefinitely, windowing helps in segmenting the stream into manageable chunks, thereby enabling more precise and temporal analysis of data. This section lays the groundwork for understanding various types of windowed operations and their significance in stream processing applications.

Windowed operations effectively handle time-sensitive data scenarios by grouping records that share certain temporal characteristics. This segmentation is crucial for tasks requiring aggregation, joining, or any operation that benefits from an isolated time frame. For instance, calculating hourly averages, detecting trends in user session activity, or maintaining stateful transformations become feasible through windowed operations.

The key notions involve:

- Defining window boundaries.
- Determining the inclusion of records within those boundaries.
- Handling window state and retention policies.

Defining Window Boundaries: Windows are defined based on time-based criteria such as fixed durations (e.g., every minute or hour), sessions determined by idle periods, or sliding intervals. These boundaries are essential for segmenting continuous data into discrete chunks.

Determining Record Inclusion: Once boundaries are established, the next step involves determining which records fall within those boundaries. This determination is based on the timestamp associated with each record. Kafka Streams allows customization in this regard, letting users specify how timestamps are extracted from incoming messages.

Handling Window State and Retention: Each window maintains a state that includes all records falling within its boundaries. The window state needs efficient management, including retention and expiration policies to ensure that the system does not run out of resources while maintaining historical accuracy.

To illustrate the importance and utilization of windowed operations, consider a real-time traffic monitoring application. This application might need to compute the average speed of vehicles passing through a certain junction every minute. Using windowed operations, one can segment the continuous stream of speed data into minute-long windows and perform the average calculation for each window separately.

```
import org.apache.kafka.streams.kstream.TimeWindows;
import org.apache.kafka.streams.kstream.KStream;

KStream<String, Long> trafficData = ...; // Input stream of traffic data (speed)

KStream<Windowed<String>, Long> avgSpeedPerMinute = trafficData
    .groupByKey()
    .windowedBy(TimeWindows.of(Duration.ofMinutes(1)))
    .reduce(
        (aggValue, newValue) -> (aggValue + newValue) / 2
    );
```

In the above code snippet, the stream trafficData is windowed by minute-long periods using the TimeWindows.of(Duration.ofMinutes(1)) construct. The reduce operation then computes the average speed for each window.

When employing windowed operations, it is also important to manage late-arriving data, which are records that arrive after the window they belong to has been closed. Kafka Streams handles this by allowing the specification of grace periods, during which late records can still be processed and included in the appropriate windows. This ensures robustness in scenarios where network latency or other factors might delay data transmission.

Consider a scenario where a traffic sensor uploads its speed data with sporadic delays due to network conditions. If a grace period of two minutes is set, it ensures that the records arriving late within these extra two minutes are still considered in their respective windows.

```
KStream<String, Long> trafficData = ...; // Input stream of traffic data (speed)

KStream<Windowed<String>, Long> avgSpeedWithGrace = trafficData
    .groupByKey()
    .windowedBy(TimeWindows.of(Duration.ofMinutes(1))
    .grace(Duration.ofMinutes(2)))
    .reduce(
        (aggValue, newValue) -> (aggValue + newValue) / 2
    );
```

By incorporating a grace period via the .grace(Duration.ofMinutes(2)) method, the windowing process remains flexible, accounting for potential delays in data arrival without compromising data integrity.

In summary, windowed operations in Kafka Streams enable efficient and meaningful time-based processing of continuous data streams. By comprehending the fundamentals outlined here, ranging from defining window boundaries to managing late-arriving data, users can harness the full potential of windowed stream processing in their real-time applications. The subsequent sections will delve deeper into specific types of windows, their implementations, and advanced customization techniques.

7.2 Time-Based Windows

Time-based windows in Kafka Streams partition data based on time intervals. These windows segment streams into finite chunks, allowing operations to be performed over these discrete segments. By using time-based windows, one can capture and process meaningful subsets of a continuous stream over specified intervals. This section will cover the key concepts of time-based windows, including their definition, application, and configuration in Kafka Streams.

A time-based window is defined by a fixed duration, during which events are grouped together. The primary types of time-based windows are tumbling windows and hopping windows. Tumbling windows divide the stream into non-overlapping, contiguous time intervals of fixed length, while hopping windows allow for overlapping intervals based on a specified hop size.

To illustrate the use of time-based windows in Kafka Streams, consider the following example that processes a stream of sensor readings. The goal is to compute the average sensor reading every minute.

```
KStream<String, String> sensorReadings = builder.stream("sensor-input");

TimeWindows timeWindows = TimeWindows.of(Duration.ofMinutes(1));

KTable<Windowed<String>, Double> avgReadings = sensorReadings
    .groupByKey()
    .windowedBy(timeWindows)
    .aggregate(
        () -> 0.0,
        (aggKey, newValue, aggValue) -> (aggValue + Double.parseDouble(newValue))
            / 2,
        Materialized.<String, Double, WindowStore<Bytes, byte[]>>as("avg-readings-
            store")
          .withValueSerde(Serdes.Double())
    );

avgReadings.toStream().to("sensor-output");
```

In this code, the stream "sensor-input" is read, and a one-minute time window is defined using ‘TimeWindows.of(Duration.ofMinutes(1))‘. The windowed aggregation calculates the average sensor reading for each minute, storing the results in a KTable which is then written back to the "sensor-output" topic.

An important consideration when working with time-based windows is window alignment. Since windows are defined by fixed durations, each window starts at an epoch-aligned timestamp. For example, if the window duration is one minute, the windows will start at 00:00:00, 00:01:00, 00:02:00, and so on. This alignment ensures consistency in windowing across different instances of the Kafka Streams application.

Time-based windows also support grace periods, which allow late-arriving data to be accounted for within a certain time frame after the window has ended. This is crucial for ensuring accuracy in environments where data can arrive out of order. The grace period can be configured using the 'grace' method of the 'TimeWindows' class.

```
TimeWindows timeWindows = TimeWindows.of(Duration.ofMinutes(1))
                                     .grace(Duration.ofSeconds(30));
```

In the above example, a 30-second grace period is set for one-minute windows, allowing events arriving within 30 seconds after the window end to still be included in the calculation.

Handling late-arriving data effectively is a crucial aspect of time-based windowing. By configuring an appropriate grace period, the windowed aggregation can maintain accuracy even in the presence of delayed events. However, setting the grace period too long can increase the resource usage and latency of the stream processing system. Therefore, a balance must be struck based on the specific characteristics and requirements of the data stream being processed.

To further cement the understanding of time-based windows, let's explore a more complex scenario where multiple streams are joined using time-based windows. Consider two streams, one for sensor readings and another for calibration data, and the objective is to join these streams on a common key within the same one-minute time window.

```
KStream<String, String> sensorReadings = builder.stream("sensor-readings");
KStream<String, String> calibrationData = builder.stream("calibration-data");

KStream<Windowed<String>, String> joinedStream = sensorReadings.join(
    calibrationData,
    (sensorValue, calibrationValue) -> sensorValue + " calibrated with " +
         calibrationValue,
    JoinWindows.of(Duration.ofMinutes(1))
);

joinedStream.to("joined-output");
```

In this join operation, the two streams "sensor-readings" and "calibration-data" are joined using a one-minute time window as specified by 'JoinWindows.of(Duration.ofMinutes(1))'. The windowed join ensures that records from both streams with matching keys and timestamps within the same one-minute window are combined.

Effectively utilizing time-based windows requires a thorough understanding of the timing characteristics of the streams being processed. This includes not only the duration of the windows and the alignment but also the frequency and potential delay of incoming events. Careful tuning of these parameters is essential to optimize the performance and accuracy of Kafka Streams applications using time-based windows.

7.3 Session Windows

Session windows are an essential concept within the realm of stream processing in Kafka Streams as they enable the grouping of records that arrive close together in time. Unlike fixed-size time windows, session windows have dynamic boundaries defined by periods of activity followed by periods of inactivity. This ability to dynamically adjust to the flow of events makes session windows especially useful for capturing user sessions or any intermittent activity over a stream.

A session window is created with a configuration that specifies an inactivity gap, often referred to as the sessionTimeout. This gap determines the threshold of inactivity after which the current window concludes and a new session begins. When a new record arrives beyond this inactivity gap, it triggers the start of a new session window.

```
KStream<String, String> inputStream = builder.stream("input-topic");

KTable<Windowed<String>, Long> sessionizedStream = inputStream
    .groupByKey()
    .windowedBy(SessionWindows.with(Duration.ofMinutes(5)))
    .count();
```

In the example above, a session window of 5 minutes is defined, meaning that if no new records for a particular key arrive within a 5-minute interval, the current session will end, and subsequent records will begin a new session. The result is a KTable keyed by a Windowed object containing the session's start and end times.

Session windows also facilitate merging, which is critical when new records arrive within the inactivity gap of an existing session. Kafka Streams merges these overlapping sessions to form a single, extended session window. The internal mechanics involve tracking session boundaries and extending them as necessary when new records are added.

```
KStream<String, Long> sessionizedStream = builder.stream("input-topic")
    .groupByKey()
    .windowedBy(SessionWindows.with(Duration.ofMinutes(5)))
    .count()
    .toStream()
    .map((key, value) -> new KeyValue<>(key.key(), value));
```

In the above code, we perform a typical session window operation followed by a transformation to extract the key from the Windowed object, leaving just the windowed count result.

Session windows require efficient handling of state, particularly when multiple sessions can overlap. The state store for session windows is more complex than for simple time-based windows. It must maintain not only the count of records but also the session boundaries for potential merging operations. Kafka Streams uses an advanced state management system to ensure that these operations remain performant and correct.

To handle late-arriving data, session windows can be configured with a grace period. This grace period allows windows to remain open for a specified amount of time, ensuring that records arriving slightly after the inactivity gap are still considered part of the session.

```
KStream<String, String> inputStream = builder.stream("input-topic");

KTable<Windowed<String>, Long> sessionizedStream = inputStream
    .groupByKey()
    .windowedBy(SessionWindows.with(Duration.ofMinutes(5)).grace(Duration.
        ofMinutes(1)))
    .count();
```

Here, a 1-minute grace period is added to the session window configuration. This ensures that late-arriving records within that 1-minute grace period are included in the session window.

One critical aspect of session windows is their flexibility in handling real-world use cases. For instance, user activity on a website, customer transactions in a shopping application or even sensor readings in IoT applications, can all benefit significantly from the dynamic nature of session windows.

Considerations when using session windows include the appropriate selection of the inactivity gap, balancing the need for timely session closure against the risk of splitting logical sessions due to brief inactivity. Another consideration is the system's ability to process the required state information, especially in high-throughput scenarios where numerous session windows may need to be tracked simultaneously.

Session windows prove integral when modeling time-dependent interactions or activities as opposed to fixed-length time windows. This flexible windowing capability enhances the precision and relevance of stream processing results, allowing developers to construct more effective and efficient applications within the Kafka Streams framework.

7.4 Tumbling Windows

Tumbling windows are a fundamental concept in the domain of streaming data processing within Kafka Streams. These windows split the continuous stream of data into fixed-size, non-overlapping intervals. Each record from the stream is assigned to one specific window based on its occurrence time, and these windows do not overlap or allow for any gaps between them. Tumbling windows enable straightforward time-based divisions of the data, making it easier to perform time-constrained operations.

To create a tumbling window in Kafka Streams, the 'TimeWindows' class must be utilized. The TimeWindows.of method helps define the window size. The window size is the duration of the tumbling window, determining how long each window will collect data before closing and a new one begins.

```
// Create a KStream from the input topic
KStream<String, Long> stream = builder.stream("input_topic");

// Specify a tumbling window of 5 minutes
KTable<Windowed<String>, Long> tumblingWindowCounts = stream
  .groupByKey()
  .windowedBy(TimeWindows.of(Duration.ofMinutes(5)))
  .count();
```

In the example above, records from the input topic are grouped by key and aggregated using a tumbling window of 5 minutes. The count method is applied to count the number of records in each window.

An important characteristic of tumbling windows is that every record belongs to exactly one window. This property simplifies window management as there is no overlap, and the computation for each window is isolated.

Determining window boundaries in tumbling windows is governed by the window size. For a window size of t time units, window boundaries can be understood as:

$$[\text{Start time}, \text{End time}) = [n \cdot t, (n+1) \cdot t)$$

for $n \in \mathbb{Z}$. Each window spans this interval, with the start time inclusive and the end time exclusive. This ensures that records falling at the boundary are systematically assigned to the subsequent window.

Consider a tumbling window size of 5 minutes, starting from epoch time $00{:}00$. The window intervals would be:

```
[00:00, 00:05)
[00:05, 00:10)
[00:10, 00:15)
...
```

These intervals are consistent across the timeline without overlap or gaps.

Tumbling windows utilize event time, which is the timestamp attached to each record. Event time is crucial for accurately aligning records with their respective windows. Kafka Streams processes records with their timestamps in consideration of the defined window boundaries.

In the presence of late-arriving data, it is essential to configure the grace period to manage records that arrive after the window's end but should still be considered. The 'grace' period provides a buffer for late records to be included within the proper window, ensuring accurate counts and aggregations.

```
// Define a tumbling window with a grace period
KTable<Windowed<String>, Long> tumblingWindowCountsWithGrace = stream
  .groupByKey()
  .windowedBy(TimeWindows.of(Duration.ofMinutes(5))
          .grace(Duration.ofMinutes(1)))
  .count();
```

In the provided code snippet, a grace period of 1 minute ensures that records arriving within 1 minute after the window's end are still counted within the respective 5-minute window.

Tumbling windows are effectively used in scenarios where data segmentation into fixed duration aggregates is required. Examples include:

1. Computing hourly sales totals in an e-commerce platform.
2. Monitoring system metrics per minute to detect performance changes.
3. Aggregating click counts in a web analytics scenario.

The non-overlapping nature of tumbling windows permits aggregating data over fixed time intervals, aligning with various analytical and monitoring requirements.

When configuring tumbling windows, several parameters need attention:

- **Window Size:** Define based on the use case requirements.

- **Grace Period:** Ensure that late-arriving data is accounted for without significantly delaying window processing.

- **State Store Configuration:** Optimize state store retention for the span of interest, balancing between memory usage and retrieval efficiency.

Careful consideration of these parameters ensures that the processing of tumbling windows is accurate and efficient, furthering the analytical capabilities inherent to stream processing applications in Kafka Streams.

7.5 Hopping Windows

Hopping windows, also known as sliding windows, are a fundamental concept in stream processing and provide a versatile mechanism to segment a data stream into overlapping time intervals. This type of windowing is particularly useful when there is a need to perform frequent computations over overlapping subsets of data. Unlike tumbling windows, which are non-overlapping, hopping windows can cover a data point multiple times, allowing for more granular analysis over time.

A hopping window is defined by two parameters: the window size and the advance interval. The window size specifies the duration of each window, while the advance interval determines how frequently a new window starts. This structure means that each data point can belong to multiple windows, depending on how the windows overlap.

For instance, consider a stream of sensor data where we need to compute the average temperature every minute over the last three minutes. In this case, the window size would be 3 minutes, and the advance interval would be 1 minute. This configuration results in overlapping windows, each one-minute apart, covering three-minute durations. Formally, if W is the window size and A is the advance interval, the nth window starts at $W_n = nA$ and ends at $W_n + W$.

```
|-----|-----|-----|-----|-----|-----|-----|-----|
0     1     2     3     4     5     6     7     8
      Window 1
   [---3 minute window---]
         Window 2
   [---3 minute window---]
               Window 3
   [---3 minute window---]
```

In Kafka Streams, hopping windows are implemented using the TimeWindows.of(...) method combined with the advanceBy(...) method. Below is a program snippet that demonstrates setting up a hopping window to compute rolling aggregate metrics over the data stream:

```
KStream<String, Long> inputStream = builder.stream("input-topic");

KTable<Windowed<String>, Long> aggregatedStream = inputStream
    .groupByKey()
    .windowedBy(TimeWindows.of(Duration.ofMinutes(3)).advanceBy(Duration.
        ofMinutes(1)))
    .reduce((aggValue, newValue) -> aggValue + newValue, Materialized.as("hopping-
        window-aggregation"));

aggregatedStream.toStream().to("output-topic", Produced.with(WindowedSerdes.
    timeWindowedSerdeFrom(String.class), Serdes.Long()));
```

In the above code, we first create a stream from the Kafka topic "input-topic". The stream is then grouped by key for aggregation purposes. The windowing behavior is specified using the windowedBy method, where TimeWindows.of(Duration.ofMinutes(3)) sets the window size and advanceBy(Duration.ofMinutes(1)) sets the advance interval. The reduce method is used to perform the aggregation, in this case, summing the values. The results are materialized using a state store named "hopping-window-aggregation" and forwarded to the "output-topic".

This approach allows for granular and detailed analysis of streams, making hopping windows an excellent fit for use cases where continuous monitoring and timely insights are crucial. Typical applications include financial services, sensor networks, and any situation where the temporal locality of data is significant.

The choice of window size and advance interval is critical and depends on the specific requirements of the application. Larger windows may smooth out short-term fluctuations but can introduce latency. Conversely, smaller windows provide more immediate insights but may be more volatile. Similarly, the advance interval determines how often computations are triggered and affects both the timeliness and the computational overhead of the processing.

By leveraging hopping windows, it is possible to balance these trade-offs effectively, ensuring that the resulting stream processing logic satisfies both performance and accuracy criteria.

7.6 Windowed Joins

Windowed joins in Kafka Streams enable the correlation of records between two or more streams over a defined time window. This operation is crucial when dealing with streaming data where synchronization and temporal relationships between records are important. Windowed joins ensure that data elements from different streams align temporally, enabling meaningful, context-aware combinations of these records.

To perform a windowed join, each stream's events are first grouped into windows using a common key, and the join operation is applied to the events within each window.

There are three primary types of windowed joins in Kafka Streams: windowed inner join, windowed left join, and windowed outer join. Each of these has specific use cases and behavior concerning the inclusion of records depending on their presence in the joining streams.

- **Windowed Inner Join**: A windowed inner join includes only the records that have matching keys in both streams within the defined time window. If a key does not find a match in the other stream, it is excluded from the result set.

```
KStream<String, String> leftStream = builder.stream("left-topic");
KStream<String, String> rightStream = builder.stream("right-topic");

KStream<String, String> joinedStream = leftStream
    .join(rightStream,
        (leftValue, rightValue) -> leftValue + ":" + rightValue,
        JoinWindows.of(Duration.ofMinutes(5))
    );
```

  In this example, records from leftStream and rightStream are joined if their keys match and occur within a five-minute window. The JoinWindows.of(Duration.ofMinutes(5)) function defines the window size.

- **Windowed Left Join**: A windowed left join includes all records from the left stream and matches them with records from the right stream within the window. If a record from the left stream does not find a match in the right stream, it is still included in the result set, paired with a null value.

```
KStream<String, String> leftStream = builder.stream("left-topic");
KStream<String, String> rightStream = builder.stream("right-topic");

KStream<String, String> joinedStream = leftStream
    .leftJoin(rightStream,
```

```
        (leftValue, rightValue) -> leftValue + ":" + (rightValue != null ?
                rightValue : "null"),
        JoinWindows.of(Duration.ofMinutes(5))
    );
```

Here, all records from leftStream are included in joinedStream. If there is no match in rightStream, the value from rightStream will be null.

- **Windowed Outer Join**: A windowed outer join includes all records from both streams. For unmatched records, the non-matching side will pair with a null value.

```
KStream<String, String> leftStream = builder.stream("left-topic");
KStream<String, String> rightStream = builder.stream("right-topic");

KStream<String, String> joinedStream = leftStream
    .outerJoin(rightStream,
        (leftValue, rightValue) -> (leftValue != null ? leftValue : "null") + ":" +
                (rightValue != null ? rightValue : "null"),
        JoinWindows.of(Duration.ofMinutes(5))
    );
```

Both streams contribute completely to the joinedStream. The handling of null values ensures that all records from both streams are reflected in the output.

- **Advanced Topics and Customization**: While defining windowed joins, Kafka Streams allows for further customization such as specifying grace periods and window retention times. These options provide fine-grained control over how late-arriving data and window expiration are managed.

  For instance, the grace period determines how long late-arriving records are allowed to update a window after its official close time. This can be crucial for use-cases where data latency is variable and not all events arrive in time.

```
KStream<String, String> leftStream = builder.stream("left-topic");
KStream<String, String> rightStream = builder.stream("right-topic");

JoinWindows joinWindows = JoinWindows.of(Duration.ofMinutes(5))
    .grace(Duration.ofMinutes(1));

KStream<String, String> joinedStream = leftStream
    .outerJoin(rightStream,
        (leftValue, rightValue) -> (leftValue != null ? leftValue : "null") + ":" +
                (rightValue != null ? rightValue : "null"),
        joinWindows
    );
```

In this snippet, the joinWindows object specifies a five-minute window with an additional one-minute grace period. This means that records arriving within one minute after the window's end will still contribute to the join result.

- **Execution Output Example**: To comprehend the behavior of windowed joins, consider the following output produced by running the above code:

```
(leftKey,value1) -> (leftKey,value1:rightValue)
(leftKey,value2) -> (leftKey,value2:null)
(rightKey,value3) -> (null,rightKey:value3)
```

  In these examples, the output shows how different records from left and right streams combine based on the stated window. We observe both matched pairs and records with null values due to unmatched keys, showcasing the nature of windowed joins effectively.

7.7 Windowed Aggregations

Windowed aggregations in Kafka Streams enable the computation of aggregates such as counts, sums, averages, and more, over finite time intervals known as windows. Aggregation operations are essential for summarizing and analyzing streaming data efficiently. This section delves into the principles of windowed aggregations, illustrating how to implement them effectively in Kafka Streams.

When performing windowed aggregations, the window itself defines the scope of data considered for each aggregation operation. Different window types can be employed based on use-case requirements, such as time-based, session, tumbling, and hopping windows. Each type has unique characteristics and is suitable for different scenarios.

To implement a windowed aggregation, the primary steps include defining the window characteristics, specifying the aggregation operation, and handling the resulting output. Consider the following code snippet where we compute the count of events within a tumbling window of five minutes:

```
KStream<String, String> input = builder.stream("input-topic");

input.groupByKey()
    .windowedBy(TimeWindows.of(Duration.ofMinutes(5)))
    .count()
    .toStream()
    .map((windowedKey, count) -> new KeyValue<>(windowedKey.key(), count))
```

```
    .to("output-topic", Produced.with(Serdes.String(), Serdes.Long()));
```

In this example:

- We first create a stream from the input topic.
- The stream is then grouped by key, which prepares it for windowed operations.
- The windowedBy method specifies a TimeWindows of five minutes, indicating that we want to count the events within successive five-minute intervals.
- The count method performs the actual aggregation by counting the number of events in each window.
- We then convert the windowed key to a plain key-value pair and send the results to an output topic. The Produced.with method ensures proper serialization of keys and values.

Windowed aggregations can also be more complex, involving computation of sums, averages, or custom aggregates. An example of calculating the sum of values over a session window is shown below:

```
KStream<String, Long> input = builder.stream("input-topic", Consumed.with(Serdes.
    String(), Serdes.Long()));

input.groupByKey()
    .windowedBy(SessionWindows.with(Duration.ofMinutes(5)))
    .aggregate(
        () -> 0L,
        (aggKey, newValue, aggValue) -> aggValue + newValue,
        (aggKey, aggOne, aggTwo) -> aggOne + aggTwo,
        Materialized.with(Serdes.String(), Serdes.Long()))
    .toStream()
    .map((windowedKey, sum) -> new KeyValue<>(windowedKey.key(), sum))
    .to("output-topic", Produced.with(Serdes.String(), Serdes.Long()));
```

Here:

- The input stream is created with key-value pairs where values are of type Long.
- The SessionWindows.with method indicates that we will aggregate events within session windows of five minutes.
- The aggregate method is used to sum the values. The initializer () -> 0L sets the initial aggregate to zero.

- The adder (aggKey, newValue, aggValue) -> aggValue + newValue updates the aggregate for each new record in the window.
- The merger (aggKey, aggOne, aggTwo) -> aggOne + aggTwo combines two aggregates when sessions merge.
- Finally, the results are written to an output topic, similar to the previous example.

Kafka Streams also supports reducing and custom aggregation operations. For instance, to compute the maximum value in tumbling windows, one can use:

```
input.groupByKey()
    .windowedBy(TimeWindows.of(Duration.ofMinutes(5)))
    .reduce(Long::max, Materialized.with(Serdes.String(), Serdes.Long()))
    .toStream()
    .map((windowedKey, max) -> new KeyValue<>(windowedKey.key(), max))
    .to("output-topic", Produced.with(Serdes.String(), Serdes.Long()));
```

In the above code:

- The reduce method is used to specify the reduction operation, which in this case finds the maximum value (Long::max).

Outputs of windowed aggregations are typically enriched with metadata about the window, including the start and end times. This can be crucial for downstream processing and for understanding the temporal context of the aggregated data. By default, the aggregation result's key in Kafka Streams includes the original key and the window metadata wrapped in a Windowed object. This can be customized if needed.

Handling late-arriving data is a significant aspect of windowed aggregations, ensuring accurate results even when data arrives out of order. This is managed through a grace period, allowing late data to be incorporated into the correct window as long as it arrives within the specified interval.

The retention and expiration of windowed state stores also impact aggregation operations. Proper configuration of retention periods is essential for managing resources and ensuring timely data processing without excessive memory or storage usage. Applications must balance between retaining enough data to handle late arrivals and expiring windows promptly to free up resources.

The versatility of windowed aggregations in Kafka Streams supports a wide array of real-time data analytics and processing demands. Proper understanding and implementation of these operations are paramount for robust stream processing applications.

7.8 Custom Windowing

Kafka Streams' flexibility allows developers to define custom windowing strategies, providing fine-grained control over the behavior of windowed operations. Custom windows enable the application to adapt to specific requirements that predefined window types might not meet adequately. This section elucidates the process of creating custom windows, emphasizing the associated configurations and practical examples.

Custom windows in Kafka Streams are constructed by extending the Window class. The crucial element in defining a custom window is the WindowBytesStoreSupplier, which specifies how the window store should behave. The key procedures involve defining the size of the windows, the grace period for late-arriving data, and the retention policy. Here is an exemplary approach to implementing a custom window:

```
public class CustomWindow extends Window {
    private final long sizeMs;

    public CustomWindow(long startMs, long sizeMs) {
        super(startMs, startMs + sizeMs);
        this.sizeMs = sizeMs;
    }

    @Override
    public boolean overlap(Window other) {
        return other.end() > this.start() && other.start() < this.end();
    }
}
```

The above code provides a simple example to define a custom window, where the CustomWindow class extends the Window class, specifying the size and overlap behavior of the windows.

Next, we must configure a WindowBytesStoreSupplier:

```
public class CustomWindowBytesStoreSupplier implements WindowBytesStoreSupplier
     {
    private final long retentionPeriodMs;
    private final long windowSizeMs;
    private final boolean retainDuplicates;

    public CustomWindowBytesStoreSupplier(long retentionPeriodMs, long
          windowSizeMs, boolean retainDuplicates) {
        this.retentionPeriodMs = retentionPeriodMs;
        this.windowSizeMs = windowSizeMs;
```

```
        this.retainDuplicates = retainDuplicates;
    }

    @Override
    public String name() {
        return "custom-window-store";
    }

    @Override
    public WindowStore<Bytes, byte[]> get() {
        return Stores.windowStoreBuilder(
            Stores.persistentWindowStore(name(), retentionPeriodMs, windowSizeMs,
                retainDuplicates),
            Serdes.Bytes(),
            Serdes.ByteArray()
        ).build();
    }

    @Override
    public long retentionPeriod() {
        return retentionPeriodMs;
    }

    @Override
    public boolean retainDuplicates() {
        return retainDuplicates;
    }

    @Override
    public long windowSize() {
        return windowSizeMs;
    }
}
```

The CustomWindowBytesStoreSupplier class provides an implementation for managing the storage properties of the custom window, encompassing retention period and window size configurations.

Integrating a custom window in a Kafka Streams application requires building a windowed aggregation or join operation with the custom window supplier:

```
StreamsBuilder builder = new StreamsBuilder();

KStream<String, String> inputStream = builder.stream("input-topic");

Materialized<String, Long, WindowStore<Bytes, byte[]>> materialized = Materialized
    .<String, Long>as(new CustomWindowBytesStoreSupplier(60000, 10000, true))
    .withKeySerde(Serdes.String())
    .withValueSerde(Serdes.Long());

inputStream
    .groupByKey()
    .windowedBy(new TimeWindows(10_000))
    .aggregate(
        Initializer<Long>() {
            @Override
            public Long apply() {
                return 0L;
```

```
            }
        },
        Aggregator<String, String, Long>() {
            @Override
            public Long apply(String key, String value, Long aggregate) {
                return aggregate + 1;
            }
        },
        materialized
    ).toStream()
    .to("output-topic", Produced.with(WindowedSerdes.timeWindowedSerdeFrom(
        String.class), Serdes.Long()));
```

The example demonstrated above shows how to define a windowed aggregation using the custom window supplier. The parameters illustrate key configurations for window size (10 seconds) and retention period (60 seconds), contributing to the custom behavior.

Developing a well-defined custom window strategy in Kafka Streams facilitates sophisticated event-time processing tailored to specific application needs. The flexibility of custom windows ensures robust handling of scenarios where predefined windows might fall short, offering granular control over data processing and retention policies, thus empowering developers to meet the precise requirements of their streaming applications.

7.9 Late-Arriving Data

In real-time stream processing, late-arriving data presents a significant challenge that must be systematically addressed to ensure the accuracy and reliability of computations. This section examines the strategies and mechanisms employed in Kafka Streams to handle late-arriving data effectively.

Late-arriving data refers to events that reach the processing pipeline after their associated time window has either partially or fully closed. The reasons for this delay can vary, including network latency, out-of-order event production, or lag in upstream data sources. Ignoring late-arriving data can lead to discrepancies in aggregations, windowed joins, and other time-sensitive operations.

Kafka Streams manages late-arriving data through a combination of watermarking, graceful window extensions, and reprocessing mechanisms.

Watermarking

Watermarks in Kafka Streams play a crucial role in marking the progress of event time within a stream. They help delineate the boundary between on-time and late-arriving events. A watermark is essentially a timestamp which signifies that any event with a timestamp less than the watermark is considered late. Kafka Streams permits the definition of watermarks to address out-of-order events and manage their state accurately.

The following example demonstrates the configuration of watermarks within a Kafka Streams topology:

```
TimeWindows timeWindows = TimeWindows.of(Duration.ofMinutes(5)).grace(
    Duration.ofMinutes(1));

KStream<String, Integer> stream = builder.stream("input-topic");
KTable<Windowed<String>, Long> table = stream
  .groupByKey()
  .windowedBy(timeWindows)
  .count();

// Custom watermark strategy
Topology topology = builder.build(new Properties() {{
    put(StreamsConfig.
        WINDOW_STORE_CHANGE_LOG_ADDITIONAL_RETENTION_MS_CONFIG
        , 60000L);
}});
```

In this example, a 'TimeWindows' object is configured with a five-minute window size and a one-minute grace period. The grace period signifies the allowance for late-arriving events to be included in the current window before being regarded as tardy.

Window Grace Period

The grace period provides a window of tolerance for late events to be processed within their designated time window before finalizing the window's state. This enables Kafka Streams to incorporate late data, avoiding premature window closures and resulting inaccuracies in aggregated results.

The implication of setting a grace period in Kafka Streams is critical for processing pipelines where data timeliness varies. An adequately configured grace period can substantially enhance the precision of windowed operations. However, extending grace periods also increases the memory footprint due to prolonged state retention.

Handling Late-Arriving Data in Aggregations

In scenarios involving windowed aggregations, late-arriving data can be seamlessly integrated within the grace period. The internal state store updates to reflect the new counts or sums, ensuring that the aggregated values are consistent and inclusive of late entries. Beyond the grace period, late events are typically dropped to maintain system performance and avoid excessive state retention.

Consider an example where we count events within a ten-second window and handle late-arriving data during this interval.

```
TimeWindows timeWindow = TimeWindows.of(Duration.ofSeconds(10)).grace(
        Duration.ofSeconds(5));

KStream<String, Long> eventStream = builder.stream("events");

KTable<Windowed<String>, Long> counts = eventStream
    .groupByKey()
    .windowedBy(timeWindow)
    .count(Materialized.as("event-counts-store"));
```

Setting a five-second grace period captures late arrivals and updates the 'event-counts-store' state within the window.

Reprocessing Mechanism

Kafka Streams provides capabilities for reprocessing to address late-arriving data beyond grace periods or in cases requiring reintegration. By leveraging the event log, applications can trigger reprocessing of specific partitions or entire topics to reevaluate windows with late data.

Reprocessing is achieved using the KStreamBuilder configuration, which involves defining new topologies or adjusting existing ones to incorporate late data.

```
builder.stream("input-topic")
  .mapValues(value -> performNecessaryTransformation(value))
  .to("output-topic");

// Rebuild and start the topology
KafkaStreams streams = new KafkaStreams(builder.build(), properties);
streams.cleanUp();
streams.start();
```

This way, reprocessing aids in recalibrating the state, ensuring that the late-arriving data contributes correctly to windowed computations.

Performance Considerations

Handling late-arriving data imposes additional computational and storage overheads. Grace periods, watermarking, and reprocessing systematically address late data, but each comes at a cost:

- Memory Usage: Prolonged state retention necessitates increased memory allocation for state stores.

- Processing Latency: Incorporating late-arriving data may introduce latency due to extended window periods and additional state updates.

- Storage Costs: Storage requirements grow when applications retain logs and state data over longer durations to accommodate late arrivals.

Configuring these mechanisms requires a balance between data accuracy and system performance, ensuring timely and precise results while managing resource utilization.

Understanding and managing late-arriving data within Kafka Streams enable resilient and accurate stream processing pipelines capable of handling real-world data inconsistencies and latencies. The strategies discussed form the bedrock of robust, time-sensitive data processing essential for a multitude of real-time applications.

7.10 Window Retention and Expiration

In the context of stream processing with Kafka Streams, window retention and expiration are crucial aspects to manage memory consumption and ensure timely data processing. Retention pertains to how long the state stores associated with windows are kept, while expiration deals with the removal of these state stores after their relevance has elapsed.

The Kafka Streams API allows fine-tuning of retention policies via window specifications. Understanding these retention semantics enables the efficient use of resources and avoids potential pitfalls, such as memory overflow or premature data deletion.

Window Retention

Retention time is the period for which Kafka Streams retains the window state stores. This duration should be long enough to account for events arriving out-of-order and to support late-arriving data. The retention time is adjustable and is specified when defining a window.

Consider a time window with a duration of 5 minutes. To handle late arrivals effectively, we may decide to retain the window state for an additional 5 minutes beyond the window's duration. This can be achieved using the grace period in Kafka Streams, specifying how long windows retain the state for late-arriving records.

```
TimeWindows.ofSizeWithNoGrace(Duration.ofMinutes(5))
    .grace(Duration.ofMinutes(5));
```

In this example, the window retains data for an additional 5 minutes beyond its designated 5-minute window size. This inclusion ensures that any late events falling within the grace period are appropriately processed.

Window Expiration

Window expiration is the process through which the window state store is purged after the retention period elapses. Kafka Streams manages this automatically, based on the specified retention time. It's essential to strike a balance when setting the retention period; too short a duration may lead to loss of late-arriving data, whereas an overly lengthy retention may result in excessive memory usage.

The key parameters influencing window expiration are the window size and the grace period. Together, these define the total retention time:

$$\text{Retention Time} = \text{Window Size} + \text{Grace Period}$$

For example, with a window size of 5 minutes and a grace period of 5 minutes, the effective retention time totals 10 minutes. This means Kafka Streams will purge the window state store 10 minutes after the initial creation of the window.

Impact of Retention on State Stores

State stores in Kafka Streams track the current state of the windows. Each windowed operation (e.g., joins, aggregations) relies on persistent state stores to maintain window contents across data streams. Efficient retention management is crucial to uphold performance and scalability.

When a retention period expires, Kafka Streams triggers the removal of outdated state segments. This expulsion process is handled internally but can be tailored via the window definition:

```
Materialized.as("windowed-store")
    .withRetention(Duration.ofMinutes(10));
```

Here, a state store named windowed-store is created with a custom retention period of 10 minutes. This parameter ensures that despite varying window sizes, the data remains in the store only as long as necessary to process relevant late events.

Handling Late-Arriving Data

Late-arriving data can impinge on the accuracy of windowed computations. Kafka Streams' retention configuration helps mitigate this impact by maintaining the state store beyond the window duration. When a record arrives after the defined window period but within the grace period, it is still processed and included in the window computations.

To configure the window to handle late-arriving data, one can adjust the grace period appropriately:

```
SessionWindows.with(Duration.ofMinutes(5))
    .grace(Duration.ofMinutes(2));
```

This configuration sets a session window of 5 minutes with an additional grace period of 2 minutes, allowing Kafka Streams to account for any late events arriving up to 2 minutes after the window closes.

Memory Considerations

Efficient memory usage is directly linked to setting appropriate retention and expiration periods. Excessively long retention periods can lead to substantial memory allocations, potentially degrading performance. Conversely, very short periods might preclude the processing of valid late-arriving data. Therefore, it is imperative to balance the retention period based on specific application requirements and data arrival patterns.

Practical Example

Consider an application monitoring transaction data, where a typical transaction window might be 10 minutes. To accommodate network delays or processing lags, a grace period of 3 minutes is specified. The configuration is as follows:

```
TimeWindows.ofSizeWithNoGrace(Duration.ofMinutes(10))
    .grace(Duration.ofMinutes(3))
    .withRetention(Duration.ofMinutes(13));
```

This approach ensures that the windowed state store retains the data for 13 minutes (window size + grace period), providing a buffer to process late-arriving transactions.

Understanding and carefully configuring window retention and expiration in Kafka Streams is crucial for robust stream processing. Proper settings maintain system performance while ensuring data accuracy, especially in time-sensitive applications.

Chapter 8

Error Handling and Logging

This chapter discusses error handling and logging in Kafka Streams applications, beginning with common error types and their causes. It covers strategies for handling deserialization, serialization, and processing errors, along with configuring error handling mechanisms within Kafka Streams. The chapter also delves into logging practices, setting up and configuring logging, and monitoring applications using metrics to detect errors. These topics ensure robust error management and maintainability of Kafka Streams applications.

8.1 Introduction to Error Handling in Kafka Streams

Kafka Streams is a powerful framework for building real-time, scalable, and fault-tolerant stream processing applications. However, as with any complex system, errors are inevitable. Effective error handling is essential to ensure the reliability and robustness of Kafka Streams applications. This section introduces the foundational concepts of error handling within the context of Kafka Streams, setting the stage for detailed discussions on specific error types and handling strategies in subsequent sections.

Error handling in Kafka Streams encompasses several facets, including deserialization and serialization errors, processing errors, and commit failures. Each category of error arises from different stages of the data processing pipeline and requires tailored handling mechanisms. By understanding these error types and their causes, developers can implement sophisticated error management systems to handle failures gracefully and maintain seamless data processing.

- **Deserialization and Serialization Errors:** Errors during deserialization and serialization occur when data is converted from one format to another. Deserialization errors typically happen when incoming data cannot be correctly interpreted, often due to schema mismatches, data corruption, or unexpected data formats. Serialization errors, on the other hand, occur when data cannot be transformed from an object format back into a byte stream for transmission or storage. Kafka Streams provides configurable mechanisms for handling such errors, allowing applications to specify fallback behaviors or handle exceptions programmatically.

- **Processing Errors:** Processing errors occur during the execution of the application's business logic. These might be due to issues like logical bugs, network problems, external service failures, or unexpected input data. Handling these errors efficiently is critical to maintaining the application's stability and throughput. Kafka Streams offers several constructs, such as the try-catch blocks in processor code, to manage processing errors. Additionally, retries, backoffs, and circuit breakers are commonly used strategies to mitigate intermittent issues.

- **Commit Failures:** Commit failures happen when Kafka Streams cannot successfully commit the processing status of a record. This often results from issues such as communication problems with the Kafka broker, timeouts, or resource limitations. Properly handling commit failures ensures that data processing remains idempotent and no records are lost or processed multiple times.

Understanding and implementing robust error handling strategies necessitates a thorough comprehension of Kafka Streams' configuration options and the API's error handling capabilities. Configurable properties such as default.deserialization.exception.handler and default.production.exception.handler enable applications to define specific behaviors when errors occur.

Below is an example of configuring a custom deserialization exception handler in Kafka Streams:

```
public class CustomDeserializationExceptionHandler
    implements DeserializationExceptionHandler {

    @Override
    public DeserializationHandlerResponse handle(
        ProcessorContext context,
        ConsumerRecord<byte[], byte[]> record,
        Exception exception
    ) {
        // Log the exception and skip the problematic record
        System.err.printf("Deserialization error: %s, record: %s%n",
                          exception.getMessage(),
                          record);
        return DeserializationHandlerResponse.CONTINUE;
    }

    @Override
    public void configure(Map<String, ?> configs) {
        // No configuration needed for this example
    }
}
```

Configuration of this handler in the Kafka Streams application properties:

```
Properties props = new Properties();
props.put(StreamsConfig.APPLICATION_ID_CONFIG, "example-app");
props.put(StreamsConfig.BOOTSTRAP_SERVERS_CONFIG, "localhost:9092");
props.put(StreamsConfig.
    DEFAULT_DESERIALIZATION_EXCEPTION_HANDLER_CLASS_CONFIG,
        CustomDeserializationExceptionHandler.class.getName());

// Additional properties ...
```

Kafka Streams also supports built-in exception handlers for common error scenarios. For instance, the LogAndContinueExceptionHandler logs the error and skips the record, continuing processing. Alternatively, the LogAndFailExceptionHandler logs the error and fails the task, useful for scenarios where data integrity cannot be compromised.

Error handling strategies must be chosen based on the application's specific requirements, such as data integrity needs, performance considerations, and fault tolerance levels. Combining appropriate error handling mechanisms ensures that Kafka Streams applications can continue operating smoothly even in the presence of unexpected issues, thereby enhancing their reliability and robustness.

8.2 Understanding Common Errors

In Kafka Streams applications, errors can occur at various stages of the stream processing pipeline. Recognizing these errors and their contexts is crucial in implementing robust error handling strategies. This section categorizes and elaborates on common error types encountered in Kafka Streams applications to prepare developers for effective mitigation.

Deserialization Errors

Deserialization errors typically occur when converting the raw byte data from Kafka topics into objects that the Kafka Streams application can process. These errors are often symptoms of schema mismatches or corrupted data. Common causes include:

- *Schema Evolution Issues*: When the schema of the data changes (e.g., through adding or removing fields), consumers expecting the old schema may fail to deserialize records.
- *Data Corruption*: Records may become corrupted during transmission or storage, leading to failure in converting raw bytes back to objects.
- *Invalid Data Types*: Mismatched types, such as trying to deserialize string-encoded data as integers, result in deserialization errors.

```
private static final String INPUT_TOPIC = "input-topic";

props.put(StreamsConfig.
    DEFAULT_DESERIALIZATION_EXCEPTION_HANDLER_CLASS_CONFIG,
    LogAndContinueExceptionHandler.class);

StreamsBuilder builder = new StreamsBuilder();
KStream<String, String> inputStream = builder.stream(INPUT_TOPIC);

inputStream.foreach((key, value) -> System.out.println(value));
```

In the above snippet, setting DEFAULT_DESERIALIZATION_EXCEPTION_HANDLER_CLASS_CONFIG to LogAndContinueExceptionHandler allows the application to log and skip over the problematic messages, continuing processing without interruption.

Serialization Errors

Serialization errors occur when converting objects back into byte data for transmission to Kafka topics. Common causes include:

- *Unsupported Data Types*: Certain serializers may not support specific data types, causing failures during serialization.
- *Schema Evolution Issues*: Similar to deserialization, if schema changes are not managed correctly, serialization errors can occur.

```
private static final String OUTPUT_TOPIC = "output-topic";

props.put(StreamsConfig.
    DEFAULT_SERIALIZATION_EXCEPTION_HANDLER_CLASS_CONFIG,
    LogAndFailExceptionHandler.class);

KStream<String, String> outputStream = ...;

outputStream.to(OUTPUT_TOPIC);
```

When an error occurs, the LogAndFailExceptionHandler logs the error and terminates the application to prevent the dissemination of potentially corrupt data.

Processing Errors

Processing errors arise during the actual computation stages of a Kafka Streams application and can be due to various factors:

- *Business Logic Bugs*: Errors in user-defined functions that carry out business logic.
- *Resource Constraints*: Insufficient resources such as memory or CPU can lead to failures in processing.
- *Time Window Issues*: Operations involving time windows may encounter problems if the window is not correctly defined or if the data stream is not appropriately handled within its time bounds.

```
KStream<String, Integer> processedStream = inputStream
    .mapValues(value -> {
        try {
            return Integer.parseInt(value);
        } catch (NumberFormatException e) {
            // Handle or log the error
            return -1;
        }
    });

processedStream.to(OUTPUT_TOPIC);
```

In this example, an attempt to convert a string value to an integer may fail, resulting in a NumberFormatException. Handling this within the map function allows the application to continue processing.

Configuration Errors

Configuration errors are often encountered during the setup phase of a Kafka Streams application. These errors can include:

- *Incorrectly Set Properties*: Typos or incorrect values in configuration properties.
- *Improper Application Settings*: Incompatible settings between the producer/consumer clients and the Kafka Streams application.

For example, setting an invalid value for replication factor or retention period in topic configuration can lead to startup failures or stability issues.

```
Properties props = new Properties();
props.put(StreamsConfig.APPLICATION_ID_CONFIG, "invalid-application");
props.put(StreamsConfig.BOOTSTRAP_SERVERS_CONFIG, "localhost:9092");
props.put(StreamsConfig.DEFAULT_KEY_SERDE_CLASS_CONFIG, Serdes.String()
    .getClass().getName());
props.put(StreamsConfig.DEFAULT_VALUE_SERDE_CLASS_CONFIG, Serdes.
    String().getClass().getName());

StreamsBuilder builder = new StreamsBuilder();
KStream<String, String> inputStream = builder.stream("input-topic");
```

```
Exception in thread "main" org.apache.kafka.common.config.ConfigException: Invalid value invalid-application
for configuration application.id: Value must be non-empty string.
```

This snippet highlights a scenario where an invalid application ID is provided, resulting in a ConfigException.

Transient Errors

Transient errors refer to temporary issues that resolve themselves, often related to network latency, temporary broker unavailability, or short-lived resource limitations. Common examples include:

- *Broker Unavailability*: Kafka brokers might be temporarily unavailable due to maintenance or network partitions.
- *Network Latency*: High network latency can cause timeouts and disconnections.

Retry mechanisms and idempotent processing guarantees in Kafka Streams can help mitigate the effects of these transient issues.

By understanding these common error categories, developers can design Kafka Streams applications more resilient to failures, ensuring higher reliability and stability in their data processing systems.

8.3 Deserialization and Serialization Errors

Within Kafka Streams, the processes of deserialization and serialization are of paramount importance for the smooth transformation of data across different stages of stream processing. Errors in these stages can lead to significant disruptions in data processing pipelines. Understanding these errors and their potential causes is critical for developing robust Kafka Streams applications.

Serialization is the process of converting an object into a byte stream, while deserialization is the reverse process—converting a byte stream back into an object. These processes allow data to be transmitted across different nodes in a distributed system.

Deserialization and serialization errors usually occur due to the following reasons:

- Incompatible Data Formats: When the schema of the incoming data does not match the expected schema.
- Corrupt Data: Occurs when the data being read is malformed or has been corrupted during storage or transmission.
- Incorrect Configurations: Configuration issues such as incorrect serializers or deserializers specified in the application's properties.

```
Properties props = new Properties();
props.put(StreamsConfig.DEFAULT_KEY_SERDE_CLASS_CONFIG, Serdes.String()
    .getClass().getName());
props.put(StreamsConfig.DEFAULT_VALUE_SERDE_CLASS_CONFIG, Serdes.
    String().getClass().getName());
```

The above lines of code ensure that both the keys and values are serialized and deserialized as Strings. Misconfiguration here can lead to runtime errors when Kafka Streams attempts to process the data.

Deserialization Errors are particularly problematic since they often signal that the incoming data cannot be interpreted as expected. When a message is consumed from a Kafka topic, the deserializer tries to convert the byte stream into a Java object. If the deserializer fails because the byte stream does not match any valid format, an exception is thrown.

One of the common deserialization errors is the 'SerializationException'. This normally indicates that the data read by the consumer is not in a format that can be deserialized by the deserializer. Below is a typical example of handling this error within a consumer application:

```
Consumer<String, String> consumer = new KafkaConsumer<>(props);
try {
    while (true) {
        ConsumerRecords<String, String> records = consumer.poll(Duration.ofMillis
            (100));
        for (ConsumerRecord<String, String> record : records) {
            // Process records
        }
    }
} catch (SerializationException e) {
    // Handle exception, log or notify, possibly skip the problematic record
    System.err.printf("Failed to deserialize message: %s%n", e.getMessage());
} finally {
    consumer.close();
}
```

On the producer side, *Serialization Errors* can occur if the object being serialized does not conform to the expected structure or if there is an issue with the serializer itself. If this happens, the producer is unable to convert the object to a byte stream suitable for transmission over Kafka.

Consider the following simplified example where a basic serializer is implemented:

```
public class CustomSerializer implements Serializer<MyObject> {
    @Override
    public byte[] serialize(String topic, MyObject data) {
        if (data == null) {
            return null;
        }
        ByteArrayOutputStream out = new ByteArrayOutputStream();
        try (ObjectOutputStream os = new ObjectOutputStream(out)) {
            os.writeObject(data);
        } catch (IOException e) {
            throw new SerializationException("Error when serializing MyObject to byte[]
                ", e);
        }
        return out.toByteArray();
    }
}
```

In this example, the 'serialize' method converts 'MyObject' into a byte array. Any errors encountered during this process, such as issues in writing the object stream, are captured and raised as a 'SerializationException'. Good practice involves catching and handling these exceptions gracefully to ensure that system stability is maintained.

Proper error handling strategies for these issues include:

- Implementing custom serializers and deserializers to handle specific data formats or schema evolutions.

- Logging detailed error messages to facilitate tracing and diagnosis.
- Configuring dead-letter topics to redirect problematic records for further analysis without disrupting the main data flow.

By preemptively addressing these serialization and deserialization concerns, highly resilient Kafka Streams applications can be engineered, maintaining the fidelity and integrity of data while ensuring continuous processing even in the presence of errant data.

8.4 Handling Processing Errors

In Kafka Streams applications, processing errors are those that occur during the execution of stream transformations and processing logic. These errors can be induced by a variety of factors including, but not limited to, invalid input data, unexpected state transitions, and logic bugs in the processing code. Properly handling these errors is crucial to maintaining the correctness, reliability, and robustness of your streaming application.

A processing error in Kafka Streams is usually manifested through exceptions thrown during the execution of the user-defined processing logic. Kafka Streams provides several mechanisms to handle these errors gracefully, ensuring that the streaming application can recover or terminate in a controlled manner.

1. Catching Exceptions in Processors

One approach to handling processing errors is to catch exceptions within the processor logic. This can be done within the process method of a custom processor. By catching exceptions directly within the processor, you can implement specific error handling logic such as logging the error, skipping the faulty record, or redirecting it to a dead-letter topic for further investigation.

```
public class ErrorHandlingProcessor implements Processor<String, String> {
  private ProcessorContext context;

  @Override
  public void init(ProcessorContext context) {
    this.context = context;
  }
```

```
  @Override
  public void process(String key, String value) {
    try {
      // User-defined processing logic
    } catch (Exception e) {
      // Handle the processing error
      context.forward(key, value, To.child("error-topic"));
      context.commit();
    }
  }

  @Override
  public void close() {
    // Clean-up resources
  }
}
```

In this example, any exceptions thrown during the processing logic are caught, and the problematic record is forwarded to an error topic. This allows you to separate erroneous records from the main processing stream and handle them independently.

2. Use of Deserialization Exceptions Handlers

Kafka Streams provides built-in Deserialization Exception Handlers that can be configured to handle exceptions that occur during the deserialization of records. While this is specifically for deserialization errors, it also encompasses a broader error handling context within stream processing.

The built-in deserialization handlers include LogAndFailExceptionHandler, LogAndContinueExceptionHandler, and LogAndSkipOnInvalidTimestamps. These handlers can be configured in the StreamsConfig property.

```
Properties props = new Properties();
props.put(StreamsConfig.
     DEFAULT_DESERIALIZATION_EXCEPTION_HANDLER_CLASS_CONFIG,
          LogAndContinueExceptionHandler.class);
KafkaStreams streams = new KafkaStreams(topology, props);
streams.start();
```

In the above example, the application is set to log the error and continue processing other records when a deserialization error occurs, allowing for seamless continuity of the stream.

3. The Use of the try-catch Wrapper in Stream DSL

For handling errors in the Kafka Streams DSL, wrapping the processing logic within a try-catch block can effectively catch and manage exceptions. The recovered records can be directed to a specified topic as shown below:

```
KStream<String, String> sourceStream = builder.stream("input-topic");
sourceStream.foreach((key, value) -> {
  try {
    // Processing logic
  } catch (Exception e) {
    // Handle processing error
    // For example, forwarding the record to an error topic
    KStream<String, String> errorStream = sourceStream
      .mapValues(value -> "Error: " + e.getMessage());
    errorStream.to("error-topic");
  }
});
```

This method clearly separates erroneous records from the main processing logic and routes them to a designated error topic, ensuring no data is lost.

4. Global State Error Handling

Kafka Streams applications often require management of stateful transformations, employing local and global state stores. Errors can arise when interacting with these state stores, such as during read/write operations or state restoration. Handling these errors involves implementing a fallback mechanism to recover or reroute the records causing failures.

```
public class StatefulProcessor implements Processor<String, String> {
  private KeyValueStore<String, String> stateStore;

  @Override
  public void init(ProcessorContext context) {
    this.stateStore = (KeyValueStore<String, String>) context.getStateStore("
        stateStore");
  }

  @Override
  public void process(String key, String value) {
    try {
      // State interaction logic
      stateStore.put(key, value);
    } catch (Exception e) {
      // Handle state store error
      context.forward(key, value, To.child("error-topic"));
      context.commit();
    }
  }

  @Override
  public void close() {
    // Clean-up resources
  }
}
```

By catching exceptions in the state interaction logic, the application ensures that state-related errors do not propagate unchecked, allowing for controlled handling and logging.

5. Handling Errors in Aggregations and Joins

Complex stream processing often involves operations such as aggregations and joins which can also introduce processing errors. Handling these errors requires catching and appropriately managing exceptions in the aggregation's supplier functions or transformations.

```
KStream<String, String> sourceStream = builder.stream("input-topic");
KTable<String, Long> aggregatedTable = sourceStream
  .groupByKey()
  .aggregate(
    () -> 0L,
    (key, value, aggregate) -> {
      try {
        return aggregate + Long.parseLong(value);
      } catch (NumberFormatException e) {
        // Handle error in aggregation
        // Log or forward erroneous data
        return aggregate;
      }
    },
    Materialized.<String, Long, KeyValueStore<Bytes, byte[]>>as("aggregation-store")
  );
```

This example shows how to handle errors in an aggregation function where invalid data could cause a number format exception. The erroneous record is handled by maintaining the current state, without allowing the error to disrupt the overall aggregation process.

Handling processing errors in Kafka Streams is a multi-faceted task requiring a combination of strategies to ensure robustness and reliability of the streaming application. By catching exceptions, configuring deserialization handlers, and managing stateful interactions appropriately, developers can create resilient stream processing logic capable of withstanding and recovering from various types of runtime errors.

8.5 Error Handling Strategies

Error handling in Kafka Streams applications plays a critical role in ensuring the stability and reliability of data processing pipelines. An effective error handling strategy addresses various potential issues that may arise during runtime, preventing application crashes and data inconsistencies. This section outlines different strategies to manage errors within Kafka Streams applications, focusing on practical implementations and configurations.

- **Retry Mechanism**

One common strategy for error handling is implementing a retry mechanism. This involves retrying operations that have failed due to transient issues, such as temporary network glitches or partitions being momentarily unavailable.

```
RetryPolicy retryPolicy = RetryPolicy.createFixedBackoff(3, Duration.ofSeconds(10));
KafkaStreams streams = new KafkaStreams(builder.build(), streamsConfiguration);
streams.setUncaughtExceptionHandler((thread, throwable) -> {
    // Logic for retrying the failed operation
});
```

This snippet illustrates the configuration of a simple retry policy where operations are retried up to three times with a 10-second interval between retries.

- **Dead Letter Queue (DLQ)**

When retries fail, it is often useful to route the problematic data to a Dead Letter Queue (DLQ) for further inspection and manual handling. This ensures that erroneous data does not impede the processing of valid records.

```
public void process(ConsumerRecord<String, String> record) {
    try {
        // Attempt to process the record
    } catch (Exception e) {
        // Send to DLQ
        ProducerRecord<String, String> dlqRecord = new ProducerRecord<>("dead-
            letter-queue", record.key(), record.value());
        producer.send(dlqRecord);
    }
}
```

In this example, when an exception is caught during the processing of a record, the record is sent to a designated "dead-letter-queue" topic for storage and analysis.

- **Graceful Degradation**

In some scenarios, it might be better to degrade the quality of service gracefully instead of failing entirely. This approach ensures that essential parts of the service remain operational even when some components experience errors.

```
public void processRecord(ConsumerRecord<String, String> record) {
    try {
```

```
        // Try processing normally
    } catch (NonCriticalException e) {
        // Handle non-critical errors gracefully
        logger.warn("Non-critical error occurred, defaulting to fallback logic", e);
        // Fallback logic
    } catch (CriticalException e) {
        // Handle critical errors, possibly halting the service
        logger.error("Critical error occurred, stopping the service", e);
        // Stop the service or alert the support team
    }
}
```

This code segment demonstrates handling non-critical exceptions by employing fallback logic while critical exceptions are handled in a manner that might involve stopping the service or alerting support teams.

- **Logging and Monitoring**

Logging and monitoring errors play essential roles in identifying and responding to issues in Kafka Streams applications. Logging provides detailed insights into the operational flow and error occurrences, while monitoring tools can automatically alert developers or operations teams about abnormalities.

```
log4j.properties:
log4j.rootLogger=INFO, stdout, file
log4j.appender.stdout=org.apache.log4j.ConsoleAppender
log4j.appender.stdout.layout=org.apache.log4j.PatternLayout
log4j.appender.stdout.layout.ConversionPattern=%d{ISO8601} %-5p %c{1}:%L - %m%
    n
log4j.appender.file=org.apache.log4j.RollingFileAppender
log4j.appender.file.File=logs/kafka-streams.log
log4j.appender.file.MaxFileSize=10MB
log4j.appender.file.MaxBackupIndex=10
log4j.appender.file.layout=org.apache.log4j.PatternLayout
log4j.appender.file.layout.ConversionPattern=%d{ISO8601} %-5p %c{1}:%L - %m%n
```

This configuration ensures that logs are written to both the console and a file, providing a persistent record of events and errors.

- **Metrics-Driven Alerts**

Utilizing Kafka Streams' integrated metrics can drive automated alerts and proactive management of errors. By monitoring specific metrics, it is possible to detect anomalies and initiate corrective actions without manual intervention.

```
public class MetricsReporter implements Runnable {

    private final KafkaStreams streams;
```

```
    public MetricsReporter(KafkaStreams streams) {
        this.streams = streams;
    }

    @Override
    public void run() {
        while (true) {
            for (Map.Entry<MetricName, ? extends Metric> entry : streams.metrics().
                 entrySet()) {
                MetricName metricName = entry.getKey();
                Metric metric = entry.getValue();
                // Analyze metrics and send alerts if necessary
                System.out.printf("Metric Name: %s, Metric Value: %f%n", metricName.
                        name(), metric.metricValue());
            }
            try {
                Thread.sleep(60000); // Fetch metrics every minute
            } catch (InterruptedException e) {
                Thread.currentThread().interrupt();
                break;
            }
        }
    }
}
```

This example provides a basic implementation of a metrics reporter that regularly fetches and prints the metrics, which could be extended to trigger alerts based on specific metric values.

By integrating these strategies—retries, dead letter queues, graceful degradation, logging, and metrics-driven alerts—Kafka Streams applications can achieve robust and resilient error handling, ensuring intermediate issues do not lead to significant service disruptions or data loss.

8.6 Configuring Error Handling in Kafka Streams

Understanding how to configure error handling in Kafka Streams is an essential aspect of building resilient stream processing applications. Ensuring that errors are managed effectively can prevent data loss and service interruption. This section outlines the process of configuring error handling by leveraging specific Kafka Streams configuration parameters and methods.

Stream Configuration Parameters

Kafka Streams provides several configuration parameters that influence error handling behavior. These configurations can be specified when creating a StreamsConfig object. Key parameters include:

- default.deserialization.exception.handler
- default.production.exception.handler

The parameter default.deserialization.exception.handler allows the developer to specify a custom deserialization exception handler class. This is useful for addressing errors that occur during the deserialization of records. The parameter default.production.exception.handler configures a handler for errors that arise during the production of records to Kafka topics.

```
Properties props = new Properties();
props.put(StreamsConfig.APPLICATION_ID_CONFIG, "error-handling-app");
props.put(StreamsConfig.BOOTSTRAP_SERVERS_CONFIG, "localhost:9092");
props.put(StreamsConfig.
    DEFAULT_DESERIALIZATION_EXCEPTION_HANDLER_CLASS_CONFIG,
      MyDeserializationExceptionHandler.class.getName());
props.put(StreamsConfig.
    DEFAULT_PRODUCTION_EXCEPTION_HANDLER_CLASS_CONFIG,
      MyProductionExceptionHandler.class.getName());
```

In this snippet, custom exception handlers MyDeserializationExceptionHandler and MyProductionExceptionHandler are assigned to handle deserialization and production errors respectively.

Deserialization Exception Handler

When handling deserialization errors, implementing the DeserializationExceptionHandler interface is necessary. This interface requires the implementation of the handle method, which defines the action to take when a deserialization error occurs.

```
public class MyDeserializationExceptionHandler implements
    DeserializationExceptionHandler {

  @Override
  public DeserializationHandlerResponse handle(ProcessorContext context,
                                               ConsumerRecord<byte[], byte[]> record,
                                               Exception exception) {
    // Implement custom deserialization error handling logic
    log.warn("Deserialization error for record: {}", record, exception);
    // Example action: Skip the corrupted record
    return DeserializationHandlerResponse.CONTINUE;
  }

  @Override
  public void configure(Map<String, ?> configs) {
    // Configuration logic if needed
  }
}
```

In the example above, the handler logs a warning message and then skips the problematic record by returning DeserializationHandlerResponse.CONTINUE.

Production Exception Handler

Production errors occur when failing to produce records to Kafka topics. To handle these errors, one must implement the ProductionExceptionHandler interface. This interface demands the implementation of the handle method, to determine the response when such errors take place.

```
public class MyProductionExceptionHandler implements ProductionExceptionHandler {


    @Override
    public ProductionExceptionHandlerResponse handle(final ProducerRecord<byte[],
            byte[]> record,
                                                     final Exception exception) {
        // Implement custom production error handling logic
        log.error("Production error for record: {}", record, exception);
        // Example action: Fail the stream processing by stopping the application
        return ProductionExceptionHandlerResponse.FAIL;
    }

    @Override
    public void configure(Map<String, ?> configs) {
        // Configuration logic if needed
    }
}
```

Here, the handler logs an error message for the failed production attempt and then stops the stream processing by returning ProductionExceptionHandlerResponse.FAIL.

Default Production Exception Handler

Kafka Streams provides a default production exception handler—DefaultProductionExceptionHandler. This handler can be configured to either ignore or log and fail the process based on the error.

To leverage the default handler or customize its behavior, set the configuration property accordingly:

```
props.put(StreamsConfig.
      DEFAULT_PRODUCTION_EXCEPTION_HANDLER_CLASS_CONFIG,
          DefaultProductionExceptionHandler.class.getName());
props.put(StreamsConfig.
      DEFAULT_PRODUCTION_EXCEPTION_HANDLER_RESPONSE, "fail");
```

Retriable Errors and Backoff Strategy

For retriable errors, configuring a backoff strategy can be valuable. The backoff settings define the retry interval and maximum retry attempts before failing.

```
props.put(StreamsConfig.RETRIES_CONFIG, 10);
props.put(StreamsConfig.RETRY_BACKOFF_MS_CONFIG, 1000);
```

This configuration attempts to retry up to 10 times with a 1-second interval between retries.

Processing Error Handlers

Handling processing errors, such as those occurring during stream processing, requires intercepting errors within Processors or Transformers. One technique is to encapsulate processing logic within try-catch blocks:

```
public class ErrorHandlingProcessor implements Processor<String, String> {

    private ProcessorContext context;

    @Override
    public void init(ProcessorContext context) {
        this.context = context;
    }

    @Override
    public void process(String key, String value) {
        try {
            // Main processing logic
        } catch (Exception e) {
            // Error handling logic
            log.error("Processing error for record (key={}, value={}):", key, value, e);
            // Decide to skip the record, send to DLQ, or stop processing
        }
    }

    @Override
    public void close() {
        // Close resources if needed
    }
}
```

Embedding the processing logic within a try-catch block facilitates tailored error handling based on the nature and severity of the processing error.

Dead Letter Queue (DLQ)

Sending erroneous records to a Dead Letter Queue (DLQ) is a common practice. This approach ensures that problematic records are not lost and can be reprocessed or analyzed later.

Setting up a DLQ involves configuring a secondary Kafka topic where failed records are sent. This can be achieved as follows:

```
public class MyDLQProcessor implements Processor<String, String> {

    private Producer<String, String> producer;
```

```
    private String dlqTopic;

    @Override
    public void init(ProcessorContext context) {
        producer = new KafkaProducer<>(context.appConfigs());
        dlqTopic = "dlq-topic";
    }

    @Override
    public void process(String key, String value) {
        try {
            // Main processing logic
        } catch (Exception e) {
            // Error handling logic
            ProducerRecord<String, String> dlqRecord = new ProducerRecord<>(
                    dlqTopic, key, value);
            producer.send(dlqRecord);
            log.error("Record sent to DLQ (key={}, value={}):", key, value, e);
        }
    }

    @Override
    public void close() {
        if (producer != null) {
            producer.close();
        }
    }
}
```

In this configuration, erroneous records are produced to the specified DLQ topic for subsequent inspection and retry.

Configuring error handling in Kafka Streams ensures the robustness and reliability of stream processing applications. Using appropriate handlers for deserialization, production, and processing errors, along with strategies like backoff, retry, and dead letter queues, creates a comprehensive error management system. Proper implementation and configuration of these elements are critical for maintaining resilient Kafka Streams applications.

8.7 Introduction to Logging in Kafka Streams

Logging is a fundamental aspect of developing and maintaining robust Kafka Streams applications. It enables developers and operators to capture essential runtime information, debug issues, track application behavior, and ensure that the streams processing pipeline operates as expected. Proper logging not only aids in troubleshooting but also plays a critical role in monitoring the health and performance of the application. This section delves into the principles and practices of logging within Kafka Streams, focusing on how to implement and configure effective logging mechanisms.

In Kafka Streams, logging is typically carried out using the SLF4J (Simple Logging Facade for Java) API, which acts as an abstraction for various logging frameworks such as Log4j, Logback, and java.util.logging. This allows developers to plug in the desired logging framework without changing the Kafka Streams application code. Below is an illustrative example of configuring SLF4J with Logback in a Kafka Streams application.

```
import org.slf4j.Logger;
import org.slf4j.LoggerFactory;

public class KafkaStreamsApp {
    private static final Logger logger = LoggerFactory.getLogger(KafkaStreamsApp.
         class);

    public static void main(String[] args) {
        // Application code
        logger.info("Starting Kafka Streams Application");

        try {
            // Create and start Kafka Streams application
        } catch (Exception e) {
            logger.error("Exception caught during Kafka Streams execution", e);
        }
    }
}
```

Here, the 'Logger' instance is created using the 'LoggerFactory' which associates the logger with the 'KafkaStreamsApp' class. This instance is used to log messages at various levels—INFO, ERROR, WARN, DEBUG, TRACE—enabling a detailed and hierarchical logging mechanism.

The log levels are crucial for controlling the granularity of log output. They can be adjusted according to the needs of the deployment environment. For example, in a development environment, a more verbose level like DEBUG might be appropriate to trace detailed execution paths, whereas, in a production environment, INFO or WARN levels might suffice to reduce the noise in log records.

Configuring the logging framework, such as Logback, typically involves setting up an XML configuration file named 'logback.xml'. Below is an example configuration file for Logback.

```
<configuration>
    <appender name="CONSOLE" class="ch.qos.logback.core.ConsoleAppender">
        <encoder>
            <pattern>%d{yyyy-MM-dd HH:mm:ss} %-5level %logger{36} - %msg%n</
```

```
            pattern>
        </encoder>
    </appender>

    <root level="info">
        <appender-ref ref="CONSOLE" />
    </root>

    <logger name="org.apache.kafka.streams" level="debug"/>
    <logger name="org.apache.kafka.clients" level="debug"/>
</configuration>
```

This configuration sets up a console appender, which writes log messages to the console output. The log pattern specifies the output format, including the timestamp, log level, logger name, and the actual message. Additionally, the log level for the root logger is set to INFO, while specific loggers for ‘org.apache.kafka.streams‘ and ‘org.apache.kafka.clients‘ are set to DEBUG to capture detailed runtime information specific to Kafka Streams and clients.

An effective logging strategy requires thoughtful consideration of what events to log and at what level. Below are some recommended practices for logging in Kafka Streams applications:

- **Log initialization parameters and configurations**: At the start of the application, log important configuration settings and parameters that affect the runtime behavior. This includes Kafka Streams configuration properties, topology structure, and state store configurations.

- **Log state transitions and lifecycle events**: Including the start, shutdown, and rebalance events within the Kafka Streams lifecycle. This informs when the application undergoes significant state changes.

- **Log key processing milestones**: Ensure critical steps within the processing pipeline are logged, such as the creation of streams, joins, aggregations, and window operations.

- **Use appropriate log levels**: Avoid overusing ERROR level logs for recoverable issues or expected exceptions. These should be logged at INFO or WARN levels. Reserve ERROR levels for unexpected failures that require immediate attention.

- **Avoid logging sensitive data**: Ensure that logs do not include sensitive information that might be exposed to unauthorized individuals. Use masking or redaction techniques if necessary.

- **Implement log rotation and archival mechanisms**: To manage the volume of logs generated over time, configure log rotation, and archival policies to preserve disk space while maintaining access to historical logs for analysis.

By adopting these logging practices, developers can enhance the observability and maintainability of Kafka Streams applications, ensuring that issues are quickly identified and resolved. Effective logging enables a proactive approach to application management, helping maintain optimal performance and reliability in production environments.

8.8 Configuring Logging in Kafka Streams

In Kafka Streams, logging plays a crucial role in debugging and monitoring the state of an application. Properly configured logging aids in tracing and understanding the flow of data, tracking errors, and maintaining overall application health. Kafka Streams leverages the Apache Log4j logging framework by default, although it can be configured to use other logging libraries such as SLF4J (Simple Logging Facade for Java).

To set up and configure logging in Kafka Streams, consider the following steps:

- **1. Add Logging Dependencies**

Ensure that the necessary logging dependencies are included in your project's build configuration. For a Maven-based project, include the following dependencies in your pom.xml file:

```
<dependency>
  <groupId>org.apache.logging.log4j</groupId>
  <artifactId>log4j-core</artifactId>
  <version>2.14.1</version>
</dependency>
<dependency>
  <groupId>org.apache.logging.log4j</groupId>
  <artifactId>log4j-slf4j-impl</artifactId>
  <version>2.14.1</version>
</dependency>
```

For a Gradle-based project, include the following in your build.gradle file:

```
implementation 'org.apache.logging.log4j:log4j-core:2.14.1'
implementation 'org.apache.logging.log4j:log4j-slf4j-impl:2.14.1'
```

- **2. Create Log Configuration File**

Log4j configurations are typically defined in an external configuration file, such as log4j2.xml. Place this file in the src/main/resources directory of your project. Below is an example configuration that sets different logging levels for various packages:

```
<?xml version="1.0" encoding="UTF-8"?>
<Configuration status="WARN">
  <Appenders>
    <Console name="Console" target="SYSTEM_OUT">
      <PatternLayout pattern="%d{HH:mm:ss.SSS} [%t] %-5level %logger{36} - %msg
          %n"/>
    </Console>
  </Appenders>
  <Loggers>
    <Logger name="org.apache.kafka" level="WARN" additivity="false">
      <AppenderRef ref="Console"/>
    </Logger>
    <Logger name="org.apache.kafka.streams" level="INFO" additivity="false">
      <AppenderRef ref="Console"/>
    </Logger>
    <Root level="ERROR">
      <AppenderRef ref="Console"/>
    </Root>
  </Loggers>
</Configuration>
```

This configuration directs all Kafka-related logs to the console, setting log levels to WARN for the general Kafka framework and INFO for Kafka Streams-specific logs. The root logger is set to ERROR to capture any severe issues.

- **3. Configure Logging Programmatically**

While external configuration files are commonly used, logging configurations can also be set programmatically within the Kafka Streams application. This is useful for dynamic logging level adjustments or for initial configurations. Example code is provided below:

```
import org.apache.logging.log4j.LogManager;
import org.apache.logging.log4j.Logger;
import org.apache.logging.log4j.core.config.Configurator;

public class LoggingConfig {
    private static final Logger logger = LogManager.getLogger(LoggingConfig.class);

    public static void configureLogging() {
        // Programmatically set the logging level to INFO for Kafka Streams
        Configurator.setLevel("org.apache.kafka.streams", org.apache.logging.log4j.Level.
            INFO);

        logger.info("Kafka Streams logging configured to INFO level.");
    }
```

```
}
```

Call the configureLogging() method at the start of your application to ensure that the logging configuration is applied when the application initializes.

- **4. Use Logging in Kafka Streams Application**

Within the Kafka Streams application, utilize the logging framework to log messages at appropriate logging levels (DEBUG, INFO, WARN, ERROR). For example:

```
public class KafkaStreamsApp {
    private static final Logger logger = LogManager.getLogger(KafkaStreamsApp.class);

    public static void main(String[] args) {
        // Configure logging
        LoggingConfig.configureLogging();

        // Application code
        logger.info("Starting Kafka Streams Application");

        // Additional code such as setting up streams etc.

        try {
            // Kafka Streams processing
        } catch (Exception e) {
            logger.error("An error occurred during stream processing", e);
        }

        logger.info("Kafka Streams Application stopped");
    }
}
```

Here, logging statements are added at critical points in the application workflow to capture useful information and any potential errors.

- **5. Adjust Logging Levels Dynamically**

In production environments, you might need to adjust the logging levels based on runtime conditions. The Log4j configuration allows for dynamic changes to the logging level. This feature can be especially useful for diagnostics and performance tuning. To change the logging level dynamically, use:

```
import org.apache.logging.log4j.LogManager;
import org.apache.logging.log4j.core.config.Configurator;

public class DynamicLogging {
    public static void setLogLevel(String loggerName, String level) {
        Configurator.setLevel(loggerName, org.apache.logging.log4j.Level.toLevel(level));
```

```
    }
}
```

Invoke the setLogLevel method with the desired logger name and log level to adjust the logging settings during runtime.

Properly configuring logging in Kafka Streams is vital for the effective management and monitoring of your applications. It provides visibility into application behavior, assists in debugging issues promptly, and supports the maintenance of application health and performance.

8.9 Monitoring Kafka Streams Applications

Effective monitoring of Kafka Streams applications is critical for detecting and addressing issues, ensuring operational stability, and optimizing performance. Kafka Streams provides a set of built-in metrics that enable us to gather, aggregate, and analyze various aspects of the application. This section elaborates on the essential elements and best practices for monitoring Kafka Streams applications.

Kafka Streams metrics are categorized into several domains, including:

- **Thread-level metrics**: These metrics provide insights into the state and performance of individual stream threads, such as the number of active threads, commit latency, and task processing rates.
- **Task-level metrics**: These metrics focus on the performance of tasks within the stream processing, including processing latency, punctuate rates, and record processing time.
- **Caching metrics**: These metrics monitor the caching layer used for aggregating and reducing records before writing them back to the state store.
- **Store-level metrics**: These metrics detail the performance of state stores, including read/write latency and request rates.

To access these metrics, Kafka Streams applications utilize the JMX (Java Management Extensions) framework. JMX provides a standard way to instrument, monitor, and manage applications. Kafka Streams exposes all of its metrics via JMX, which can then be polled or pushed to a monitoring system for analysis.

The first step to monitor a Kafka Streams application is to enable JMX. This can be done by setting the JMX_PORT environment variable when starting the application:

```
export JMX_PORT=9999
kafka-streams-application-start.sh
```

In this example, the Kafka Streams application will listen on port 9999 for JMX connections. You can use JConsole, VisualVM, or any JMX-compliant monitoring tool to connect to this port and visualize the metrics.

Here is a simple example to connect to the JMX endpoint using JConsole:

```
jconsole localhost:9999
```

After connecting to the Kafka Streams application, navigate to the kafka.streams domain within the JMX hierarchy to explore the available metrics.

Metrics Configuration

Kafka Streams applications offer several configurations to customize metrics collection. The StreamsConfig.METRICS_RECORDING_LEVEL_CONFIG setting allows you to control the granularity of metrics captured. The possible values are:

- **INFO**: Provides a general overview with essential metrics.
- **DEBUG**: Captures more detailed metrics for in-depth analysis.

To set the metrics recording level to DEBUG, you would include the following configuration in your Kafka Streams application:

```
Properties props = new Properties();
props.put(StreamsConfig.APPLICATION_ID_CONFIG, "my-streams-app");
props.put(StreamsConfig.BOOTSTRAP_SERVERS_CONFIG, "localhost:9092");
props.put(StreamsConfig.METRICS_RECORDING_LEVEL_CONFIG, "DEBUG");

KafkaStreams streams = new KafkaStreams(builder.build(), props);
streams.start();
```

Implementing a Custom Metrics Reporter

For more advanced monitoring requirements, you might want to push Kafka Streams metrics to an external system such as Prometheus, Grafana, or Datadog. Kafka Streams allows you to implement custom metrics reporters by extending the org.apache.kafka.common.metrics.

MetricsReporter interface.

Here is an example of a simple custom metrics reporter that logs metric values:

```
import org.apache.kafka.common.metrics.KafkaMetric;
import org.apache.kafka.common.metrics.MetricsReporter;
import java.util.List;

public class LoggingMetricsReporter implements MetricsReporter {

    @Override
    public void init(List<KafkaMetric> metrics) {
        for (KafkaMetric metric : metrics) {
            System.out.println("Initialized metric: " + metric.metricName());
        }
    }

    @Override
    public void metricChange(KafkaMetric metric) {
        System.out.println("Metric changed: " + metric.metricName() + " = " + metric.
              metricValue());
    }

    @Override
    public void metricRemoval(KafkaMetric metric) {
        System.out.println("Metric removed: " + metric.metricName());
    }

    @Override
    public void close() {
        // Clean up resources if necessary
    }

    @Override
    public void configure(Map<String, ?> configs) {
        // Configure the reporter if needed
    }
}
```

To use this custom metrics reporter, include it in the Kafka Streams configuration:

```
Properties props = new Properties();
props.put(StreamsConfig.APPLICATION_ID_CONFIG, "my-streams-app");
props.put(StreamsConfig.BOOTSTRAP_SERVERS_CONFIG, "localhost:9092");
props.put(StreamsConfig.METRIC_REPORTER_CLASSES_CONFIG,
      LoggingMetricsReporter.class.getName());

KafkaStreams streams = new KafkaStreams(builder.build(), props);
streams.start();
```

Monitoring Practices

- **Baseline Metrics**: Establish baseline metrics during normal operations to identify what constitutes typical performance. This helps in recognizing deviations that indicate problems.

- **Alerting**: Set up alerting mechanisms for critical metrics such as commit failures, elevated processing latency, and dropped records. Use thresholds aligned with your performance SLAs.
- **Dashboards**: Create dashboards in tools like Grafana or Kibana to visualize real-time and historical metrics. This aids in quickly diagnosing issues and observing long-term trends.
- **Log Aggregation**: Combine logs and metrics in central aggregation tools like Elasticsearch and Kibana to correlate application behavior with performance metrics.

Example Metrics Analysis

Below is an example of a metric that might be of interest when monitoring Kafka Streams applications: record-rate. This metric indicates the rate at which records are consumed by a stream thread. Analyzing this metric helps to ensure that the application is operating within expected throughput levels and can handle the incoming data volume.

```
$ kafka-run-class kafka.tools.JmxTool --object-name kafka.streams:type=stream-metrics,thread-id=StreamThread-1,metric=record-rate --jmx-url service:jmx:rmi:///jndi/rmi://localhost:9999/jmxrmi
```

This command fetches the record-rate metric for StreamThread-1 from the application's JMX output.

Monitoring Kafka Streams applications effectively ensures that you can maintain optimal performance, quickly respond to anomalies, and perform proactive maintenance based on observed trends. This is indispensable for developing highly available and performant stream processing applications in production environments.

8.10 Using Metrics for Error Detection

Metrics offer a quantitative means to monitor and diagnose the health and performance of Kafka Streams applications. They provide valuable insights into various components and processes, which can be instrumental in identifying and correcting errors. This section focuses on utilizing metrics for error detection in Kafka Streams, examining key metrics, their configurations, and practical use cases.

Kafka Streams integrates with the Java Management Extensions (JMX) framework, enabling access to numerous metrics that detail the performance and state of the streaming application. These metrics can be classified into several categories, such as processing metrics, producer and consumer metrics, as well as state store metrics. Each category serves a specific purpose in monitoring the Kafka Streams system and ensuring its smooth operation.

Processing metrics are crucial for understanding how efficiently the stream processing tasks are being executed. Key metrics in this category include:

- **total-processed-records**: Indicates the total count of records that have been processed successfully.
- **total-failed-records**: Represents the number of records that failed during processing.
- **avg-latency**: Average latency of processing records, useful for detecting performance degradation.

These metrics are particularly useful for diagnosing bottlenecks or identifying points where the stream processing may be encountering issues. Sudden spikes in total-failed-records or increases in avg-latency can signify underlying problems that need to be investigated.

For example, the following configuration code snippet enables JMX reporting for Kafka Streams:

```
Properties props = new Properties();
props.put("application.id", "my-application");
props.put("bootstrap.servers", "localhost:9092");
props.put("default.key.serde", Serdes.String().getClass());
props.put("default.value.serde", Serdes.String().getClass());
props.put("metric.reporters", "org.apache.kafka.common.metrics.JmxReporter");
KafkaStreams streams = new KafkaStreams(builder.build(), props);
```

Producer and consumer metrics provide insights into the interaction with Kafka brokers. Important metrics include:

- **record-error-rate**: The rate at which record send errors occur.
- **records-lag**: The number of records lagging behind, indicative of consumer performance.
- **record-retry-total**: Total number of retry attempts for sending records.

Monitoring these metrics helps in identifying issues related to the network, broker configurations, or Kafka cluster performance. For instance, a high record-error-rate may point to network issues or misconfiguration, while a significant records-lag value indicates potential consumer inefficiencies.

Additionally, state store metrics are key to monitoring the stateful computations within Kafka Streams applications:

- **put-latency-avg**: Average latency of put operations in state stores.
- **get-latency-avg**: Average latency of get operations, indicating performance of state lookups.
- **persistent-store-size**: The size of the persistent store, useful for capacity planning and detecting anomalies.

Regularly checking these metrics ensures that stateful operations are efficient and not contributing to performance issues. For instance, a surge in put-latency-avg may suggest that the state store is undergoing stress and could potentially lead to processing delays.

To collect and visualize these metrics, various tools such as Prometheus, Grafana, and Confluent Control Center can be employed. Prometheus, for instance, can scrape JMX metrics using the JMX exporter, allowing for detailed monitoring and alerting on specific thresholds. An exemplary Prometheus configuration might look like:

```
global:
  scrape_interval: 15s

scrape_configs:
  - job_name: 'kafka_streams'
    static_configs:
      - targets: ['localhost:7071']
```

Once configured, these metrics can be visualized on Grafana dashboards, offering real-time insights and alerting mechanisms. Alerts can be set up to notify if specific metrics exceed defined thresholds, ensuring proactive error detection and resolution.

Finally, it is important to note that metrics are not static and should be reviewed periodically to align with the application's evolving nature. Metrics thresholds that made sense during initial low-load testing might need adjustments under heavy production traffic. Therefore, continuous monitoring, along with periodic assessment and tuning, forms the backbone of effective metrics-based error detection in Kafka Streams applications.

Chapter 9

Testing Kafka Streams Applications

This chapter provides a comprehensive guide to testing Kafka Streams applications. It begins with unit testing using the TopologyTestDriver, and covers testing both stateless and stateful transformations. The chapter explores integration testing techniques, error handling tests, and performance testing. Additionally, it discusses strategies for mocking Kafka Streams, test automation best practices, and effective debugging methods to ensure application reliability and correctness.

9.1 Introduction to Testing Kafka Streams Applications

Testing Kafka Streams applications is a critical aspect of ensuring their reliability and correctness. Given the complex and distributed nature of these stream processing applications, a structured approach to testing is necessary. This section introduces the foundational concepts and methodologies employed in testing Kafka Streams applications, providing a brief overview of the available tools and strategies that will be elaborated upon in subsequent sections.

Kafka Streams is a client library designed specifically for building robust, scalable, and fault-tolerant stream processing applications. These applications process and transform data streams using various transformations and stateful operations. Ensuring that each component of a Kafka Streams application operates as expected under different conditions requires a mix of unit tests, integration tests, and performance tests.

Unit Testing with Kafka Streams typically involves validating individual components of the stream processing topology without the need to interact with a real Kafka cluster. The TopologyTestDriver is a powerful tool in this context, enabling developers to simulate Kafka topics and perform assertions on outputs based on controlled inputs. This form of testing is crucial for verifying the correctness of transformations, such as map, flatMap, filter, and joins.

For testing stateless transformations, wherein the processing of each message is independent of others, the TopologyTestDriver can inject input records into the topology and compare the actual output with the expected results. Stateless transformations are typically simpler to test because their output is purely a function of the current input message.

Stateful transformations, on the other hand, introduce additional complexity due to their reliance on state stores, which retain data across message boundaries. Testing these transformations requires managing and asserting the state of the store before and after processing records. The TopologyTestDriver supports various types of state stores, such as in-memory key-value stores, window stores, and session stores. Properly testing stateful transformations ensures that the logic handling state updates and retrievals is functioning correctly.

Integration Testing extends the scope of testing beyond individual components, validating the interactions between different parts of the Kafka Streams application and potentially other external services. These tests often involve spinning up an embedded Kafka cluster, complete with topics, producers, and consumers, to mimic a real-world environment closely. Tools such as TestContainers assist in managing and orchestrating these embedded clusters, ensuring consistent and isolated test environments.

Handling errors gracefully is another critical aspect of a resilient Kafka Streams application. **Testing Error Handling** involves simulating various failure scenarios, such as message deserialization errors, processing exceptions, and downstream service failures, to ensure that the application can recover or retry operations as expected. Implementing robust error handling and testing these mechanisms ensures minimal disruption in the processing workflow.

In scenarios where interacting with an actual Kafka cluster is impractical or slow, **Mocking Kafka Streams** components provides a viable alternative. Various mocking frameworks can be employed to simulate Kafka producers, consumers, and state stores, allowing for isolation of the component under test. This approach helps simulate specific conditions and edge cases that might be challenging to reproduce in a live environment.

Performance Testing is essential to ascertain the throughput and latency characteristics of a Kafka Streams application under different loads. Benchmarking the application involves generating a large volume of test data and measuring the system's performance metrics. Tools like KafkaProducerPerformance and KafkaConsumerPerformance can be instrumental in this process.

Test Automation Best Practices advocate for integrating testing into the continuous integration and continuous deployment (CI/CD) pipelines. Automated test suites ensure that any changes to the codebase do not introduce regressions, maintaining a high level of confidence in the application's integrity. Effective test case management, comprehensive test coverage, and regular test execution are key components of a robust test automation strategy.

Debugging Kafka Streams Applications often involves identifying and resolving discrepancies between expected and actual application behavior. Effective debugging techniques include thorough logging, use of breakpoints in development environments, and inspection of state stores and intermediate outputs. Leveraging the APIs provided by Kafka Streams for querying state stores and monitoring metrics can aid significantly in this process.

Building an extensive suite of tests for Kafka Streams applications ensures a higher degree of reliability and maintainability. It allows developers to address issues proactively, enhance application resilience, and ultimately deliver robust stream processing solutions. Subsequent sections of this chapter will delve deeper into specific testing methodologies, tools, and best practices for comprehensive validation of Kafka Streams applications.

9.2 Unit Testing with TopologyTestDriver

Unit testing is an essential aspect of developing reliable Kafka Streams applications. The TopologyTestDriver is a key tool for this purpose, providing the means to test Kafka Streams topologies in isolation. This section delves into the core concepts and practices of utilizing TopologyTestDriver to ensure the correctness of your Kafka Streams logic.

TopologyTestDriver facilitates the testing of streams without requiring a running Kafka cluster. By creating a mock environment, it allows developers to simulate data input and output, enabling thorough examination and validation of the stream processing logic.

Setting Up TopologyTestDriver

To begin testing with TopologyTestDriver, you need to create a topology and configure it using the StreamsBuilder and Topology classes. Subsequently, instantiate TopologyTestDriver with this topology and a set of properties that mimic a real Streams configuration.

```
Properties props = new Properties();
props.setProperty(StreamsConfig.APPLICATION_ID_CONFIG, "test-application");
props.setProperty(StreamsConfig.BOOTSTRAP_SERVERS_CONFIG, "dummy:1234")
    ;

StreamsBuilder builder = new StreamsBuilder();
// Define your topology here
KStream<String, String> stream = builder.stream("input-topic");
stream.filter((key, value) -> value.contains("test"))
    .to("output-topic");

Topology topology = builder.build();
TopologyTestDriver testDriver = new TopologyTestDriver(topology, props);
```

In this setup, the application ID is specified as test-application, and a dummy bootstrap server is used since the TopologyTestDriver does not connect to an actual Kafka broker.

Piping Input Records

To test the topology, you need to send records to the input topics. This is accomplished by creating test input topics and piping data into them:

```
TestInputTopic<String, String> inputTopic = testDriver.createInputTopic(
    "input-topic",
    Serdes.String().serializer(),
    Serdes.String().serializer()
);

inputTopic.pipeInput("key1", "value1");
inputTopic.pipeInput("key2", "test-value2");
```

In this example, two records are sent to the input-topic. The second record contains the string *"test"*, so it is expected to pass the filter condition defined in the topology.

Verifying Output Records

Once the data is piped into the input topic, the next step is to verify the output records from the output topics. The OutputVerifier class, part of the Kafka Streams test utilities, enables convenient assertion of the output records' correctness.

```
TestOutputTopic<String, String> outputTopic = testDriver.createOutputTopic(
    "output-topic",
    Serdes.String().deserializer(),
    Serdes.String().deserializer()
);

OutputVerifier.compareKeyValue(outputTopic.readKeyValue(), "key2", "test-value2");
assertTrue(outputTopic.isEmpty());
```

The first assertion checks that the output topic produced a key-value pair ("key2", "test-value2"), which matches the expected result as it satisfies the filter condition. The second assertion ensures that no other records are present in the output topic, validating that the filtering logic operates correctly.

Testing Stateful Operations

When testing stateful operations, such as aggregations or joins, it is crucial to verify the interaction with state stores. Create and initialize the required state stores in the topology setup, and use the TopologyTestDriver to inspect their state.

```
Stores.KeyValueFactory<String, Long> keyValueStoreFactory = Stores.
      keyValueStoreBuilder(
    Stores.inMemoryKeyValueStore("counts-store"),
    Serdes.String(),
    Serdes.Long()
);

builder.addStateStore(keyValueStoreFactory);
// Define stateful topology
KStream<String, String> statefulStream = builder.stream("input-topic");
statefulStream.groupByKey()
            .count(Materialized.<String, Long>as("counts-store"))
            .toStream()
            .to("output-topic");

// Pipe records to input topic
inputTopic.pipeInput("key1", "one");
inputTopic.pipeInput("key1", "one more");

// Verify state store contents
ReadOnlyKeyValueStore<String, Long> store = testDriver.getKeyValueStore("counts-
      store");

assertEquals(Long.valueOf(2), store.get("key1"));
```

Here, input records with the same key are aggregated, and the counts are stored in a state store named "counts-store". Piping records with the key "key1" results in a count of 2, which is then asserted by accessing the internal state store.

TopologyTestDriver also supports advance-time operations, which are necessary when dealing with time-sensitive logic such as windowed operations. By advancing the mock time, you can simulate real-world scenarios and ensure that the topology responds as expected to time-based events.

Understanding how to effectively leverage TopologyTestDriver is fundamental for writing robust and reliable Kafka Streams applications. Its ability to test in isolated conditions with precise control over inputs and outputs makes it an indispensable tool for developers.

9.3 Testing Stateless Transformations

Stateless transformations are a fundamental aspect of Kafka Streams, performing transformations on each record independently. This ensures that the processing of one record is not influenced by any previous records. Common stateless transformations include map, filter, flatMap, and branch. This section elaborates on how to effectively test these transformations using the TopologyTestDriver, ensuring the correctness and reliability of your Kafka Streams application.

A TopologyTestDriver provides a mock environment for running a Kafka Streams topology. It allows you to simulate input and verify output records without needing a running Kafka cluster. This isolation facilitates focused testing on specific parts of the topology, promoting granular verification of functionality.

To begin, a simple Kafka Streams topology involving a stateless transformation can be constructed and tested as follows:

```
import org.apache.kafka.streams.StreamsBuilder;
import org.apache.kafka.streams.TopologyTestDriver;
import org.apache.kafka.streams.test.ConsumerRecordFactory;
import org.apache.kafka.streams.test.OutputVerifier;
import org.apache.kafka.common.serialization.Serdes;
import org.apache.kafka.streams.KeyValue;

public class StatelessTransformationTest {
    public void testMapTransformation() {
        // Define the topology
        StreamsBuilder builder = new StreamsBuilder();
        builder.stream("input-topic", Consumed.with(Serdes.String(), Serdes.String()))
                .map((key, value) -> KeyValue.pair(key, value.toUpperCase()))
                .to("output-topic");
```

```
        // Create TopologyTestDriver
        TopologyTestDriver testDriver = new TopologyTestDriver(builder.build(), new
            Properties());

        // Define input and output record factories
        ConsumerRecordFactory<String, String> recordFactory = new
            ConsumerRecordFactory<>(Serdes.String().serializer(), Serdes.String().
            serializer());

        // Pipe input record
        testDriver.pipeInput(recordFactory.create("input-topic", "key", "value"));

        // Verify output record
        OutputVerifier.compareKeyValue(testDriver.readOutput("output-topic", Serdes.
            String().deserializer(), Serdes.String().deserializer()), "key", "VALUE");

        // Close test driver
        testDriver.close();
    }
}
```

In this example, the topology reads from an input topic input-topic, applies a map transformation converting the value to uppercase, and writes to the output topic output-topic. The TopologyTestDriver is then utilized to simulate the input record and verify the output.

Testing filter Transformation

The filter transformation is used to retain records that satisfy a predicate. Here's how you can test it:

```
public void testFilterTransformation() {
    StreamsBuilder builder = new StreamsBuilder();
    builder.stream("input-topic", Consumed.with(Serdes.String(), Serdes.String()))
            .filter((key, value) -> value.length() > 3)
            .to("output-topic");

    TopologyTestDriver testDriver = new TopologyTestDriver(builder.build(), new
        Properties());
    ConsumerRecordFactory<String, String> recordFactory = new
        ConsumerRecordFactory<>(Serdes.String().serializer(), Serdes.String().
        serializer());

    testDriver.pipeInput(recordFactory.create("input-topic", "key1", "abcd"));
    testDriver.pipeInput(recordFactory.create("input-topic", "key2", "ab"));

    OutputVerifier.compareKeyValue(testDriver.readOutput("output-topic", Serdes.
        String().deserializer(), Serdes.String().deserializer()), "key1", "abcd");
    assertNull(testDriver.readOutput("output-topic", Serdes.String().deserializer(),
        Serdes.String().deserializer()));

    testDriver.close();
}
```

In this filter test, the topology processes records with values longer than three characters. The test inputs two records, verifying that only the appropriate record is emitted to the output topic.

Testing flatMap Transformation

flatMap is used to transform each input record into zero or more output records. Below is an example test:

```
public void testFlatMapTransformation() {
    StreamsBuilder builder = new StreamsBuilder();
    builder.stream("input-topic", Consumed.with(Serdes.String(), Serdes.String()))
            .flatMap((key, value) -> {
                List<KeyValue<String, String>> result = new ArrayList<>();
                for (char c : value.toCharArray()) {
                    result.add(KeyValue.pair(key, String.valueOf(c)));
                }
                return result;
            })
            .to("output-topic");

    TopologyTestDriver testDriver = new TopologyTestDriver(builder.build(), new
        Properties());
    ConsumerRecordFactory<String, String> recordFactory = new
        ConsumerRecordFactory<>(Serdes.String().serializer(), Serdes.String().
        serializer());

    testDriver.pipeInput(recordFactory.create("input-topic", "key", "abcd"));

    OutputVerifier.compareKeyValue(testDriver.readOutput("output-topic", Serdes.
        String().deserializer(), Serdes.String().deserializer()), "key", "a");
    OutputVerifier.compareKeyValue(testDriver.readOutput("output-topic", Serdes.
        String().deserializer(), Serdes.String().deserializer()), "key", "b");
    OutputVerifier.compareKeyValue(testDriver.readOutput("output-topic", Serdes.
        String().deserializer(), Serdes.String().deserializer()), "key", "c");
    OutputVerifier.compareKeyValue(testDriver.readOutput("output-topic", Serdes.
        String().deserializer(), Serdes.String().deserializer()), "key", "d");
    assertNull(testDriver.readOutput("output-topic", Serdes.String().deserializer(),
        Serdes.String().deserializer()));

    testDriver.close();
}
```

This test for flatMap ensures that the input "abcd" is transformed into four records, each containing a single character. The assertions validate that all expected output records are produced correctly.

Verification of Complex Stateless Transformations

Complex stateless transformations might incorporate a sequence of multiple operations. Testing such sequences involves verifying the intermediate as well as the final results. Here is an example showcasing the testing of a combination of filter and map:

```
public void testComplexTransformation() {
    StreamsBuilder builder = new StreamsBuilder();
    builder.stream("input-topic", Consumed.with(Serdes.String(), Serdes.String()))
            .filter((key, value) -> value.startsWith("a"))
            .map((key, value) -> KeyValue.pair(key, value.toUpperCase()))
            .to("output-topic");

    TopologyTestDriver testDriver = new TopologyTestDriver(builder.build(), new
```

```
        Properties());
    ConsumerRecordFactory<String, String> recordFactory = new
        ConsumerRecordFactory<>(Serdes.String().serializer(), Serdes.String().
        serializer());

    testDriver.pipeInput(recordFactory.create("input-topic", "key1", "apple"));
    testDriver.pipeInput(recordFactory.create("input-topic", "key2", "banana"));

    OutputVerifier.compareKeyValue(testDriver.readOutput("output-topic", Serdes.
        String().deserializer(), Serdes.String().deserializer()), "key1", "APPLE");
    assertNull(testDriver.readOutput("output-topic", Serdes.String().deserializer(),
        Serdes.String().deserializer()));

    testDriver.close();
}
```

This test checks that an input "apple" is filtered and then mapped to "APPLE", while "banana" is filtered out. End-to-end verification ensures both transformations work in conjunction without errors.

For each transformation test, the TopologyTestDriver provides a controlled environment ensuring reproducibility and isolation from external systems, paramount for thorough testing of Kafka Streams applications. By rigorously applying these testing methodologies, developers can ensure their stateless transformations exhibit the desired behavior under various input scenarios, significantly enhancing the application's robustness and reliability.

9.4 Testing Stateful Transformations

Stateful transformations in Kafka Streams involve operations that depend on some form of state, such as aggregations, joins, and windowed computations. These transformations persist intermediate results for further processing, necessitating specialized testing techniques to ensure both functional correctness and statefulness. We will use TopologyTestDriver to test these stateful operations robustly.

Utilizing TopologyTestDriver for Stateful Operations

When testing stateful transformations, we must emphasize verifying the state stores' contents. The TopologyTestDriver simplifies this by providing access to state stores, allowing us to inspect their values as part of the testing process.

Consider a Kafka Streams application that performs a windowed aggregation. Our task is to verify that the state store correctly aggregates the input records over the defined windows.

```
public class WindowedAggregationTest {

    private TopologyTestDriver testDriver;
    private TestInputTopic<String, Long> inputTopic;
    private TestOutputTopic<String, Long> outputTopic;

    @Before
    public void setup() {
        StreamsBuilder builder = new StreamsBuilder();

        // Define windowed aggregation
        KStream<String, Long> input = builder.stream(”input-topic”);
        KTable<Windowed<String>, Long> aggregated = input
            .groupByKey()
            .windowedBy(TimeWindows.of(Duration.ofMinutes(5)))
            .reduce(Long::sum, Materialized.as(”aggregated-store”));

        // Define output topic
        aggregated.toStream().to(”output-topic”, Produced.with(WindowedSerdes.
              timeWindowedSerdeFrom(String.class), Serdes.Long()));

        Properties config = new Properties();
        config.put(StreamsConfig.APPLICATION_ID_CONFIG, ”test-application”);
        config.put(StreamsConfig.BOOTSTRAP_SERVERS_CONFIG, ”dummy:1234”);
        config.put(StreamsConfig.DEFAULT_KEY_SERDE_CLASS_CONFIG, Serdes.
              String().getClass().getName());
        config.put(StreamsConfig.DEFAULT_VALUE_SERDE_CLASS_CONFIG,
              Serdes.Long().getClass().getName());

        testDriver = new TopologyTestDriver(builder.build(), config);

        inputTopic = testDriver.createInputTopic(”input-topic”, new StringSerializer(),
              new LongSerializer());
        outputTopic = testDriver.createOutputTopic(”output-topic”, new
              TimeWindowedDeserializer<>(new StringDeserializer()), new
              LongDeserializer());
    }

    @Test
    public void shouldAggregateValuesOverWindow() {
        // Publish input records
        inputTopic.pipeInput(”key”, 1L, Instant.ofEpochMilli(0L));
        inputTopic.pipeInput(”key”, 2L, Instant.ofEpochMilli(1L));

        // Read and assert output records
        TestRecord<Windowed<String>, Long> output = outputTopic.readRecord();

        assertEquals(”key”, output.key().key());
        assertEquals(3L, output.value().longValue());
        assertTrue(output.key().window().start() < output.timestamp());
        assertTrue(output.key().window().end() >= output.timestamp());
    }

    @After
    public void tearDown() {
        testDriver.close();
    }
}
```

In this code snippet, we define a test case for an application performing a windowed aggregation. We set up the TopologyTestDriver, create input and output topics, and verify that the state store accumulates the values correctly within the specified window.

Accessing and Inspecting State Stores

Beyond verifying the output, it is crucial to inspect the state store contents directly to ensure they are correctly maintained throughout the application lifecycle. Here is a method to access and validate the stateful stores:

```
@Test
public void shouldMaintainStateCorrectly() {
    // Publish input records
    inputTopic.pipeInput("key1", 10L, Instant.ofEpochMilli(0L));
    inputTopic.pipeInput("key1", 20L, Instant.ofEpochMilli(1000L));

    // Access state store
    ReadOnlyWindowStore<String, Long> windowStore = testDriver.getWindowStore(
        "aggregated-store");
    KeyValueIterator<Windowed<String>, Long> iterator = windowStore.fetchAll(
        Instant.ofEpochMilli(0L), Instant.ofEpochMilli(5000L));

    // Validate store contents
    List<KeyValue<Windowed<String>, Long>> storeEntries = new ArrayList<>();
    while (iterator.hasNext()) {
        storeEntries.add(iterator.next());
    }
    iterator.close();

    assertEquals(1, storeEntries.size());
    assertEquals("key1", storeEntries.get(0).key.key());
    assertEquals(30L, storeEntries.get(0).value.longValue());
}
```

This test validates that the state store, identified by the name "aggregated-store", contains the expected aggregated result. The fetchAll method on the store retrieves all entries within the specified time range, which we then verify.

Handling Stream Joins

Testing stream joins involves combining records from multiple streams. Here, it is essential to ensure both streams' state stores reflect the correct joined records.

```
public class StreamJoinTest {

    private TopologyTestDriver testDriver;
    private TestInputTopic<String, String> leftInputTopic;
    private TestInputTopic<String, String> rightInputTopic;

    @Before
    public void setup() {
        StreamsBuilder builder = new StreamsBuilder();

        // Define two streams
        KStream<String, String> leftStream = builder.stream("left-topic");
```

```
        KStream<String, String> rightStream = builder.stream("right-topic");

        // Perform join operation
        KStream<String, String> joinedStream = leftStream.join(
            rightStream,
            (leftValue, rightValue) -> leftValue + "-" + rightValue,
            JoinWindows.of(Duration.ofMinutes(5)),
            StreamJoined.with(Serdes.String(), Serdes.String(), Serdes.String())
        );

        joinedStream.to("output-topic");

        Properties config = new Properties();
        config.put(StreamsConfig.APPLICATION_ID_CONFIG, "test-application");
        config.put(StreamsConfig.BOOTSTRAP_SERVERS_CONFIG, "dummy:1234");
        config.put(StreamsConfig.DEFAULT_KEY_SERDE_CLASS_CONFIG, Serdes.
              String().getClass().getName());
        config.put(StreamsConfig.DEFAULT_VALUE_SERDE_CLASS_CONFIG,
              Serdes.String().getClass().getName());

        testDriver = new TopologyTestDriver(builder.build(), config);

        leftInputTopic = testDriver.createInputTopic("left-topic", new StringSerializer(),
               new StringSerializer());
        rightInputTopic = testDriver.createInputTopic("right-topic", new
              StringSerializer(), new StringSerializer());
    }

    @Test
    public void shouldJoinRecordsCorrectly() {
        // Publish input records
        leftInputTopic.pipeInput("key", "leftValue", Instant.ofEpochMilli(0L));
        rightInputTopic.pipeInput("key", "rightValue", Instant.ofEpochMilli(1L));

        // Read and assert output records
        TestOutputTopic<String, String> outputTopic = testDriver.createOutputTopic(
              "output-topic", new StringDeserializer(), new StringDeserializer());
        TestRecord<String, String> outputRecord = outputTopic.readRecord();

        assertEquals("key", outputRecord.key());
        assertEquals("leftValue-rightValue", outputRecord.value());
    }

    @After
    public void tearDown() {
        testDriver.close();
    }
}
```

This example tests a join between two streams using the TopologyTestDriver. We verify that the joined stream produces the expected output records, combining values from both input streams based on the join logic.

Careful inspection of state stores and validating the intermediate states are crucial in ensuring the correctness of stateful transformations. Through rigorous testing with TopologyTestDriver, developers can confidently assess the behavior and reliability of stateful Kafka Streams applications.

9.5 Integration Testing

Integration testing aims to verify that various components or subsystems of an application work together as expected. For Kafka Streams applications, this involves testing how different stream processing components—such as sources, processors, and sinks—interact with each other and external systems like Kafka brokers and databases.

Unlike unit testing, integration testing involves testing the application in a more realistic environment, which includes actual network communication and external dependencies. This type of testing is crucial for identifying issues that might not be apparent when testing individual components in isolation.

To perform integration tests on Kafka Streams applications, you need a real or simulated Kafka cluster, as well as any other external systems your application interacts with. Below, we will discuss the steps involved, tools, and best practices.

Setting Up a Kafka Cluster

A Kafka cluster consists of one or more Kafka brokers that manage the communication between producers and consumers. For integration testing, you may opt to use a single-node Kafka cluster, which simplifies the setup process while still providing a realistic testing environment.

You can set up a local Kafka cluster using tools like Docker. For instance, the following docker-compose.yml file sets up a single-node Kafka cluster:

```
version: '2'
services:
  zookeeper:
    image: wurstmeister/zookeeper:3.4.6
    ports:
      - "2181:2181"
  kafka:
    image: wurstmeister/kafka:latest
    ports:
      - "9092:9092"
    environment:
      KAFKA_ADVERTISED_LISTENERS: INSIDE://kafka:9093,OUTSIDE://
          localhost:9092
      KAFKA_LISTENER_SECURITY_PROTOCOL_MAP: INSIDE:PLAINTEXT,
          OUTSIDE:PLAINTEXT
      KAFKA_INTER_BROKER_LISTENER_NAME: INSIDE
      KAFKA_ZOOKEEPER_CONNECT: zookeeper:2181
      ALLOW_PLAINTEXT_LISTENER: "yes"
```

```
volumes:
  - /var/run/docker.sock:/var/run/docker.sock
```

To start the Kafka cluster, execute the following command:

```
docker-compose up -d
```

Writing Integration Tests

JUnit, along with additional libraries like Kafka's EmbeddedKafka and TestContainers, can facilitate writing integration tests for Kafka Streams applications. The example below demonstrates how to set up an integration test using TestContainers to start a Kafka cluster within a test.

```
import org.apache.kafka.streams.*;
import org.apache.kafka.streams.test.*;
import org.junit.*;
import org.springframework.kafka.test.context.EmbeddedKafka;
import org.springframework.kafka.test.utils.*;
import static org.assertj.core.api.Assertions.*;

@EmbeddedKafka(partitions = 1, topics = {"input-topic", "output-topic"})
public class KafkaStreamsIntegrationTest {

    private static EmbeddedKafkaBroker embeddedKafkaBroker;
    private KafkaStreams kafkaStreams;
    private Properties streamsConfig;

    @BeforeClass
    public static void setUpClass() {
        embeddedKafkaBroker = new EmbeddedKafkaBroker(1, true, 1, "input-topic", "
                output-topic");
        embeddedKafkaBroker.afterPropertiesSet();
    }

    @Before
    public void setUp() {
        streamsConfig = new Properties();
        streamsConfig.put(StreamsConfig.APPLICATION_ID_CONFIG, "test-
                integration");
        streamsConfig.put(StreamsConfig.BOOTSTRAP_SERVERS_CONFIG,
                embeddedKafkaBroker.getBrokersAsString());
        streamsConfig.put(StreamsConfig.DEFAULT_KEY_SERDE_CLASS_CONFIG,
                Serdes.String().getClass().getName());
        streamsConfig.put(StreamsConfig.
                DEFAULT_VALUE_SERDE_CLASS_CONFIG, Serdes.String().getClass
                ().getName());

        Topology topology = ... // build your topology here
        kafkaStreams = new KafkaStreams(topology, streamsConfig);
    }

    @Test
    public void testKafkaStreamProcessing() {
        // Start the Kafka Streams instance
        kafkaStreams.start();

        // Produce input data
        embeddedKafkaBroker.consumeFromAnEmbeddedTopic("input-topic", "test-key"
                , "test-value");
```

```
        // Verify the output
        ConsumerRecords<String, String> receivedRecords =
            KafkaTestUtils.getRecords(consumer);
        Assertions.assertThat(receivedRecords).isNotEmpty();
        // Add more assertions to verify your processing logic

        // Cleanup
        kafkaStreams.close();
    }
}
```

In the code above, a Kafka broker is instantiated using EmbeddedKafkaBroker. The integration test initializes the Kafka Streams instance, produces input data, and verifies the output to ensure the stream processing works correctly.

Best Practices for Integration Testing

- **Isolation of Tests:** Ensure that each test runs in isolation by setting unique application IDs or using separate topics for different tests. This prevents data leakage between tests and ensures that tests are repeatable and independent.
- **Managing External Resources:** Use tools like TestContainers and EmbeddedKafka to programmatically manage Kafka clusters and other external resources. This approach ensures a consistent testing environment.
- **Assertions and Verifications:** Use robust assertion libraries like AssertJ to validate the output comprehensively. Ensure that your tests cover various edge cases and scenarios.
- **Teardown and Cleanup:** Always close the Kafka Streams instance and clean up any Kafka topics and clusters used for testing to avoid resource leaks and ensure a clean state for subsequent tests.
- **Realistic Data Loads:** Simulate realistic data loads in your tests to uncover performance and scalability issues. Utilize tools like Apache Kafka's load generator or custom scripts to produce significant volumes of data.

Integration testing is a critical aspect of ensuring the reliability and correctness of Kafka Streams applications when interacting with complex ecosystems. Through diligent setup, robust tools, and best practices, comprehensive integration tests can effectively validate the entire processing pipeline.

9.6 Testing Error Handling

Handling errors in Kafka Streams applications is a critical aspect to ensure the robustness and reliability of data processing workflows. This section delves into the nuances of testing error handling mechanisms within Kafka Streams applications, covering common scenarios such as invalid input data, serialization and deserialization issues, uncaught exceptions during processing, and recovery strategies for stateful operations.

Error handling in Kafka Streams can be tested through a combination of unit tests using 'TopologyTestDriver' and integration tests. These tests ensure that the application can gracefully handle errors and continue processing or halt execution as appropriate.

Before diving into specific examples, it is important to understand the key components involved in error handling within Kafka Streams:

- Deserialization Exceptions: These occur when the application cannot convert byte arrays from Kafka records into their respective Java objects.
- Processing Exceptions: These are runtime exceptions that occur during the stream processing logic.
- Serialization Exceptions: These happen when serialized output from the stream cannot be transformed back into bytes to send to another Kafka topic.
- State Store Exceptions: These exceptions may arise from operations related to stateful transformations involving local state stores.

```
StreamsConfig config = new StreamsConfig();
config.put(StreamsConfig.
    DEFAULT_DESERIALIZATION_EXCEPTION_HANDLER_CLASS_CONFIG,
    LogAndContinueExceptionHandler.class.getName());
config.put(StreamsConfig.
    DEFAULT_PRODUCTION_EXCEPTION_HANDLER_CLASS_CONFIG,
    DefaultProductionExceptionHandler.class.getName());
```

The configuration above specifies how to handle deserialization and production exceptions using provided exception handlers.

To test the handling of deserialization errors, we use the 'TopologyTestDriver' to simulate invalid input data. The test should validate that the application can either skip the problematic record and continue processing or stop the application as configured.

```
public void testDeserializationErrorHandling() {
    Properties config = new Properties();
    config.put(StreamsConfig.APPLICATION_ID_CONFIG, "test-app");
    config.put(StreamsConfig.BOOTSTRAP_SERVERS_CONFIG, "dummy:9092");
    config.put(StreamsConfig.DEFAULT_KEY_SERDE_CLASS_CONFIG, Serdes.
        String().getClass().getName());
    config.put(StreamsConfig.DEFAULT_VALUE_SERDE_CLASS_CONFIG, Serdes.
        Integer().getClass().getName());
    config.put(StreamsConfig.
        DEFAULT_DESERIALIZATION_EXCEPTION_HANDLER_CLASS_CONFIG
        , LogAndContinueExceptionHandler.class.getName());

    Topology topology = createTopology();
    try (TopologyTestDriver testDriver = new TopologyTestDriver(topology, config)) {
        TestInputTopic<String, String> inputTopic = testDriver.createInputTopic("
            input-topic", new StringSerializer(), new StringSerializer());
        TestOutputTopic<String, Integer> outputTopic = testDriver.createOutputTopic
            ("output-topic", new StringDeserializer(), new IntegerDeserializer());

        inputTopic.pipeInput("key", "invalid integer");

        assertTrue(outputTopic.isEmpty());
    }
}
```

The example demonstrates a test case where an invalid integer string is provided, and the deserialization should be gracefully handled by logging and continuing without producing any output.

Processing errors can be simulated by injecting faulty logic within the processing routine. Such tests ensure that uncaught exceptions do not crash the application and that appropriate fallback mechanisms are in place.

```
public void testProcessingErrorHandling() {
    StreamsBuilder builder = new StreamsBuilder();
    KStream<String, String> stream = builder.stream("input-topic");
    stream.mapValues(value -> {
        if ("error".equals(value)) {
            throw new RuntimeException("Processing error");
        }
        return value.toUpperCase();
    }).to("output-topic");

    Properties config = new Properties();
    config.put(StreamsConfig.APPLICATION_ID_CONFIG, "test-app");
    config.put(StreamsConfig.BOOTSTRAP_SERVERS_CONFIG, "dummy:9092");

    Topology topology = builder.build();
    try (TopologyTestDriver testDriver = new TopologyTestDriver(topology, config)) {
        TestInputTopic<String, String> inputTopic = testDriver.createInputTopic("
            input-topic", new StringSerializer(), new StringSerializer());
        TestOutputTopic<String, String> outputTopic = testDriver.createOutputTopic(
            "output-topic", new StringDeserializer(), new StringDeserializer());

        inputTopic.pipeInput("key", "error");
```

```
        inputTopic.pipeInput("key", "valid");

        assertEquals(outputTopic.readValue(), "VALID");
        assertTrue(outputTopic.isEmpty());
    }
}
```

In this example, an intentional processing error is induced by providing the input "error", thus testing if the application skips the problematic record and continues processing subsequent valid records.

Serialization errors are tested by ensuring that the output records match the expected format and type. If serialization fails, the error handling strategy configured in the 'StreamsConfig' should be validated.

```
public void testSerializationErrorHandling() {
    Properties config = new Properties();
    config.put(StreamsConfig.APPLICATION_ID_CONFIG, "test-app");
    config.put(StreamsConfig.BOOTSTRAP_SERVERS_CONFIG, "dummy:9092");
    config.put(StreamsConfig.
            DEFAULT_PRODUCTION_EXCEPTION_HANDLER_CLASS_CONFIG,
            DefaultProductionExceptionHandler.class.getName());

    StreamsBuilder builder = new StreamsBuilder();
    KStream<String, String> stream = builder.stream("input-topic");
    stream.mapValues(value -> {
        try {
            int intValue = Integer.parseInt(value);
            return intValue * 2;
        } catch (NumberFormatException e) {
            return null;
        }
    }).to("output-topic");

    Topology topology = builder.build();
    try (TopologyTestDriver testDriver = new TopologyTestDriver(topology, config)) {
        TestInputTopic<String, String> inputTopic = testDriver.createInputTopic("
                input-topic", new StringSerializer(), new StringSerializer());
        TestOutputTopic<String, Integer> outputTopic = testDriver.createOutputTopic
            ("output-topic", new StringDeserializer(), new IntegerDeserializer());

        inputTopic.pipeInput("key", "invalid");
        inputTopic.pipeInput("key", "10");

        assertEquals(outputTopic.readValue().intValue(), 20);
        assertTrue(outputTopic.isEmpty());
    }
}
```

This unit test examines how the application handles a null return value from the 'mapValues' function due to a serialization failure. The test verifies that subsequent valid records are processed correctly.

State store exceptions can be a bit more complex, as they often involve more detailed state management and error handling logic. Testing these scenarios might involve simulating errors in state store operations, such as attempting to access a non-existent key or simulating storage failures.

```
public void testStateStoreErrorHandling() {
    Properties config = new Properties();
    config.put(StreamsConfig.APPLICATION_ID_CONFIG, "test-app");
    config.put(StreamsConfig.BOOTSTRAP_SERVERS_CONFIG, "dummy:9092");

    StreamsBuilder builder = new StreamsBuilder();
    KeyValueBytesStoreSupplier storeSupplier = Stores.inMemoryKeyValueStore("test-
        store");
    StoreBuilder<KeyValueStore<String, String>> storeBuilder = Stores.
        keyValueStoreBuilder(storeSupplier, Serdes.String(), Serdes.String());
    builder.addStateStore(storeBuilder);

    KStream<String, String> stream = builder.stream("input-topic");
    stream.transformValues(() -> new ValueTransformerWithKey<String, String, String
        >() {
        private KeyValueStore<String, String> stateStore;

        @Override
        @SuppressWarnings("unchecked")
        public void init(ProcessorContext context) {
            stateStore = (KeyValueStore<String, String>) context.getStateStore("test-
                store");
        }

        @Override
        public String transform(String readOnlyKey, String value) {
            if ("trigger-error".equals(value)) {
                throw new RuntimeException("State store error");
            }
            stateStore.put(readOnlyKey, value);
            return value;
        }

        @Override
        public void close() {}
    }, "test-store").to("output-topic");

    Topology topology = builder.build();
    try (TopologyTestDriver testDriver = new TopologyTestDriver(topology, config)) {
        TestInputTopic<String, String> inputTopic = testDriver.createInputTopic("
            input-topic", new StringSerializer(), new StringSerializer());
        TestOutputTopic<String, String> outputTopic = testDriver.createOutputTopic(
            "output-topic", new StringDeserializer(), new StringDeserializer());

        inputTopic.pipeInput("key1", "trigger-error");
        inputTopic.pipeInput("key2", "valid");

        assertEquals(outputTopic.readValue(), "valid");
        assertTrue(outputTopic.isEmpty());
    }
}
```

Here, the test case verifies that a state store error is correctly handled by the application. When "trigger-error" is processed, an exception is raised, yet the application must continue processing subsequent valid records, validating the integrity of state store operations.

This detailed approach to testing various error handling scenarios within Kafka Streams ensures that the application remains resilient and capable of dealing with real-world data inconsistencies and processing anomalies. Ensuring comprehensive error handling tests as part of your Kafka Streams application development workflow is crucial for maintaining high reliability and fault tolerance in your streaming data pipelines.

9.7 Mocking Kafka Streams

Testing Kafka Streams applications often involves interactions with external systems such as databases, other Kafka topics, or external APIs. While integration testing provides a way to test these interactions using real instances, it can be resource-intensive and time-consuming. To mitigate these issues and to achieve more controlled, faster, and reliable tests, mocking is a crucial strategy.

Mocking components allows us to create stand-ins for the real components that our Kafka Streams application interacts with. This is especially useful in unit tests, where the goal is to isolate the component under test and verify its behavior in a controlled environment. In this section, we discuss various techniques and best practices for mocking in Kafka Streams applications.

- **Mocking Kafka Producers and Consumers**

Kafka producers and consumers are fundamental to Kafka Streams applications. Mocking them ensures that we can test the application's logic without setting up real Kafka brokers.

Using the MockProducer and MockConsumer classes provided by the Kafka client library, we can simulate producing and consuming records.

```
import org.apache.kafka.clients.producer.MockProducer;
import org.apache.kafka.clients.producer.ProducerRecord;
import org.apache.kafka.clients.consumer.MockConsumer;
import org.apache.kafka.clients.consumer.ConsumerRecord;

MockProducer<String, String> mockProducer = new MockProducer<>(true, null, null
    );
MockConsumer<String, String> mockConsumer = new MockConsumer<>(
    OffsetResetStrategy.EARLIEST);

// Adding records to the mock consumer to simulate data ingestion
mockConsumer.schedulePollTask(() -> {
   mockConsumer.addRecord(new ConsumerRecord<>("input-topic", 0, 0, "key", "
        value"));
```

```
});

// Verifying the mock producer records
mockProducer.send(new ProducerRecord<>("output-topic", "key", "transformedValue"
    ));
// The records can be asserted within the unit test context
assertEquals(1, mockProducer.history().size());
```

- **Mocking External Systems**

When a Kafka Streams application interfaces with external systems such as databases or RESTful services, these systems can be mocked using frameworks such as Mockito or embedded databases like H2 for simulating database interactions. This allows us to test the stream processing logic without depending on the external system's availability and state.

```
import static org.mockito.Mockito.*;
import org.springframework.jdbc.core.JdbcTemplate;

JdbcTemplate mockJdbcTemplate = mock(JdbcTemplate.class);
when(mockJdbcTemplate.queryForObject(anyString(), any(Class.class))).thenReturn("
    mockedResult");

// Use mockJdbcTemplate in the Kafka Streams application logic
String result = mockJdbcTemplate.queryForObject("SELECT name FROM users
    WHERE id = 1", String.class);
assertEquals("mockedResult", result);
```

- **Mocking Kafka Streams State Stores**

State stores are critical components in Kafka Streams, enabling stateful processing. To test stateful transformations, we need to ensure that these stores can be mocked or instantiated in a way that simulates their behavior accurately. Kafka Streams offers the MockKeyValueStore and MockWindowStore classes for this purpose.

```
import org.apache.kafka.streams.state.internals.InMemoryKeyValueStore;
import org.apache.kafka.streams.state.KeyValueStore;
import org.apache.kafka.streams.state.Stores;

KeyValueStore<String, Long> mockKeyValueStore = Stores.keyValueStoreBuilder(
    Stores.inMemoryKeyValueStore("mockStore"),
    Serdes.String(),
    Serdes.Long()
).build();

mockKeyValueStore.put("key", 42L);
assertEquals(Long.valueOf(42), mockKeyValueStore.get("key"));
```

- **Mocking Time in Kafka Streams**

Kafka Streams applications often depend on system time for tasks such as windowed transformations or punctuate functions. Controlling and mocking time can be crucial for testing such behaviors. Kafka Streams' MockProcessorContext allows us to set and manipulate time during tests.

```
import org.apache.kafka.streams.processor.MockProcessorContext;

// Initialize a MockProcessorContext with a provided clock
MockProcessorContext context = new MockProcessorContext();
context.setCurrentSystemTime(10L * 60 * 1000); // 10 minutes in milliseconds

// Use the context in processor or transformer for testing
assertEquals(10L * 60 * 1000, context.currentSystemTime());
context.schedule(5000, PunctuationType.WALL_CLOCK_TIME, timestamp -> {
    // Punctuator code
});
```

Mocking promotes robustness in unit tests by decoupling them from variables like network latency, external system states, and resource constraints. This controlled testing environment helps in quickly identifying and fixing issues in the core logic of Kafka Streams applications.

9.8 Performance Testing

Performance testing of Kafka Streams applications involves thorough assessment to ensure the system can handle a given load efficiently while maintaining desired throughput and latency. This section delves into strategies, tools, and methodologies for conducting comprehensive performance tests.

When addressing performance testing, it is crucial to characterize both the throughput—the rate at which data is processed—and latency—the delay in data processing. This aids in identifying bottlenecks and performance limitations.

Firstly, setting up a realistic testing environment that closely mirrors the production setup is essential. This includes deploying similar hardware resources, network settings, and Kafka and Kafka Streams configurations. Only when the testing environment mirrors production can the test results be considered reliable.

1. Throughput Measurement

To measure throughput, one must determine the volume of records that Kafka Streams can process per unit time. This is typically assessed by generating a large dataset and processing it through the stream topology.

Employ tools like kafka-producer-perf-test.sh to generate test data. Example usage of the tool is shown below:

```
bin/kafka-producer-perf-test.sh \
    --topic test-topic \
    --num-records 1000000 \
    --record-size 100 \
    --throughput 100000 \
    --producer-props bootstrap.servers=localhost:9092
```

This command produces 1,000,000 records of size 100 bytes each, targeting a throughput of 100,000 records per second.

2. Latency Measurement

Message latency can be measured by instrumenting the stream processing code or by configuring Kafka's client interceptors to log the time taken for processing. For example, latency can be calculated through timestamps added at different stages of the processing pipeline:

```
KStream<String, String> stream = builder.stream("input-topic");

stream.foreach((key, value) -> {
    long startTime = System.currentTimeMillis();

    // Processing logic
    // - Transformations, aggregations, etc.

    long endTime = System.currentTimeMillis();
    long processingTime = endTime - startTime;
    log.info("Processing time for message with key {}: {} ms", key, processingTime);
});
```

3. Load Testing

Load testing aims to understand how the Kafka Streams application performs under peak load conditions. This involves gradually increasing the load until the system's limits are reached, thus exposing performance bottlenecks.

Apache JMeter is a popular load testing tool. A sampler configuration example for Kafka in JMeter is as follows:

```
Thread Group
 |
 +- Kafka Producer Sampler
    - topic: test-topic
    - partition: 0
    - key: key
    - value: ${__RandomString(100,abcdefghijklmnopqrstuvwxyz,)}
    - producer.properties
        bootstrap.servers=localhost:9092
        key.serializer=org.apache.kafka.common.serialization.StringSerializer
        value.serializer=org.apache.kafka.common.serialization.StringSerializer
```

4. Bottleneck Identification

After running throughput and load tests, it is important to analyze metrics from Kafka, Kafka Streams, and the operating environment to pinpoint bottlenecks. Tools such as Kafka's built-in testing utilities, e.g., JMX metrics, can be pivotal:

```
bin/kafka-run-class.sh kafka.tools.JmxTool --object-name kafka.server:type=
    BrokerTopicMetrics,topic=test-topic,name=MessagesInPerSec --jmx-url service:
    jmx:rmi:///jndi/rmi://localhost:9999/jmxrmi --reporting-interval 1000
```

This command monitors the rate of messages ingested in a specific topic, aiding in identifying whether the producer is sending data too quickly or the broker is handling data inefficiently.

Other useful metrics include:

- **Consumer lag**: Total lag in message consumption.
- **Commit latency**: Time taken to commit records.
- **Record processing rate**: Rate at which streams are processed.
- **State store metrics**: Access time and cache miss rate.

5. Performance Tuning

Depending on the identified bottlenecks, the following tuning strategies can help improve performance:

- **Parallelism**: Increase the number of stream threads to parallelize processing workload.

```
Properties props = new Properties();
props.put(StreamsConfig.NUM_STREAM_THREADS_CONFIG, 4);
```

- **Batching**: Adjust producer.batch.size and linger.ms to optimize the number of records sent in a single request.

```
props.put(ProducerConfig.BATCH_SIZE_CONFIG, 16384);
props.put(ProducerConfig.LINGER_MS_CONFIG, 5);
```

- **Compression**: Use compression techniques such as Snappy or LZ4 to reduce the size of records.

```
props.put(ProducerConfig.COMPRESSION_TYPE_CONFIG, "snappy");
```

- **Memory tuning**: Configure heap sizes and garbage collection settings based on memory usage patterns observed during tests.

```
export KAFKA_HEAP_OPTS="-Xms4g -Xmx4g"
```

Consistently monitoring, analyzing, and optimizing these parameters allows for achieving a Kafka Streams application that performs efficiently under various conditions. This holistic approach ensures high throughput, low latency, and reliable performance, leading to a robust and scalable streaming data processing solution.

9.9 Test Automation Best Practices

Test automation is an integral part of maintaining the reliability and efficiency of Kafka Streams applications. Adopting best practices ensures that automated tests are not only effective in identifying issues but also maintainable and scalable. This section delves into the essential practices that should be followed when automating tests for Kafka Streams applications.

Consistency in Test Environments: Ensure that test environments are consistent with production environments. This includes matching configurations for Kafka brokers, Zookeeper instances, and schema registries, if used. Inconsistent environments can lead to false positives or negatives, undermining the reliability of the tests.

Isolation of Test Cases: Each test case should be executed in isolation to prevent interference from previous tests. This can be achieved by ensuring that each test case has its own instance of the necessary components, such as Kafka brokers and state stores. For unit tests using TopologyTestDriver, ensure that it is instantiated fresh for each test. This isolation guarantees that test results are accurate and reflect the functionality being tested.

```
public class KafkaStreamsTest {
    private TopologyTestDriver testDriver;
    private TestInputTopic<String, String> inputTopic;
    private TestOutputTopic<String, String> outputTopic;

    @Before
    public void setUp() {
        Properties props = new Properties();
        props.put(StreamsConfig.APPLICATION_ID_CONFIG, "test-app");
        props.put(StreamsConfig.BOOTSTRAP_SERVERS_CONFIG, "dummy:1234");

        StreamsBuilder builder = new StreamsBuilder();
```

```
        // Define your topology here
        Topology topology = builder.build();

        testDriver = new TopologyTestDriver(topology, props);
        inputTopic = testDriver.createInputTopic("input-topic", new StringSerializer(),
             new StringSerializer());
        outputTopic = testDriver.createOutputTopic("output-topic", new
             StringDeserializer(), new StringDeserializer());
    }

    @After
    public void tearDown() {
        testDriver.close();
    }

    @Test
    public void testProcessing() {
        inputTopic.pipeInput("key", "value");
        assertThat(outputTopic.readKeyValue()).isEqualTo(KeyValue.pair("key", "
             processed-value"));
    }
}
```

Use of Fixtures for Reusable Setup: Employing fixtures can significantly reduce code duplication and ensure a consistent setup across multiple test cases. This is especially useful for setting up complex environments and initial states.

Validation of End-to-End Scenarios: While unit tests focus on individual components, end-to-end tests validate the entire data flow from ingestion to output. This ensures that all integrated components work together as expected. Use embedded Kafka clusters, such as EmbeddedKafkaCluster from spring-kafka-test, to simulate production-like environments in your integration tests.

Mock External Dependencies: Mock external dependencies that are not the focus of the test. For example, if your Kafka Streams application interacts with a database or a web service, mock these interactions to focus on testing the stream processing logic. This can be achieved using frameworks like Mockito.

```
@RunWith(MockitoJUnitRunner.class)
public class ExternalServiceKafkaStreamsTest {
    @Mock
    private ExternalService externalService;

    private KafkaStreams kafkaStreams;

    @Before
    public void setUp() {
        when(externalService.fetchData(anyString())).thenReturn("mock-data");

        StreamsBuilder builder = new StreamsBuilder();
        // Define your topology here, including interaction with externalService
```

```
        kafkaStreams = new KafkaStreams(builder.build(), new Properties());
    }

    @Test
    public void testWithMockedService() {
        // Test logic here
        verify(externalService, times(1)).fetchData(anyString());
    }
}
```

Parameterization of Tests: Parameterize your test cases to cover a wide range of scenarios without duplicating test code. JUnit provides support for parameterized tests, facilitating the execution of the same test logic with different inputs.

```
@RunWith(Parameterized.class)
public class ParameterizedKafkaStreamsTest {
    @Parameterized.Parameters
    public static Collection<Object[]> data() {
        return Arrays.asList(new Object[][] {
            { "input1", "expectedOutput1" },
            { "input2", "expectedOutput2" }
        });
    }

    private final String input;
    private final String expectedOutput;

    public ParameterizedKafkaStreamsTest(String input, String expectedOutput) {
        this.input = input;
        this.expectedOutput = expectedOutput;
    }

    @Test
    public void testProcessing() {
        // Set up the test driver and topic
        // Assert that input produces the expected output
    }
}
```

Monitoring and Reporting: Implement monitoring and reporting mechanisms to track test execution and results. Integrate with CI/CD pipelines to auto-generate reports and alerts for failures. Tools like Jenkins, GitLab CI, and Travis CI can be configured to run tests and produce comprehensive reports.

Regular Test Review and Refactoring: Periodically review and refactor your test code and cases to ensure they remain relevant and efficient as your Kafka Streams application evolves. Remove obsolete tests and update existing ones to reflect any changes in the application's functionality.

```
        pipeline {
            agent any
            stages {
```

```
        stage('Build') {
            steps {
                script {
                    // Compile and package the application
                }
            }
        }
        stage('Test') {
            steps {
                script {
                    // Run the test suite
                }
            }
        }
        stage('Report') {
            steps {
                script {
                    // Generate test reports
                }
            }
        }
    }
}
```

By adhering to these best practices, developers can create robust and maintainable test automation suites for their Kafka Streams applications. This ensures that the stream processing logic is thoroughly tested and dependable, ultimately leading to more reliable and performant applications.

9.10 Debugging Kafka Streams Applications

Effective debugging of Kafka Streams applications is critical to ensuring their reliability and correctness. This section provides detailed instructions and techniques for identifying and fixing issues in Kafka Streams applications.

Debugging in any application typically involves monitoring the application's runtime behavior, analyzing logs, and setting breakpoints to inspect states and data flows. Kafka Streams applications introduce additional complexity due to their distributed nature and stream processing paradigm. Consequently, a more structured approach is required.

1. Logging and Monitoring

Logging is a fundamental aspect of debugging. Kafka Streams leverages SLF4J (Simple Logging Facade for Java) for logging purposes. To start logging, ensure that your log4j.properties or logback.xml is correctly configured and placed in the classpath.

A typical log4j.properties configuration might look like:

```
log4j.rootLogger=DEBUG, stdout, file

log4j.appender.stdout=org.apache.log4j.ConsoleAppender
log4j.appender.stdout.layout=org.apache.log4j.PatternLayout
log4j.appender.stdout.layout.ConversionPattern=%d [%t] %-5p %c - %m%n

log4j.appender.file=org.apache.log4j.RollingFileAppender
log4j.appender.file.File=logs/kafka-streams.log
log4j.appender.file.MaxFileSize=10MB
log4j.appender.file.MaxBackupIndex=5
log4j.appender.file.layout=org.apache.log4j.PatternLayout
log4j.appender.file.layout.ConversionPattern=%d [%t] %-5p %c - %m%n
```

In Kafka Streams applications, it is crucial to log the beginning and end of major processing steps. For instance, logging the entry and exit points of your transformation logic provides insights into the data flowing through the stream.

```
import org.slf4j.Logger;
import org.slf4j.LoggerFactory;

public class MyKafkaStreamApp {
    private static final Logger logger = LoggerFactory.getLogger(MyKafkaStreamApp.
        class);

    public void processStream() {
        logger.debug("Starting Kafka Stream processing.");

        // Stream processing logic here

        logger.debug("Finished Kafka Stream processing.");
    }
}
```

2. Setting Breakpoints

For deeper inspection during development, setting breakpoints in your Integrated Development Environment (IDE) can be highly effective. Modern IDEs like IntelliJ IDEA or Eclipse provide support for remote debugging. This involves starting your Kafka Streams application with debug options and attaching a remote debugger.

Start your application with debug options:

```
java -agentlib:jdwp=transport=dt_socket,server=y,suspend=n,address=5005 -jar your-
    application.jar
```

Attach to the remote debugger: Run > Edit Configurations > Remote > Configure with the appropriate host and port.

You can now set breakpoints in your Kafka Streams code. This allows you to pause execution and inspect the state of your application at critical points.

3. Inspecting State Stores

Kafka Streams' stateful processing capabilities often use state stores to manage the application's state. Accessing state store data directly helps verify correctness and diagnose issues.

For example, assume you are using a key-value store:

```
StoreBuilder<KeyValueStore<String, Long>> storeBuilder =
    Stores.keyValueStoreBuilder(
        Stores.persistentKeyValueStore("my-state-store"),
        Serdes.String(),
        Serdes.Long()
    );
streamsBuilder.addStateStore(storeBuilder);
```

You can query the state store at runtime:

```
ReadOnlyKeyValueStore<String, Long> keyValueStore =
    streams.store(StoreQueryParameters.fromNameAndType("my-state-store",
        QueryableStoreTypes.keyValueStore()));

keyValueStore.get("some-key");
```

4. Analyzing Stream Topologies

Kafka Streams applications consist of topologies. Visualizing and analyzing these topologies assists in understanding the data flow and identifying points of failure.

Kafka Streams provides an API to expose the current topology:

```
System.out.println(streams.toString());
```

This prints the topology, showing the processors and their connections. For complex topologies, integrating with visualization tools like the ksqlDB UI provides graphical representations.

5. Debugging the Kafka Cluster

Issues sometimes stem from the Kafka cluster itself. Tools like kafka-consumer-groups.sh and kafka-topics.sh offer insights into consumer groups' states and topic configurations:

```
kafka-consumer-groups.sh --bootstrap-server localhost:9092 --describe --group my-
    consumer-group
```

This helps in identifying offsets, lag, and potential consumer issues.

6. Error Handling Configuration

Properly configuring error handlers ensures that exceptions in the stream processing do not halt your application. Kafka Streams provides mechanisms like DeserializationExceptionHandler and ProductionExceptionHandler.

For instance, to handle deserialization errors gracefully:

```
Properties props = new Properties();
props.put(StreamsConfig.
    DEFAULT_DESERIALIZATION_EXCEPTION_HANDLER_CLASS_CONFIG,
  LogAndContinueExceptionHandler.class.getName());
```

This configuration logs the error and continues processing, preventing application termination.

7. Using Debugging Libraries

Leverage libraries like kafka-streams-test-utils for unit tests, allowing assertions on expected behavior. Additionally, tools like jconsole and VisualVM monitor JVM metrics, GC behavior, and application threads.

Effective debugging of Kafka Streams applications thus involves a combination of logging, setting breakpoints, inspecting state stores, analyzing topologies, checking Kafka cluster states, configuring error handlers, and utilizing debugging libraries. Equipped with these techniques, developers can efficiently identify and resolve issues, ensuring robust stream processing applications.

Chapter 10

Performance Tuning and Optimization

This chapter focuses on performance tuning and optimization of Kafka Streams applications. It begins with understanding key performance metrics and covers optimizing Kafka producer and consumer settings. The chapter discusses tuning Kafka Streams configurations, improving threading and concurrency, and best practices for memory management. It also addresses scaling applications, monitoring performance, and includes case studies that highlight effective optimization techniques.

10.1 Introduction to Performance Tuning

Performance tuning is a critical aspect of building and maintaining high-performance Kafka Streams applications. It involves systematically identifying and modifying various parts of the system to enhance efficiency, decrease latency, and ensure optimal resource utilization. In this section, we will examine the foundational principles and methodologies that practitioners use to evaluate and improve the performance of Kafka Streams applications.

Performance tuning begins with an understanding of the key performance metrics that influence a Kafka Streams application. These metrics typically include throughput, latency, and resource utilization.

Throughput measures the number of records processed by the application per unit of time, often expressed in records per second. Latency refers to the time taken for a record to traverse the entire processing topology, from ingress to egress. Resource utilization encompasses CPU, memory, and I/O usage, which directly impacts the application's overall performance.

To effectively tune a Kafka Streams application, one must first establish a performance baseline. This baseline serves as a reference point against which all subsequent performance improvements are measured. Typically, this involves running the application under a controlled workload and measuring the initial values of the key performance metrics. Tools such as kafkacat and JConsole can be leveraged to gather these baseline metrics.

Once the baseline is established, the next step is to identify bottlenecks within the system. Bottlenecks are components that constrain the overall performance and are frequently pinpointed through profiling and monitoring tools. For instance, Apache Kafka provides a variety of metrics through its MBeans, accessible via Java Management Extensions (JMX). These metrics can be analyzed to determine which parts of the system are underperforming and are likely candidates for optimization.

One common approach to diagnosing performance issues is end-to-end tracing, which helps in visualizing the flow of records through the Kafka Streams topology. This technique involves instrumenting the application code to capture timestamps and other relevant metadata at various stages of record processing. Subsequently, by analyzing this trace data, it becomes possible to identify stages with higher-than-expected latency or throughput limitations.

With a clear understanding of the bottlenecks, the next phase involves formulating and applying optimization strategies. These strategies often target various layers within the Kafka Streams ecosystem, including producer and consumer configurations, threading models, and memory management practices.

Optimizing producer settings is pivotal as it directly influences how quickly data is ingested into Kafka topics. Key configurations such as linger.ms, batch.size, and compression.type can be adjusted to improve throughput and reduce latency. For example, increasing batch.size allows the producer to send larger batches of records, reducing the overhead associated with each network request.

Similarly, optimizing consumer settings ensures that the Kafka Streams application can efficiently pull data from Kafka topics for processing. Key settings include fetch.min.bytes, fetch.max.wait.ms, and max.poll.records. By carefully tuning these parameters, it is possible to balance the trade-offs between latency, throughput, and resource consumption.

Kafka Streams configuration parameters themselves play a crucial role in performance optimization. Parameters such as buffered.records.per.partition, commit.interval.ms, and num.stream.threads are essential levers that can be adjusted to enhance performance. For instance, increasing num.stream.threads can improve parallelism, but it must be done judiciously to avoid excessive context switching and resource contention.

Threading and concurrency optimizations are particularly significant in achieving high performance in Kafka Streams applications. By strategically assigning threads to different tasks and balancing the load across multiple instances, it is possible to maximize throughput and minimize latency. The Java Executor framework can be utilized to manage thread pools effectively, ensuring that thread allocation aligns with the workload's demands.

In addition to these considerations, memory management practices such as configuring the JVM heap size, tuning garbage collection algorithms, and leveraging off-heap memory can substantially impact performance. Proper memory management reduces the likelihood of prolonged garbage collection pauses and out-of-memory errors, leading to more predictable and stable performance.

Adopting a systematic approach to performance tuning, complemented by regular monitoring and profiling, enables practitioners to fine-tune their Kafka Streams applications continuously. The ultimate goal is to achieve a state where the application processes data efficiently, with minimal latency, and within the constraints of the available resources.

10.2 Understanding Performance Metrics

The effectiveness of tuning Kafka Streams applications fundamentally depends on accurately measuring performance through a set of well-defined metrics. These metrics provide insights into the operational aspects of a Kafka Streams application and facilitate informed decision-making for performance improvement.

A comprehensive understanding of performance metrics divides into three primary categories: throughput, latency, and resource utilization. Each of these categories encompasses further specific metrics that need to be accurately monitored and analyzed.

Throughput refers to the amount of data processed by the Kafka Streams application over a specified period. Key throughput metrics include:

- *Records Processed*: This metric counts the number of records successfully processed by the application per second. It includes both source records and intermediate records produced by intra-stream operations.
- *Bytes Processed*: Similar to records processed, this metric measures the volume of data in bytes the application processes per second. It encompasses both incoming and outgoing data flow.

Below is an illustrative code snippet to fetch and display throughput metrics using Kafka Streams' built-in metrics.

```
KafkaStreams streams = new KafkaStreams(builder.build(), config);
streams.start();

// Get all stream metrics
Metrics metrics = streams.metrics();

// Display throughput metrics
metrics.metric(new MetricName("throughput_records", "stream-metrics")).metricValue
    ();
metrics.metric(new MetricName("throughput_bytes", "stream-metrics")).metricValue();
```

Latency measures the time taken for a record to progress through the various stages of processing within the Kafka Streams pipeline. The essential latency metrics include:

- *End-to-End Latency*: Represents the total time from when a record is produced in the source topic until it is consumed and processed by the sink.
- *Processing Latency*: Time taken for a record to be processed by a particular operation or node within the stream topology.

Accurate measurement of latency entails the instrumentation of stream processing stages, often visualized through execution timing logs and performance monitoring tools. Below is an exemplar application of timing logs to track processing latency.

```
public void process(Record<K, V> record) {
    long startTime = System.nanoTime();

    // Process the record
    processRecord(record);

    long endTime = System.nanoTime();
    long processingLatency = endTime - startTime;
    log.debug("Processing latency: {} ns", processingLatency);
}
```

Resource Utilization focuses on the consumption of computational resources such as CPU, memory, and network bandwidth. Key metrics in this category comprise:

- *CPU Utilization*: Percentage of CPU resources used by the Kafka Streams application. Monitoring CPU usage helps in identifying bottlenecks caused by computational intensity.
- *Memory Usage*: Amount of JVM heap space utilized by Kafka Streams. This metric indicates memory consumption patterns and potential memory leaks.
- *Network I/O*: Volume of data transmitted and received over the network interface. It includes bytes sent to and received from Kafka brokers, crucial for understanding network traffic patterns.

The following Java Management Extensions (JMX) code demonstrates how to gather and log resource utilization metrics.

```
// Get Runtime MXBean for CPU usage
OperatingSystemMXBean osBean = ManagementFactory.getPlatformMXBean(
    OperatingSystemMXBean.class);
long cpuUsage = osBean.getSystemCpuLoad() * 100;

// Get Memory MXBean for heap memory usage
MemoryMXBean memoryBean = ManagementFactory.getMemoryMXBean();
long heapMemoryUsage = memoryBean.getHeapMemoryUsage().getUsed();

// Log the metrics
log.info("CPU Usage: {}%", cpuUsage);
log.info("Heap Memory Usage: {} bytes", heapMemoryUsage);
```

Equipped with the knowledge of these fundamental performance metrics, practitioners can embark on the performance tuning process with greater precision. By systematically monitoring throughput, latency, and resource utilization, it becomes feasible to identify potential bottlenecks and areas for optimization within Kafka Streams applications.

10.3 Optimizing Kafka Producer Settings

In optimizing Kafka Producer settings, the goal is to achieve a balance between throughput, latency, reliability, and resource consumption. Proper tuning of these settings is crucial for ensuring high performance in Kafka Streams applications. The parameters which are primarily influential include batch size, linger time, compression, acknowledgments, and retries.

Batch Size (batch.size): The batch size defines the maximum number of bytes that can be accumulated to form a single batch before sending it to a Kafka partition. Increasing the batch size can improve throughput by reducing the number of requests sent; however, it may also increase latency since data might wait in the buffer longer until the batch size threshold is reached. The default batch size is 16KB, and adjusting this parameter is particularly beneficial when dealing with small messages which can be batched together more efficiently.

```
properties.put("batch.size", 32768); // Set batch size to 32KB
```

Linger Time (linger.ms): The linger time parameter specifies the amount of time to wait for additional messages before sending a batch to the Kafka broker. By default, this is set to 0, which means records are sent as soon as they are available. Introducing a slight delay can allow the producer to batch more records together in a single request, thus increasing throughput. On the other hand, setting this too high might increase latency unnecessarily.

```
properties.put("linger.ms", 5); // Wait up to 5 ms for additional messages
```

Compression (compression.type): Kafka producer supports different types of message compression such as none, gzip, snappy, and lz4. Compression can significantly reduce the amount of data that needs to be sent over the network and stored on disk, which can enhance throughput and reduce latency. However, the trade-off is the additional CPU overhead required to compress and decompress data.

```
properties.put("compression.type", "gzip"); // Use gzip for compression
```

Acknowledge Settings (acks): The acks configuration controls the criteria determining the completion of a request. Several levels of acknowledgments are available:

- acks=0: The producer will not wait for any acknowledgment from the broker, which is the fastest but least reliable setting.

- acks=1: The producer will wait for the leader broker to acknowledge receipt of the data. This offers a balance between reliability and performance.

- acks=all or acks=-1: The producer will wait for acknowledgment from all in-sync replicas. This is the slowest but most reliable option.

Using acks=all provides the highest consistency guarantee, ensuring that the data is written to all replicas.

```
properties.put("acks", "all"); // Wait for all in-sync replicas to acknowledge
```

Retries (retries): The retries parameter specifies the number of times the producer will attempt to resend data after a transient error occurs. By default, this value is set to 0, meaning that the producer will not retry after a failure. Increasing this value can improve the reliability of message delivery, particularly in cases of intermittent network issues or broker unavailability. It is also advisable to configure the retry.backoff.ms parameter to control the time between retry attempts.

```
properties.put("retries", 3); // Retry sending messages up to 3 times
properties.put("retry.backoff.ms", 100); // Wait 100 ms between retries
```

Max In-Flight Requests (max.in.flight.requests.per.connection): This setting defines the maximum number of unacknowledged requests the client will send on a single connection before blocking. A higher number can increase throughput but might decrease reliability, as there could be more messages in-flight in the event of a retry scenario.

```
properties.put("max.in.flight.requests.per.connection", 5); // Limit of in-flight requests
```

Additional Settings: Some additional Kafka Producer settings to consider include:

- buffer.memory: This controls the total amount of memory available to the producer for buffering. Ensure the value is aligned with the environment's physical memory resources.

- max.block.ms: This determines the maximum time the producer will block when buffer memory is exhausted.

- delivery.timeout.ms: This provides an upper bound on the time to report failures.

Below is an example of a comprehensive configuration of a Kafka producer:

```
Properties properties = new Properties();
properties.put("bootstrap.servers", "kafka01:9092,kafka02:9092");
properties.put("key.serializer", "org.apache.kafka.common.serialization.StringSerializer"
    );
properties.put("value.serializer", "org.apache.kafka.common.serialization.StringSerializer
    ");
properties.put("batch.size", 32768);
properties.put("linger.ms", 5);
properties.put("compression.type", "gzip");
properties.put("acks", "all");
properties.put("retries", 3);
properties.put("retry.backoff.ms", 100);
properties.put("max.in.flight.requests.per.connection", 5);
properties.put("buffer.memory", 33554432); // 32MB buffer memory
properties.put("max.block.ms", 60000); // Block max 60 sec when buffer full
properties.put("delivery.timeout.ms", 120000); // Delivery timeout at 2 minutes
```

Optimizing Kafka Producer settings is critical for balancing the trade-offs between throughput, latency, availability, and resource utilization. By carefully tuning these parameters based on the specific use case and application requirements, one can achieve significant performance improvements in Kafka Streams applications.

10.4 Optimizing Kafka Consumer Settings

Optimizing Kafka consumer settings is crucial for improving the overall performance and efficiency of Kafka Streams applications. Proper configuration can minimize latency, maximize throughput, and ensure better resource utilization. This section examines the various Kafka consumer settings that can be adjusted to achieve optimal performance.

The fetch.min.bytes configuration setting determines the minimum amount of data that the consumer wants to receive from the broker when fetching records. The default setting is 1 byte, but by increasing this value, consumers can reduce the number of fetch requests made to the broker. This parameter helps balance latency and throughput; higher values can lead to higher throughput at the cost of increased latency, as the consumer might wait longer for the desired amount of data to be available.

```
props.put("fetch.min.bytes", 1048576); // 1 MB
```

The fetch.max.wait.ms setting works hand-in-hand with fetch.min.bytes. It specifies the maximum amount of time (in milliseconds) the broker will wait before sending data to the consumer if the minimum fetch size condition is not met. Raising this value can benefit scenarios where data production is sporadic, ensuring larger batches of data and hence, improved throughput.

```
props.put("fetch.max.wait.ms", 500); // 500 ms
```

The max.partition.fetch.bytes parameter controls the maximum amount of data fetched by the consumer in one request per partition. This parameter can be increased to allow consumers to fetch larger batches of records, hence improving throughput. However, it's important to monitor the memory usage since fetching too much data can lead to excessive memory consumption.

```
props.put("max.partition.fetch.bytes", 10485760); // 10 MB
```

The max.poll.records setting limits the number of records returned in a single poll call. By controlling the volume of records fetched per poll, one can manage the consumption rate and processing time. A higher value improves throughput but may increase processing time per poll cycle.

```
props.put("max.poll.records", 500); // 500 records per poll
```

Adjusting the session.timeout.ms setting is essential for maintaining a stable connection between the consumer and the broker. This setting specifies the amount of time the consumer can be out of contact with the broker while still considered alive. If the consumer does not send a heartbeat within this timeout, it is typically considered to have failed. The default value is usually 10 seconds, but this can be increased for environments with network delays or high processing times per poll.

```
props.put("session.timeout.ms", 30000); // 30 seconds
```

The heartbeat.interval.ms setting defines the interval at which the consumer sends heartbeats to the broker. Heartbeats are crucial for maintaining group membership and partition ownership. This value should be lower than the session.timeout.ms to ensure timely detection of failures.

```
props.put("heartbeat.interval.ms", 10000); // 10 seconds
```

Fine-tuning enable.auto.commit and auto.commit.interval.ms settings is also imperative. Setting enable.auto.commit to false provides complete control over offset management, allowing for precise control over record processing and error handling. When automatic committing is enabled, auto.commit.interval.ms determines the frequency of automatic commits. Controlling these intervals can help manage commit overhead and ensure reliable message processing.

```
props.put("enable.auto.commit", "false"); // Manual offset management
```

The isolation.level setting is relevant for transactions. It determines the visibility of transactional messages to the consumer. This can be set to read_committed to ensure that only the committed records are read, which is essential for ensuring data consistency in distributed systems.

```
props.put("isolation.level", "read_committed"); // Ensures transactional integrity
```

Lastly, auto.offset.reset is crucial for determining the behavior of the consumer when there is no initial offset or if the current offset is out of range. Setting this to earliest allows the consumer to start reading from the beginning of the partition, which can be useful in batch processing scenarios. Conversely, setting it to latest makes the consumer read from the end, thus processing only new records.

```
props.put("auto.offset.reset", "earliest"); // Start from the beginning if no offset
    present
```

Properly tuning these Kafka consumer settings can result in a more responsive and resource-efficient Kafka Streams application, capable of meeting the demands of various processing workloads efficiently.

10.5 Tuning Kafka Streams Configuration

Kafka Streams offers a range of configuration options that allow for fine-tuning performance. Properly configuring these parameters can lead to significant improvements in throughput, latency, and resource utilization. This section explores the critical configuration properties and their impact on Kafka Streams performance.

- **Batch Size:**

The commit.interval.ms configuration parameter controls how frequently Kafka Streams commits the processed records. By default, this is set to 30 seconds (30000 milliseconds). Decreasing this interval results in more frequent commits, which can reduce potential data loss during failures but increases the overhead per batch. Increasing the interval can boost throughput but at the cost of potential data loss.

```
properties.put(StreamsConfig.COMMIT_INTERVAL_MS_CONFIG, 1000); // 1
    second
```

Monitoring the trade-offs concerning batch size and commit frequency is crucial. Testing different intervals can help find the optimal balance between performance and durability according to the application's requirements.

- **Cache Size:**

Kafka Streams uses a caching mechanism to buffer records during processing, reducing the frequency of state store access. By default, this cache size is set to 10 MB per thread. It can be configured using cache.max.bytes.buffering.

```
properties.put(StreamsConfig.CACHE_MAX_BYTES_BUFFERING_CONFIG, 50 *
    1024 * 1024); // 50 MB
```

A larger cache can improve performance by reducing the load on state stores and RocksDB, but it increases memory usage. It is important to monitor and adjust the cache size based on the available resources and workload characteristics.

- **Parallelism and Threading:**

The num.stream.threads configuration property determines the number of processing threads in a Kafka Streams application. By default, it is set to 1, which means a single thread is responsible for processing all data. Increasing the number of threads can enable parallel processing of different partitions.

```
properties.put(StreamsConfig.NUM_STREAM_THREADS_CONFIG, 4); // 4 threads
```

While increasing parallelism allows better utilization of multi-core processors, it necessitates careful consideration of the workload splitting among threads and the overhead of context switching.

- **State Store Configuration:**

Kafka Streams supports persistent state stores, configured with RocksDB by default. Adjusting RocksDB configurations, like write buffer size (rocksdb.writebuffer.size) and block cache size (rocksdb.block.cache.size), can significantly influence performance.

```
rocksdbOptions.put("write_buffer_size", 64 * 1024 * 1024); // 64 MB
rocksdbOptions.put("block_cache_size", 256 * 1024 * 1024); // 256 MB
```

Optimizing these settings based on the expected state size and access patterns can result in better performance.

- **Processing Guarantees:**

The processing.guarantee parameter determines the level of processing guarantees provided by the application. It can be set to at_least_once or exactly_once. Enabling exactly-once semantics (exactly_once_v2) adds overhead due to the additional coordination needed.

```
properties.put(StreamsConfig.PROCESSING_GUARANTEE_CONFIG, StreamsConfig
    .EXACTLY_ONCE_V2);
```

While exactly-once guarantees ensure that records are processed exactly once, thereby eliminating duplicates, it comes at the cost of decreasing throughput. Choosing between these guarantees involves a trade-off between data accuracy and performance.

- **Log Configuration:**

Kafka Streams relies heavily on the underlying Kafka broker logs. Configuring appropriate log segment sizes (log.segment.bytes) and retention policies (log.retention.ms, log.cleanup.policy) can help manage log performance and storage.

```
logConfig.put("log.segment.bytes", 1073741824); // 1 GB segments
logConfig.put("log.retention.ms", 604800000); // 1 week
```

Balancing the frequency of log segment creation and the duration for which logs are retained is essential for efficiently managing disk space and I/O operations.

- **Serde Configuration:**

The choice of serializers/deserializers (Serdes) can impact the performance of a Kafka Streams application. Using efficient and compact Serdes minimizes the overhead associated with record serialization and deserialization. Configuring Serdes is essential for ensuring high performance and efficient data handling.

```
properties.put(StreamsConfig.DEFAULT_KEY_SERDE_CLASS_CONFIG, Serdes.
    String().getClass());
properties.put(StreamsConfig.DEFAULT_VALUE_SERDE_CLASS_CONFIG, Serdes.
    String().getClass());
```

For more complex data types, custom Serdes may provide optimized serialization, further enhancing performance.

- **Buffering:**

Kafka Streams uses internal buffering mechanisms to reduce the number of network requests. The buffered.records.per.partition configuration defines the maximum number of records buffered per partition.

```
properties.put(StreamsConfig.BUFFERED_RECORDS_PER_PARTITION_CONFIG,
    1000); // 1000 records
```

Increasing this value can improve throughput by allowing more records to be processed in each batch, but at the expense of increased memory usage.

- **Grace Periods:**

For windowed operations, the grace period (grace.ms) defines the time to wait for out-of-order records. Setting an appropriate grace period ensures that late-arriving data is considered while maintaining performance.

```
properties.put(StreamsConfig.
    WINDOW_STORE_CHANGE_LOG_ADDITIVE_LAG_MS_CONFIG,
    300000); // 5 minutes
```

Balancing the grace period with the stream's characteristics can minimize latency without losing critical data.

- **Metrics and Monitoring:**

Kafka Streams provides a metric system for monitoring the application's health and performance. Enabling JMX (jmx.prefix) and configuring metrics reporters gives insights into various performance aspects.

```
properties.put(StreamsConfig.METRICS_RECORDING_LEVEL_CONFIG, Sensor.
    RecordingLevel.INFO.name());
properties.put(StreamsConfig.METRICS_SAMPLE_WINDOW_MS_CONFIG, 30000)
    ; // 30 seconds
properties.put(StreamsConfig.JMX_PREFIX_CONFIG, "kafka.streams");
```

Utilizing these metrics helps in proactively identifying performance bottlenecks and ensuring the application operates within desired parameters.

Successful tuning of Kafka Streams configurations requires a comprehensive understanding of application requirements and operational context. Experimenting with different settings, analyzing performance impacts, and adjusting configurations accordingly ensures optimized resource utilization and enhanced performance.

10.6 Threading and Concurrency Optimization

Threading and concurrency are pivotal in scaling Kafka Streams applications to efficiently process high-throughput data streams. Kafka Streams leverages multi-threading capabilities to improve parallelism and throughput, thus optimizing performance. This section delineates various strategies and configurations to fine-tune threading and concurrency for optimal operation.

Kafka Streams defines threads at the client level through the application configuration parameter *num.stream.threads*. Each thread operates independently, processing different tasks from the same application instance. Properly configuring this parameter is key to achieving balanced resource utilization. For example:

```
Properties props = new Properties();
props.put(StreamsConfig.APPLICATION_ID_CONFIG, "my-app");
props.put(StreamsConfig.BOOTSTRAP_SERVERS_CONFIG, "localhost:9092");
props.put(StreamsConfig.NUM_STREAM_THREADS_CONFIG, "4");
KafkaStreams streams = new KafkaStreams(builder.build(), props);
```

In this configuration, the application runs with four threads. These threads concurrently execute tasks, enhancing the application's ability to handle larger throughputs.

However, it's essential to comprehend the implications of over-provisioning threads. Assigning more threads than available processing units (e.g., CPU cores) can lead to context switching overhead, which deteriorates performance. A balanced approach entails setting the number of threads close to the number of CPU cores available to the application.

Besides thread configuration, Kafka Streams utilizes a task management approach known as task assignment and balancing. Each stream thread is responsible for one or more tasks, and a task comprises processing one or more partitions of the input topics. Proper task management is crucial for achieving balanced load distribution across threads.

The workload of tasks can be monitored through Kafka Streams metrics. Metrics such as "Thread-level total process, punctuate, and idle ratio" provide insights into individual thread performance. Employ the following metric exposition:

```
kafka.streams:type=stream-metrics,client-id=my-app-StreamThread-1
- total-process-ratio
- total-punctuate-ratio
- total-idle-ratio
```

A thread that exhibits high idle time implies underutilization. Conversely, a consistent high processing ratio without substantial punctuate indicates the need for additional threading or rebalancing tasks across threads.

Optimization extends beyond simply adding threads; it involves task-specific strategies like parallelizing state stores. Embedded RocksDB used for stateful operations within Kafka Streams can be tuned for concurrent access. Configuration parameters such as *rocksdb.batch.size*, *rocksdb.columnfamily.block.cache.size*, and *rocksdb.max.write.buffer.number* can be fine-tuned to optimize concurrency.

Consider the following configuration for RocksDB:

```
props.put("rocksdb.batch.size", "1500");
props.put("rocksdb.max.write.buffer.number", "4");
props.put("rocksdb.columnfamily.block.cache.size", "10485760");
```

These settings enhance the concurrent read/write performance of RocksDB, facilitating faster state store operations.

Another crucial aspect of threading optimization is ensuring that stateful processing operations are thread-safe. Kafka Streams abstract these through thread-safe state stores and synchronized access patterns, minimizing concurrency issues.

The use of synchronized processors or partitioned processing paradigms is beneficial in solving concurrency challenges. For example:

```
builder.stream("input-topic")
    .transform(() -> new SynchronizedTransformer<>())
    .to("output-topic");

...
```

```
public class SynchronizedTransformer<K, V> implements Transformer<K, V,
    KeyValue<K, V>> {
  private Object lock = new Object();

  @Override
  public KeyValue<K, V> transform(K key, V value) {
    synchronized (lock) {
      // Thread-safe operation
    }
    return null;
  }
}
```

This pattern ensures that the processing logic within the 'Synchronized-Transformer' is executed safely in multi-threaded environments.

Furthermore, Kafka Streams' internal optimizations, such as co-partitioning of topics and local state management, play instrumental roles in threading efficiency. When source topics are co-partitioned—having the same number of partitions and aligned partitioning key semantics—the locality of data is maintained, reducing cross-node data shuffling and enhancing thread efficiency.

Understanding and correctly configuring thread and concurrency settings in Kafka Streams can lead to a significant performance boost. Proper utilization of threads, proficient task management, fine-tuning state stores for concurrency, and ensuring thread-safe operations collectively contribute to the overarching goal of threading and concurrency optimization.

10.7 Memory Management Best Practices

Understanding and implementing effective memory management practices are critical for ensuring that Kafka Streams applications perform optimally. Given the real-time data processing nature of Kafka Streams, poorly managed memory can lead to application crashes, increased latency, and reduced throughput. This section focuses on best practices for managing memory in Kafka Streams applications, discussing heap settings, garbage collection (GC) tuning, and leveraging state stores efficiently.

Proper heap sizing is essential for any Java application, including those running Kafka Streams. An optimal heap size depends on the application's workload, the data volume being processed, and the available system resources. The heap size configuration should balance between being large enough to accommodate the working data set and small enough to avoid excessive GC pauses. The heap size is configured using the '-Xms' and '-Xmx' JVM options, which set the initial and maximum heap size, respectively. For instance:

```
java -Xms1g -Xmx4g -jar kafka-streams-app.jar
```

In this example, the JVM starts with an initial heap size of 1GB and can grow up to a maximum of 4GB.

Garbage Collection tuning is another critical aspect of memory management. Kafka Streams applications often benefit from the G1 Garbage Collector (G1GC), which is designed to handle large heap sizes with minimal pause times. Configuration options for G1GC include:

- Setting the pause time goals
- Adjusting the size of the regions in the heap

To use G1GC and configure it for a Kafka Streams application, the following options can be added to the JVM parameters:

```
java -Xms4g -Xmx4g -XX:+UseG1GC -XX:MaxGCPauseMillis=200 -jar kafka-streams-
    app.jar
```

Here, G1GC is enabled, and the target maximum pause time for garbage collection is set to 200 milliseconds. This setting helps in reducing the latency spikes caused by GC pauses.

Kafka Streams applications make heavy use of state stores to maintain the state across various operations such as aggregations, joins, and windowing. Efficient use of state stores can significantly impact the memory footprint. RocksDB, the default persistent state store used by Kafka Streams, is highly configurable. Key configuration options include:

- Cache sizing
- Write buffer management

To configure RocksDB for optimal memory consumption, the following configuration can be set in the Kafka Streams application properties:

```
properties.put("rocksdb.config.setter", "com.example.MyRocksDBConfig");
```

The 'MyRocksDBConfig' class would then be implemented to override RocksDB default settings, as shown:

```
public class MyRocksDBConfig implements RocksDBConfigSetter {
    @Override
    public void setConfig(String storeName, Options options, Map<String, Object>
        configs) {
        options.setWriteBufferSize(64 * 1024 * 1024); // 64MB
        options.setMaxWriteBufferNumber(3);
        options.setMaxBackgroundCompactions(2);
    }
}
```

These settings adjust the memory allocation for write buffers and the number of background compaction threads, which can help in managing memory usage and ensuring smoother operation.

Monitoring and profiling tools are instrumental in managing memory effectively. The Java VisualVM tool provides real-time monitoring and profiling of the heap memory usage and enables identification of memory leaks and evaluation of GC behavior. Profiling a running Kafka Streams application with VisualVM can be initiated as follows:

```
jvisualvm
```

After starting VisualVM, connect to the Kafka Streams application process and observe its memory usage under the "Monitor" and "Visual GC" tabs. Identifying and addressing memory bottlenecks in real-time is crucial for maintaining optimal performance.

Kafka Streams also provides internal metrics that can be used to monitor memory usage, particularly the metrics related to state stores and caches. These metrics can be accessed programmatically and used to trigger alerts or automated responses in case of abnormal memory usage. For example:

```
StreamsConfig config = new StreamsConfig(properties);
KafkaStreams streams = new KafkaStreams(topology, config);

streams.setStateListener((newState, oldState) -> {
    if (newState == KafkaStreams.State.RUNNING) {
        Metric metric = streams.metrics().get(new MetricName("memory-total-bytes-
            used", "state-stores"));
        System.out.println("Memory used by state stores: " + metric.metricValue());
    }
});
```

This code snippet sets a custom state listener to log the memory usage of state stores when the Kafka Streams application transitions to the running state.

Effectively managing memory requires continual tuning and monitoring as workloads change. Employing these best practices facilitates optimal Kafka Streams application performance, minimizes latency, and maximizes throughput.

10.8 Scaling Kafka Streams Applications

Scaling Kafka Streams applications is essential to handle increasing data volume, ensure high availability, and maintain low-latency processing. Proper scaling allows Kafka Streams applications to meet the demands of large-scale, real-time data processing while ensuring resilience. This section covers various techniques and best practices for effectively scaling Kafka Streams applications.

Kafka Streams' architecture inherently supports horizontal scalability due to its distributed nature. The primary components involved in scaling are the Kafka brokers, the stream processing instances, tasks, and partitions. Proper understanding and configuration of these components ensure optimized use of resources and efficient load distribution.

1. Partitioning and Parallelism

Kafka Streams leverages Kafka's partitioned log to achieve parallel processing. Each Kafka topic can have multiple partitions, and these partitions form the unit of parallelism.

- *Partition Count:* Increase the number of partitions for a topic to enable greater parallelism. Each partition can be processed independently, distributing the load across multiple instances.
- *Task Distribution:* Kafka Streams divides the processing into tasks, with each task handling one or more partitions. By increasing the number of tasks, we enable better utilization of available processing instances.

2. Scaling Out

Scaling out involves adding more instances of Kafka Streams applications. Each instance runs independently and can process one or more stream tasks.

```
Properties props = new Properties();
props.put(StreamsConfig.APPLICATION_ID_CONFIG, "my-streams-app");
props.put(StreamsConfig.BOOTSTRAP_SERVERS_CONFIG, "kafka-broker1:9092,
    kafka-broker2:9092");
props.put(StreamsConfig.NUM_STREAM_THREADS_CONFIG, 3); // Number of
    stream threads
KafkaStreams streams = new KafkaStreams(topology, props);
```

```
streams.start();
```

In the example above, we configure the Kafka Streams application to use three threads. By deploying this application on multiple instances, we achieve horizontal scalability. It's crucial to evenly spread the instances across available physical or virtual machines to avoid single points of failure.

3. Stateful Stream Processing

Stateful operations in Kafka Streams, such as aggregations and joins, require appropriate state management to scale effectively.

- *State Store Configuration:* Optimize state stores by configuring parameters like cache size and change log topic settings to ensure efficient state management.
- *RocksDB Settings:* Kafka Streams uses RocksDB for persistent state storage. Tuning RocksDB parameters can significantly impact performance. Configure memory, write buffers, and compaction settings tailored to application requirements.

```
props.put(StreamsConfig.ROCKSDB_CONFIG_SETTER_CLASS_CONFIG,
    CustomRocksDBConfig.class);

public class CustomRocksDBConfig implements RocksDBConfigSetter {
  @Override
  public void setConfig(String storeName, Options options, Map<String,Object>
      configs) {
    options.setWriteBufferSize(64 * 1024 * 1024); // 64MB write buffer size
    options.setMaxWriteBufferNumber(3); // Number of write buffers
    options.setMaxBackgroundCompactions(4); // Max background compactions
  }
  @Override
  public void close(String storeName, Options options) {
    // Cleanup if required
  }
}
```

4. Managing Metadata

Kafka Streams applications require coordination and metadata sharing among instances. This is managed using Kafka's internal topics (e.g., *__consumer_offsets*, *__transaction_state*).

- *Internal Topics Configuration:* Internal topics used for processing management should have sufficient partitions to avoid bottlenecks.

```
props.put(StreamsConfig.NUM_STANDBY_REPLICAS_CONFIG, 2); // Number of
    standby replicas for fault tolerance
props.put(StreamsConfig.REPLICATION_FACTOR_CONFIG, 3); // Replication
    factor for internal topics
```

5. Monitoring and Autoscaling

Implement monitoring to track the performance of Kafka Streams applications. Tools like Prometheus and Grafana can be used to visualize metrics and set up alerts for scaling triggers.

- *Resource Utilization:* Monitor CPU, memory, and disk usage to identify bottlenecks and scale resources accordingly.
- *Autoscaling:* Use automation tools such as Kubernetes to manage autoscaling. Define policies based on resource utilization thresholds.

An example Kubernetes deployment configuration that supports autoscaling:

```
apiVersion: apps/v1
kind: Deployment
metadata:
  name: kafka-streams-app
spec:
  replicas: 3
  selector:
    matchLabels:
      app: kafka-streams-app
  template:
    metadata:
      labels:
        app: kafka-streams-app
    spec:
      containers:
      - name: kafka-streams-app
        image: my-streams-app:latest
        resources:
          requests:
            memory: "512Mi"
            cpu: "500m"
          limits:
            memory: "1Gi"
            cpu: "1"
---
apiVersion: autoscaling/v1
kind: HorizontalPodAutoscaler
metadata:
  name: kafka-streams-app-hpa
spec:
  scaleTargetRef:
    apiVersion: apps/v1
    kind: Deployment
    name: kafka-streams-app
```

```
minReplicas: 3
maxReplicas: 10
targetCPUUtilizationPercentage: 80
```

6. Fault Tolerance

Ensuring high availability and fault tolerance is a critical aspect of scaling.

- *Standby Replicas:* Configure standby replicas to automatically take over in case of instance failure.
- *Stateful Recovery:* Enable change logging and persistent state to recover state stores efficiently after failures.

7. Load Balancing

Effective load balancing ensures efficient resource utilization and minimizes latency.

- *Rebalancing Protocols:* Kafka Streams uses the Kafka consumer's rebalancing protocols to distribute partitions across instances dynamically.
- *Uniform Data Distribution:* Ensure data is evenly distributed among partitions to avoid hotspots.

Applying these scaling techniques ensures that Kafka Streams applications remain resilient and efficient under varying loads.

10.9 Monitoring Performance

Effective monitoring of a Kafka Streams application is crucial for identifying bottlenecks and ensuring optimal performance. By leveraging various monitoring tools and techniques, one can gain insights into the system's health, identify performance degradation, and take corrective actions proactively. This section delves into the key components and strategies for monitoring Kafka Streams applications.

Metrics Collection and Analysis: Kafka Streams provides numerous metrics that can be used to monitor different aspects of the application. These metrics can be accessed via JMX (Java Management Extensions) and are categorized into several broad groups, including:

- **Producer Metrics:** These metrics provide information about the Kafka producer's performance, such as record sending rate, error rates, and request latencies.
- **Consumer Metrics:** These metrics track the performance of Kafka consumers, including poll rates, lag, and fetch latencies.
- **Stream Processing Metrics:** These metrics cover details specific to stream processing tasks, such as processing rate, commit rate, and state store metrics.
- **Thread-Level Metrics:** These include the number of active threads, blocked threads, and task latencies per thread.
- **RocksDB Metrics:** For applications using RocksDB for state storage, these metrics provide information about the state store's I/O performance and compactions.

Setting Up JMX: To enable JMX, start the Kafka Streams application with the following JVM options:

```
-Dcom.sun.management.jmxremote
-Dcom.sun.management.jmxremote.local.only=false
-Dcom.sun.management.jmxremote.port=9010
-Dcom.sun.management.jmxremote.rmi.port=9011
-Dcom.sun.management.jmxremote.authenticate=false
-Dcom.sun.management.jmxremote.ssl=false
```

Once JMX is enabled, tools such as JConsole, VisualVM, or Prometheus can be used to collect and visualize these metrics.

Important Kafka Streams Metrics: Below are some critical Kafka Streams metrics one should monitor to ensure the application's optimal performance:

- **kafka.streams:type=stream-metrics,group=streams-metrics,name=all-committed-records**: Indicates the total number of records committed across all tasks.
- **kafka.streams:type=stream-metrics,group=streams-metrics,name=commit-time-avg**: The average time taken to commit records in milliseconds.
- **kafka.streams:type=stream-metrics,group=streams-metrics,name=process-time-avg**: The average time taken to process records.

- **kafka.streams:type=stream-metrics,group=threads,name=thread-start-time-total**: Total time spent by threads in the start state.
- **kafka.streams:type=stream-metrics,group=caches,name=cache-size-bytes**: The size of the in-memory state cache in bytes.

Integrating with Monitoring Systems: Kafka Streams applications can be integrated with enterprise-grade monitoring systems like Prometheus and Grafana for more sophisticated monitoring and alerting. Below is an example of how to expose Kafka Streams metrics to Prometheus using the JMX Exporter.

Configuring JMX Exporter: Install the JMX Exporter as an agent to your Kafka Streams application JVM by adding the following parameters:

```
-javaagent:/path/to/jmx_prometheus_javaagent-0.16.1.jar=8080:/path/to/config.yaml
```

Here is a sample config.yaml for the JMX Exporter:

```
rules:
  - pattern: kafka.streams<type=(.+), name=(.+)><> (value=.
  - name: "kafka_streams_$1_$2"
    type: GAUGE
    attrNameSnakeCase: true
```

Alerting and Dashboarding: Once the metrics are available in Prometheus, Grafana dashboards can be set up to visually monitor the application's performance. You can define alerts in Prometheus or Grafana based on specific metric thresholds to notify you when certain performance parameters exceed acceptable limits.

Log-Based Monitoring: Logs are another crucial element for monitoring Kafka Streams applications. Here are key logs to monitor:

- **Producer Logs:** These logs can help diagnose issues related to message production, such as message drops or retries.
- **Consumer Logs:** These logs provide insight into consumer lag, rebalances, and other consumer-related issues.
- **Stream Thread Logs:** Monitoring logs produced by stream threads can help in understanding processing delays, errors, and thread-state transitions.
- **State Store Logs:** These provide details on state store operations, especially useful for debugging state-related issues.

Using Log Aggregation Tools: Centralizing logs using log aggregation tools like Elasticsearch, Logstash, and Kibana (commonly known as the ELK stack) or Splunk enables easier querying and visualization of log data. Configurations to push logs from Kafka Streams applications to these systems generally involve:

- Setting up log appenders in log4j.properties or log4j2.xml.
- Ensuring log messages are structured (e.g., as JSON) to facilitate parsing and querying.

Example Log4j Configuration: An example log4j configuration for sending logs to Elasticsearch:

```
log4j.rootLogger=INFO, ELASTIC

log4j.appender.ELASTIC=org.apache.log4j.ElasticsearchAppender
log4j.appender.ELASTIC.Endpoint=https://es-host:9200
log4j.appender.ELASTIC.Index=app-logs
log4j.appender.ELASTIC.Layout=org.apache.log4j.PatternLayout
log4j.appender.ELASTIC.Layout.ConversionPattern=%d{ISO8601} %p %t %c - %m%n
```

Such configurations enable efficient real-time log monitoring, aiding in quick diagnosis and troubleshooting. By building robust monitoring and alerting mechanisms, Kafka Streams applications can achieve high reliability and performance.

10.10 Case Studies: Performance Optimization

This section delves into practical examples of how performance optimization can be effectively implemented in Kafka Streams applications. We will analyze real-world scenarios to illustrate various techniques and strategies, covering a spectrum of challenges and solutions. These case studies aim to provide a comprehensive understanding of the methods discussed in previous sections by applying them to actual use cases.

Case Study 1: Real-Time Log Processing

In this scenario, a company processes millions of log entries generated by their web applications in real time. The Kafka Streams application is designed to aggregate logs and detect anomalies.

The initial deployment faced latency issues, with processing times frequently exceeding acceptable limits. To address this, several optimization strategies were applied:

Understanding the Issue

- Problem: High end-to-end latency
- Initial Metrics: Average latency = 500ms, Maximum latency = 1200ms

Optimizations Implemented

1. **Kafka Producer Settings:**

```
Properties producerProps = new Properties();
producerProps.put("acks", "all");
producerProps.put("retries", 3);
producerProps.put("batch.size", 16384);
producerProps.put("linger.ms", 5);
```

   Adjusting the acks parameter to "all" ensures higher reliability at the cost of slightly increased latency, which was acceptable in this case for the sake of consistency.

2. **Kafka Consumer Settings:**

```
Properties consumerProps = new Properties();
consumerProps.put("fetch.min.bytes", 50000);
consumerProps.put("fetch.max.wait.ms", 100);
```

   Increasing the fetch.min.bytes parameter reduced the number of fetch requests, thereby lowering latency by optimizing the consumer throughput.

3. **Threading and Concurrency:**

```
StreamsConfig config = new StreamsConfig(properties);
config.put(StreamsConfig.NUM_STREAM_THREADS_CONFIG, 4);
```

   Configuring multiple stream threads helped distribute the processing load more evenly and efficiently across available CPU cores.

4. **Scaling with Kafka Streams Configuration:**

```
Properties streamProps = new Properties();
streamProps.put(StreamsConfig.
    BUFFERED_RECORDS_PER_PARTITION_CONFIG, 10000);
```

Increasing the buffer size for each partition allowed more records to be processed in memory before being committed downstream.

Results

- Post-Optimization Metrics: Average latency = 200ms, Maximum latency = 600ms
- Outcome: The latency issues were mitigated, achieving a significant performance boost.

Case Study 2: Financial Transaction Processing

In this use case, a financial institution needs to process legal and regulatory checks on transaction data. The Kafka Streams application performs computations on transaction amounts and flags any suspicious transactions in real time.

The initial application encountered bottlenecks due to high memory usage and frequent garbage collection pauses, leading to performance degradation.

Understanding the Issue

- Problem: High memory consumption and excessive GC pauses
- Initial Metrics: Heap usage above 80%, GC Pause Time = 120ms per minute

Optimizations Implemented

1. **Memory Management Best Practices:**

```
Properties streamProps = new Properties();
streamProps.put(StreamsConfig.
    CACHE_MAX_BYTES_BUFFERING_CONFIG, 10240);
```

   Reducing the cache size helped to minimize memory footprint and prevent excessive garbage collection.

2. **Tuning RocksDB Settings:** As Kafka Streams uses RocksDB for local storage, tuning its configuration was crucial.

```
Properties rocksDBProps = new Properties();
rocksDBProps.put("write_buffer_size", 1024 * 1024 * 64);
rocksDBProps.put("max_write_buffer_number", 3);
streamsConfig.put(StreamsConfig.
    ROCKSDB_CONFIG_SETTER_CLASS_CONFIG,
        "com.example.CustomRocksDBConfig");
```

Adjusting the write_buffer_size and max_write_buffer_number parameters optimized RocksDB for the high-write workload.

3. **Threading and Concurrency:**

```
StreamsConfig config = new StreamsConfig(properties);
config.put(StreamsConfig.NUM_STREAM_THREADS_CONFIG, 6);
```

Scaling up the number of threads utilized the processing power more effectively and distributed tasks more efficiently.

Results

- Post-Optimization Metrics: Heap usage around 55%, GC Pause Time = 40ms per minute
- Outcome: Improved memory management significantly reduced pauses due to garbage collection, enhancing overall performance.

Case Study 3: Social Media Analytics

A social media platform analyzes user interactions to generate real-time insights. The Kafka Streams application aggregates and computes metrics, such as user engagement and popular content.

The platform initially struggled with throughput limitations due to inefficient configuration settings and suboptimal message batching.

Understanding the Issue

- Problem: Low throughput limiting real-time capabilities
- Initial Metrics: Throughput = 1000 messages/second

Optimizations Implemented

1. **Kafka Producer Settings:**

```
Properties producerProps = new Properties();
producerProps.put("batch.size", 32768);
producerProps.put("linger.ms", 10);
```

Increasing the batch.size and linger.ms improved throughput by allowing the producer to process larger batches of messages at a time.

2. **Kafka Consumer Settings:**

```
Properties consumerProps = new Properties();
consumerProps.put("fetch.max.bytes", 52428800);
consumerProps.put("max.poll.records", 1000);
```

Optimizing the fetch.max.bytes and max.poll.records parameters enabled more efficient data consumption.

3. **Tuning Kafka Streams Configuration:**

```
Properties streamProps = new Properties();
streamProps.put(StreamsConfig.NUM_STREAM_THREADS_CONFIG,
     8);
```

Increasing the number of stream threads took advantage of multi-core processors, enhancing parallel processing capabilities.

4. **Monitoring and Feedback Loop:** Continuous monitoring facilitated adaptive tuning, resulting in dynamic adjustments based on real-time metrics.

Results

- Post-Optimization Metrics: Throughput = 3500 messages/second
- Outcome: Substantial throughput improvement enabled real-time analytics, enhancing the platform's functional effectiveness.

These case studies demonstrate various techniques applied to optimize Kafka Streams applications, emphasizing the significance of tailored configurations for distinct scenarios. By systematically addressing specific bottlenecks and fine-tuning parameters, substantial performance enhancements can be achieved.

Made in the USA
Monee, IL
05 November 2026

67911517R00144